ETHNICITY IN HELLENISTIC EGYPT

STUDIES IN
HELLENISTIC CIVILIZATION

Edited by Per Bilde,
Troels Engberg-Pedersen, Lise Hannestad,
and Jan Zahle

III

ETHNICITY
IN HELLENISTIC EGYPT

Edited by Per Bilde,
Troels Engberg-Pedersen, Lise Hannestad,
and Jan Zahle

AARHUS UNIVERSITY PRESS

Printed on acid-free paper by Rosendahls Bogtrykkeri, Esbjerg
ISBN 87 7288 359 6

AARHUS UNIVERSITY PRESS
Aarhus University, DK-8000 Aarhus C

CONTENTS

6

PREFACE

This volume, the third in the series Studies in Hellenistic Civilization, owes its origin to the second international conference organized by the Danish research project on the Hellenistic period and sponsored by the Danish Research Council for the Humanities. The project was launched in 1988-89 and is planned to last for a five-year period (1989-93). It defines its field of research as the cultural development from Alexander the Great to the middle of the second century AD, with special emphasis on the formative period, i.e. the period traditionally labelled "Hellenistic", from Alexander to Augustus. The aim of the project is to stimulate Danish research in the Hellenistic period through grants to younger scholars, topical one-day seminars for experts in a single field, and longer seminars on broader issues, where contacts are being developed with scholars from Scandinavia and abroad.

The special profile of the project lies in its interdisciplinary character. At present, when traditional stereotypes in the account of the Hellenistic period are increasingly being questioned as a result of scholars' adopting post-"classicist" and post-"colonial" perspectives on the period, one way forward towards reaching a new interpretation of general trends in the period lies in attempting to bring into a single pool as many relevant disciplines as possible. From archaeology to the history of philosophy and religion: from Greek-oriented disciplines to scholarly disciplines traditionally based on "the other side" (be it Near-Eastern in its many forms or Egyptian): what trends and patterns emerge from a close comparative study of results reached in these various disciplines?

Against this general background two international conferences were held in 1990 at Fuglsang Manor in southern Denmark: one (in January) on Religion and Religious Practice in the Seleucid Kingdom (see Studies in Hellenistic Civilization vol. 1) and one (in August) on The Ptolemaic Kingdom and Alexandria, with the participation of about 30 foreign and Danish scholars, among whom were the authors of the contributions to the present volume. The theme of the Ptolemaic conference was specified as follows: the process of acculturation between

Egyptians, Macedonians-Greeks and Jews as reflected in the Macedonian-Greek creation, and the historical development of central political, economic, cultural and religious institutions and in any significant local reactions to them.

Many of these institutions (the army, Ptolemaic administration, the Alexandrian Museum and Library, the Isis-Sarapis, cult etc.) have been investigated in detail during the twentieth century partly on the basis of newly found material from papyri and inscriptions, but the aim of the conference was to consider their role as part of a wider process of acculturation. Thus the formulation of the conference theme was intended to focus attention on the following more general issues: (1) an aspect which has not yet received its proper due in the exploration of Ptolemaic Egypt, viz. the social one or the question of the role played by the interplay of various institutions in the everyday life of the ordinary citizen; (2) the role of the various institutions in holding together a heterogeneous society across ethnical boundaries: their integrating or segregating character and the role they were intended to play within an overall political scheme; (3) the overall character of the Macedonian-Greek conquest of Egypt (exploitation, co-operation etc.?); and finally (4), the changes undergone by Ptolemaic society during the Hellenistic period.

As it happened, the conference came to have a rather more sharply defined focus by concentrating attention on the concept of ethnicity and the relationship between ethnicity and acculturation in the Ptolemaic kingdom. This was to a large extent due to two contributions to the conference, by Uffe Østergaard and Koen Goudriaan, who formulated particularly clearly a conception of ethnicity that has recently been developed by the leading Norwegian anthropologist Fredrik Barth. In this conception (see below) the notion of an "ethnic strategy" becomes very important, and this is reflected, in many different ways, in the other essays contained in this volume. One important result that came out of the conference was the shared realization that the theme of acculturation in a multi-ethnic society like Ptolemaic Egypt requires for its proper treatment work along two complementary axes: (i) a historical stock-taking both of the facts concerning the actual interaction between what appear in the sources to be treated as different ethnic groups and also of the origin and actual intermingling of any cultural elements that went into any apparent case of acculturation and (ii) focus on the very many different ways in which the social agents in the cultural interaction themselves construed the differences between themselves and the others, i.e. their ethnic strategies. In the present volume the essays by Dorothy J. Thompson, Jerker

Blomqvist, Aryeh Kasher and Jørgen Podemann Sørensen work mainly along the first line, those by Koen Goudriaan, Peder Borgen and Carl R. Holladay along a combination of the first and second lines. By mixing the essays in an order that reflects differences in subject matter and cultural perspective (mainly Greek for Thompson and Blomqvist, Jewish for Goudriaan, Kasher, Borgen and Holladay, and Egyptian for Podemann Sørensen), the editors hope that readers of the volume will appreciate the movements back and forth between the two axes.

The Barthian conception of ethnicity is set forth in the following way by Østergaard and Goudriaan. Discussing the kind of "primitive ethnography" that one finds in Herodotus, Plato and Aristotle, Østergaard pinpoints the essence of Barth's suggestion as follows: "Some of us have come to believe that identity [including ethnic identity] is only what we say it is, no more no less." Barth has proposed "a social interaction model of ethnic identity that does not posit a fixed 'character' or 'essence' for the group, but examines the perceptions of its members which distinguish them from other groups." "The primary characteristic of ethnic boundaries is attitudinal" and since attitudes may shift, ethnicity too is "a bundle of shifting interactions rather than a nuclear component of social organization." Changing the focus of the investigation from the internal characteristics of the group to its self-perceived boundaries is, as Østergaard admits, "only a start towards an examination of ethnicity in history." And it is a change which, if anything, only makes the historical investigation more complex. Still, for conceptual reasons the change is necessary.

Goudriaan sets out the Barthian conception in six points. (1) "Ethnicity is looked at from the inside." (2) "Ethnicity, as a way of organizing cultural differences, implies that specific features of culture ... are singled out as ethnically significant, whilst others are neutral." (3) "Ethnicity is an independent dimension of social life" not reducible to any of those cultural features that serve as boundary marks (religion, occupation, mode of life, language). (4) Survival of the ethnic identity group depends on the continued interest on the part of its members in maintaining boundaries. Thus "one might describe the history of an ethnic group as the outcome of the combined ethnical strategies of its members and of those with whom they are in contact." (5) "Ethnicity is a normal feature of social life," which does not automatically entail tension between the ethnic groups. (6) Finally, ethnicity is a universal trait of human experience and so the concept may appropriately be used for analysis of the ancient world too. Throughout his essay, Goudriaan also insists on the difference between "culture" and "ethnicity" implied in the third point above (cf. also the two axes mentioned earlier). And he suggests that this distinction may help to reach a better conceptualization of some age-old problems concerning the Hellenistic period, e.g. that we move away from characterizing that period, with Claire Préaux, in terms of an "etancheite des cultures" (separateness of cultures). Rather, whereas the cultures of East and West did fuse to a large degree, what we find instead is an "étancheité des ethnies".

As already noted, the individual essays move along the two complementary axes distinguished above in different ways. Uffe Østergaard (Aarhus University) was invited to present an inaugural paper to the conference on the notion of ethnicity and its relevance for investigating the Hellenistic world. Starting his essay ("What is National and Ethnic Identity?") very much from the modern period, Østergaard sketches the history of the rise of the modern nation-state, showing the relative novelty of the identification of state, nation and people. He also sketches the history of modern, mainly North American, research since the 1930's on national character and national identity in order to raise the question (much discussed in modern anthropology, sociology and political science) whether the modern phenomenon of nationalism may at all be usefully brought into an analysis of pre-modern societies like the ancient ones. Against the modern "functionalists", who deny this (e.g. Ernest Gellner), stand the "primordialists" or "perennialists", who see nations as simply larger, updated versions of pre-modern ties and sentiments, and those who try to mediate between the two (Anthony Smith, Benedict Anderson), e.g. (Smith) by concentrating on the ethnie preceding the modern nation-states. Developing a point made by Anderson concerning the "imagined" quality of national identity, Østergaard finally arrives at the Barthian conception of ethnic identity. His message is that, so construed, the concept of ethnicity may in fact be fruitfully employed in the analysis of ancient societies too, even though this use is widely different from the one made by the ancients themselves of the concept of ethnos.

Plunging directly into the rich source material, Dorothy J. Thompson (Cambridge University) discusses in her essay ("Language and Literacy in Early Hellenistic Egypt") the ways in which, in the first hundred years of Ptolemaic rule, Greeks came to be part of Egyptian life, as evidenced by the spread of the Greek language in the country, with the effects of this upon the society and the relation of the two peoples within it. On the basis of the papyri and other literary remains (e.g. Manetho), Thompson argues for an extensive interdependence and cooperation in the early years between the Greek-speaking conquerors and members of the Egyptian literate classes, including the priests. When this was followed by a widespread programme of education and schooling in Greek, possibly on royal initiative, the result was the eventual acceptance by educated Egyptians of Greek for administrative purposes, with a considerable long-term impact under the Romans. Thus in the early years the Egyptian literate classes adapted themselves to a change of regime through collaboration and Hellenization. Thompson ends by suggesting, however, that the process was not in fact so much one of Hellenization as of integration. Here, then, is a historical stocktaking which implicitly supports the point made by Goudriaan that there may be a gradual fusion of cultures which does not, however, necessarily break down the separateness of the ethnies.

In his essay ("Alexandrian Science: The Case of Eratosthenes"), Jerker Blomqvist (Lund University) moves from the programme of elementary education in Greek discussed by Thompson to the polymath Eratosthenes, who was in charge of that institution of the highest available learning also created and supported by the Ptolemaic kings, the Library and Museum in Alexandria. Having sketched Eratosthenes' career and scientific profile, Blomqvist addresses the issue of Eratosthenes' relations with the Egyptians. Are there any traces in his work of Egyptian learning or experience? Blomqvist argues for a negative answer. The inhabitants of the learned institutions of Alexandria seem to have had little contact with the native Egyptians or for that matter with the Greeks of Egypt either. They formed a closed circle with little interest in their Egyptian surroundings, whether Greek or indigenous. Conversely, these surroundings went about their own business and ignored the scientists. On Blomqvist's reading, then, what went on in the learned institutions in Alexandria, at least as represented by the case of Eratosthenes, did not enter into any kind of cultural interaction, nor did it play any role as part of an ethnic strategy except possibly negatively. (For a somewhat different suggestion concerning contact between Eratosthenes and Jewish scholars, see Holladay's essay.)

Koen Goudriaan (Free University, Amsterdam) takes the reader from material reflecting the Macedonian-Greek perspective to Jewish issues. In a searching attempt to apply Barthian insights into ethnicity, Goudriaan's essay ("Ethnical Strategies in Graeco-Roman Egypt") analyses the source material (mainly Philo) for the 38 AD progrom in Alexandria with a view to identifying the interplay between historical facts underlying this event and the ethnic construal given to it by the social agents themselves. One striking observation concerns the way in which both the Jews (as represented by Philo) and their Alexandrian opponents employed the same third party, the Egyptians, in their attempt to denigrate each other. For Philo his Alexandrian opponents were mere Egyptians, for the Alexandrians it was the Jews who were. Still, the basic demarcation line along which all issues that may have gone into the clash were organized was, as Goudriaan shows, the ethnic one of Jew versus non-Jew. In his discussion of the question why this was so and why it happened exactly in the early Roman period, Goudriaan suggests two answers which distinguish the Roman period from the preceding, Ptolemaic one. First, by now all other allochthnous ethnic entities had vanished, leaving only the Egyptians, the Greeks and the Jews. Secondly, the Roman policy of introducing fiscal difference between various groups within the population (the *laographia*) strengthened ethnic boundaries and made them more rigorous. In this latter respect, Goudriaan argues, the Romans differed from the Ptolemies who, he claims, "simply took no notice of ethnicity." "It seems probable that the Ptolemaic government, at least during the first two centuries of its existence, did not use ethnicity as a factor in governing the country otherwise than for identification purposes."

This view is partly problematized in the essay ("The Civic Status of the Jews in Ptolemaic Egypt") by Aryeh Kasher (Tel-Aviv University), who aims to relate the Jews in Egypt to the four classes of (1) full citizens of the Greek poleis (Alexandria, Ptolemais, Naucratis), (2) the permanent residents in those poleis without citizenship (*metoikoi*), (3) foreigners who settled in the *chora* and were employed in government service (army and civilian administration), (4) and finally the Egyptian "natives" (*laoi*). On the one hand, he insists on what he calls "the Ptolemies' dual policy as regards their Hellenic and native subjects," viz. "a distinct segregation between the two classes." On the other hand, he implicitly shows how these social boundaries were permeated in a number of ways, not least by the Egyptian Jews, who were found among the last three of the four groups distinguished. As for the first group, however, Kasher argues that Jews who were, from an administrative point of view, treated as Greeks were not in fact full Greek citizens. Rather, both in the chora and, as Kasher specifically argues, in Alexandria too they would at most have a status as quasi-Greek citizens, viz. as members of independent *politeumata*, parallelling but separate from the Greek *poleis*. Finally, Kasher provides an overall sketch of the position of the Jews in Egypt during the whole of the Ptolemaic period, thereby laying the historical ground-work for a consideration of whatever ethnic strategies Jews may have adopted in one or the other context during the same period.

Focusing on Philo's perception of the relationship between Jews and non-Jews, Peder Borgen (Trondheim University) in effect displays in his essay ("Philo and the Jews in Alexandria") the wide range af ethnic strategies available to an educated Jew with Philo's position and point of view. In addition to the actual fusion, at the historical level, of Greek and Jewish cultural elements that may be found in Philo's thought, there is also an attempt, at the level of what is in fact a fully developed ethnic strategy, to combine an emphasis on what Jews and Gentiles have in common with the distinctiveness of the Jewish ethnos. Thus as one example of Philo's strategy Borgen mentions his claim that what is good among non-Jews receives its full and authentic dimension in Moses and his followers, e.g. by actually being derived from him. Borgen also notes how denigration of Egyptian religion and culture constitutes one weapon in Philo's ethnic armoury. Finally, Borgen shows how Philo employs the cosmic and eschatological perspective of a special militaristic tradition derived from the Old Testament to highlight Jewish ethnic specificity. Though not noted by Borgen, this suggestion brings Philo, the Hellenistic highly educated Jew, into close similarity with apocalyptic trends in Egyptian religious texts from the Ptolemaic period. (See Podemann Sørensen below.)

The mixture between Jewish accommodation and resistance is illuminatingly discussed by Carl R. Holladay (Emory University, Atlanta, Georgia) in his essay ("Jewish Responses to Hellenistic Culture in Early Ptolemaic Egypt") on those Jewish Hellenistic writers who can with relative certainty be located in Egypt: Demetrius the Chronographer, the historian Artapanus, the poets Ezekiel the Tragedian and Philo Epicus, the philosophers Aristobulus and the author of the *Letter of Aristeas*, and finally the author of the *Third Sibylline Oracle*. From a literary point of view Holladay notes a willingness on the part of these authors to experiment with new literary forms to an extent which reveals levels of Greek literacy that presuppose more than a casual participation in the Greek educational system. Indeed, he even speaks of a "significant level of participation in Alexandrian intellectual life." Moving to the other issue of ethnic strategies, Holladay perceptively suggests that the Jewish engagement with Hellenistic culture represents an exercise in ethnic promotion as well as ethnic self-preservation. It served to "reinforce ethnic identity by providing ways for making both Jewish

scripture and tradition more credible to Jews themselves." Turning next to the
attitude towards Hellenistic religion and culture expressed in the writings, Holladay
argues that "one cannot proceed as if there were fundamentally two options:
acceptance or rejection of Greek culture." Rather, whereas some of the writings
are decisively for and others equally decisively against, most lie in between, in
complex and subtle ways that provide evidence of a number of ethnic strategies.
Finally, the same pattern may be noted when one considers the attitudes evidenced
in the writings towards Jewish ethnicity itself and towards other ethnic groups.
Summarizing, Holladay hazards the suggestion that in parallel with the Jewish
assimilation of Hellenistic culture, which had begun already in the early Ptolemaic
period, there is some evidence that the Jews also began to define ethnic boundaries
less rigidly.

   Finally, in what is unfortunately the only essay in the volume written from a
clearly Egyptian perspective ("Native Reactions to Foreign Rule and Culture in
the Religious Literature"), Jørgen Podemann Sørensen (Copenhagen University)
investigates specimens of two literary genres, the *conte prophétique* and the
magical literature, in order to trace any native responses to the new institutions
and the influx of foreign cultures imposed on the Egyptians during the Ptolemaic
period. By going back to pre-Hellenistic Egyptian religious texts and comparing
them with Hellenistic ones, he aims to detect the Egyptian cultural determinants
that were at work in the Hellenistic process of acculturation and resistance. The
result of the search is predictably complex. On the one hand, in the literary genre
of the *conte prophétique* Podemann Sørensen findes a decisive new element in
the specimens he discusses (a story in Manetho and the Oracle of the Potter), viz.
apocalypticism. On the other hand, in the magical literature Egyptian, Greek and
Jewish elements are to be found in a fusion which is complete and reveals an
altogether striking syncretism. However, Podemann Sørensen argues that this
syncretism was to a very large degree governed by a native cultural determinant
which has been called transmythological redundancy and which admitted an almost
unlimited inflow of foreign motifs while also at the same time preserving basic
Egyptian structures. (Thus this particular cultural determinant may in effect be
viewed as another ethnic strategy.) However, in the magical literature too one
meets an apocalyptic tendency, which represents a decisive innovation. And so
Podemann Sørensen ends by suggesting that the prevalence of apocalypticism in
the narratives and the magical literature of Hellenistic Egypt is to be understood

as a reaction to foreign rule and culture, i.e. both to cultural conflict and to the many and drastic social changes brought about by the Ptolemaic regime.

Superficially, this conclusion may seem to go against suggestions made in some of the other essays (e.g. that by Dorothy Thompson). However, once one remembers the complexity highlighted throughout the volume, of adaptation and resistance, of actual acculturation and strategic insistance on ethnic separateness, the impression of inconsistency should disappear. Indeed, it is a major lesson to be gained from the present volume that there are no easy answers to questions concerning acculturation and ethnicity in Hellenistic Egypt. There are differences of time, of social location of the authors studied, of genre and overall character of the source material. And finally, there is the difference between the two foci of investigation identified at the beginning of this preface: culture and ethnicity. All these differences must be taken into consideration before a complete picture can be reached.

Technically, the volume is organized with a single bibliography for all papers, to which references are made in the brief form giving only author's name and the date of publication. The volume is concluded by an index of names and an index locorum.

It remains to thank the Danish Research Council for the Humanities for generous support for the seminar and the publication of this volume.

Copenhagen and Aarhus, August 1992

The Editors

WHAT IS NATIONAL AND ETHNIC IDENTITY?

Uffe Østergård

No serious historian of nations and nationalism can be a committed political nationalist, except in the sense in which believers in the literal truth of the Scriptures, while unable to make contributions to evolutionary theory, are not precluded from making contributions to archaeology and Semitic philology. Nationalism requires too much belief in what is patently not so. (Hobsbawm 1990, 12).

Or put more bluntly,

It has proven as disastrous to leave the history of nationalism to nationalists as that of railways to railway enthusiasts. (Hobsbawm 1972, 397).

I take my point of departure from the dictum of one of the foremost scholars on nationalism and national identity, Hans Kohn. According to him, nationalism as we understand it dates from no earlier than the second half of the eighteenth century. Its first great manifestation was the French Revolution, which gave the new movement an increased dynamic force. Nationalism had become manifest, however, at the end of the eighteenth century almost simultaneously in a number of widely separated European countries (cf. Kohn 1944, 3). Nationalism, then, is a relatively recent phenomenon. But what about ethnicity and national identity? There is a huge debate on this and the opinions of the scholars involved differ enormously. As the Nestor of marxist historiography, E.J. Hobsbawm, recently put it:

the problem is that there is no way of telling the observer how to distinguish a nation from other entities *a priori*, as we can tell him or her how to recognize a bird or to distinguish a mouse from a lizard. Nation-watching would be simple if it could be like bird-watching. (Hobsbawm 1990, 5).

Apart from the fact that bird-watching is not uncomplicated either Hobsbawm is right in pointing to the ambiguous and contested nature of the facts as well as the language of national identity. The words for "nation" or "people" in most European languages are derived from the Latin words *natio* and *populus*. *Natio* is derived from the verb *nascor* (I am born), and indicates the common descent of the group. In the Middle Ages *natio* was the same as "tribe" or "clan" but it was sometimes also used for people who were simply born in the same country. In 17th and 18th century France and England "nation" gradually came to denominate inhabitants of a state. Common language had usually been connected with common descent but in Western Europe it came to be considered a characteristic of the rising state nation. During the French revolution "nation" became the repository of popular sovereignty. This "nation" was no longer a state nation, i.e. a result of the formation of dynastic territorial states of early modern Europe. The philosopher Jean-Jacques Rousseau believed it to be a collective which logically and historically predated the state. According to the political philosophers of the Enlightenment and the French Revolution, sovereignty resided with the people who could hand it over to their elected representatives (Kemiläinen 1984, 33-34).

Thus, a fundamental characteristic of the word nation and everything connected with it is its relative novelty: the novelty of the identification of state, nation and people. On this, virtually all recent scholarship agrees. In politics, though, the opposite assumption, that national identification is so natural, primary, and permanent as to precede history, is still widely held. This popular and populist assumption has been reinforced by the recent developments in Eastern Europe and in the Third World as well as by the rise of racism and xenophobia in the West. If we turn to the dictionaries, we learn that in most Western languages nation, state, and people only began to be identified with each other as late as the 1880's. The primary meaning of "nation" was political. A Dutch dictionary from 1899 explicitly notes that the French and English use the word "nation" to mean people who are citizens in a state even when they do not speak the same language (Hobsbawm 1990, 17). As late as 1908 the *New English Dictionary* pointed out that the old meaning of the word envisaged mainly an ethnic unit, but "recent usage has begun to stress the notion of political unity and independence" (quoted in Hobsbawm 1990, 18). These two definitions represent the extremes in the wide spectrum of uses of the concepts "nation" and "nationality".

At the beginning of the nineteenth century, England and France emerged from the Revolutionary and Napoleonic Wars as archetypes of the nation-state, though, as we have seen, they were innovators in two very different ways. In its turn this experience provoked other states and peoples to aspire to the same condition. First, German and Italian liberals, then Slavs, Scandinavians, and Latin Americans made it their program to attain a status comparable to that of England and France. The German nation (*Volk*), the Russian nation (*Narod*), and so on, were to inherit state powers shaped for them by their rulers. By the end of the 19th century the international world was divided into three layers. At the top six "Great Powers" competed; two of them, Russia and Austria-Hungary were not nation-states at all, whereas Britain, France, Germany and Italy claimed to be so. At the second level were several "recognized states" including the US. Under these was a world of "non-states" including the Ottoman Empire, China, and Japan (at least until 1905) which were partly left alone, partly devoured or "protected" by stronger powers.

World War I came to be perceived as caused by the unleashing of popular chauvinism within and between the Great Powers. The revolutionary consequences of this first industrialized mass war obliterated most of the differences in the development of nationhood produced in the nineteenth century. At the Versailles Conference in 1919, the principle of national independence was turned into common orthodoxy of the international political world. It meant that every member of the human race should be legally assigned to one nation state and not more than one; and that the rights of the state were conferred on it by the nation whose membership coincided with that of the state. It was translated into a legally constituted world of nation-states formally organized in the *League of Nations*; in French, *la Société des Nations*. It is a symptom of the terminological difficulties that the organization was called "The Association of Peoples" (*Folkenes Forbund*) in Danish. This system recognized eight Great Powers, though they were never all members at the same time. The USA had joined the ranks of the Great Powers because of the war effort, although, for internal political reasons she never entered the organization. The Soviet Union only joined in 1934 after Germany and Japan had left, shortly followed by Italy in 1935. Besides these were 54 other members of varying ranks.

The second World War, in many ways the logical continuation of the first, settled its scores in a more pragmatic way; it produced few new states directly, but it indirectly weakened colonialism and thereby helped create many new non-European states especially after 1960. They joined a world system of nominally independent nation-states organized in the *United Nations* (in French *Organization des Nations Unies, ONU*) which should really have been called "United States" had this name not already been occupied. Until 1989 the reality was an effective two-power situation whith the USA and USSR each surrounded by major and minor satellites and China lurking in the shadows. Outside these existed a sea of more or less reluctant camp-followers, sometimes called the non-aligned nations. The total number grew from 50 in April 1945 to 122 in 1966, 160 in 1990 and 175 in 1992.

Thus, the political reality of the world of today is characterized by the almost complete domination of the principle of independent nation-states. Yet, paradoxically, the very concepts of nation and nationality were almost run out of Western scholarly debate after World War II. Nationalism was identified with chauvinism and only considered relevant for the understanding of the Third World or the underdeveloped peripheries of Europe. The members of United Nations are defined as states rather than nations though officially they all claim to be proper nation-states. One only has to think of the number of aspiring nations without statehood in order to realize this. The fundamental political institution of today is not the nation, but the state aspiring to turn its subjects into loyal national or nationalized citizens and thus becoming a recognized nation-state. So far very few have succeeded, but those who have, have set the norm. Yet, serious research into the nature of national identity hardly existed until 50 years ago. The major exceptions were produced by two cosmopolitan historians, the American Roman Catholic, Carlton J. Hayes, and the German-Czech secular Jew, Hans Kohn, who treated most nationalisms rather negatively as leading to chauvinism and intolerance.

Like the majority of historians Hayes avoided discussing the phenomenon of national identity in his article on "Nationalism" in the *Encyclopedia of the Social Sciences* (Hayes 1933). Equally cautious, his colleague Max Hildebert Boehm refrained from giving any scholarly credit to the phenomenon of "National Character" in his rejoinder on the theoretical aspects of nationalism (Boehm 1933). Boehm observed that the most prolific writers on the subject were "scientific travellers, historians, poets, members of military expeditions, and tourists", all of whom were more than willing to comment on the peoples of the countries they visited — from an unscientific point of view, of course (Boehm 1933, 232). Admittedly, he does criticize critics of the concept of national character such as himself for not distinguishing clearly enough between the various aspects of the problem: whether clear and unmistakable characterizations of nations are possible or whether perhaps in the theoretical and practical relations between nations there is a presupposition of national character although it can never be exactly determined. (Boehm 1933, 232-233).

Personally he does not doubt

that there is at least a relative uniformity and constancy in the attitude of a nation ... The determination of national character in this sense, however, is rendered more difficult by the fact that there are also common attitudes characteristic of an age as well as of groups and individuals; national character is thus but a partial factor which cannot be isolated for observation and description. A particular difficulty in ascertaining and determining national character arises out of the fact that *it is applied not to the average but to the typical, and in a wide sense to the ideally typical, attitudes of a people*. It is therefore dependent on the social relations of the period particularly with regard to the domination of one or another social group within the nation. (Boehm 1933, 233, emphases added).

Maybe there is such a thing as national character but it changes over time and is very hard to determine. Yet, in the very same collective work where the historian Boehm wrote this obituary for the study of national character and claimed that in the nineteenth century it had been replaced by "the idea of the character of an epoch" we meet optimistic claims regarding the capacity of the behavioural sciences to characterize different national cultures. In the entry on "Personality" the anthropologist Edward Sapir concluded:

The socialization of personality traits may be expected to lead cumulatively to the development of specific psychological biases in the cultures of the world. Thus, Eskimo culture, contrasted with most North American Indian cultures, is extraverted; Hindu culture on the whole corresponds to the world of the thinking introvert; the culture of the United States is definitely extraverted in character, with a greater emphasis on thinking and intuition than on feeling; and sensational evaluations are more clearly evident in the cultures of the Mediterranean area than in those of Northern Europe. *Social scientists have been hostile to such psychological characterizations of culture but in the long run they are inevitable and necessary*. (Sapir 1933, 87, emphases added).

In the short run he turned out to be right. Though the old nationalist history was totally discredited in most European countries by the extreme chauvinism of Nazism and Fascism, American anthropologists had great success in applying social psychology to the study of "national character" during and after World War

II. They ranged from Gregory Bateson to Ruth Benedict and Margaret Mead. Their endeavours were hailed throughout the forties and fifties even by many formerly sceptical historians. A telling example of this optimism was the American historian David Potter. A sophisticated historian with a solid foundation in detailed studies of the Civil War, he was so overwhelmed by the optimistic promises of the behavioural sciences that he began his presentation of the three main interpretations of the American national character as follows:

The essential weakness that has always disabled historians in their effort to deal with the subject scientifically has been their failure to recognize that national character is not a separate phenomenon in itself but simply one specialized manifestation of group character. Group character in turn is but a composite of individual characters, and individual character is simply a pattern in that complex of human processes and qualities which are designated nowadays by the term 'personality'. The study of national character, therefore, is properly a branch of the study of group character and of personality. *Only when it is recognized as such can it make real advances*. (Potter 1954, 33 emphases added).

Nevertheless, this multidisciplinary approach had come to a halt by the end of the fifties when, in the words of David Riesman,

the psychoanalysts returned to their patients and the anthropologists to their tribes (Riesman 1961, XXV).

Riesman himself had been one of the leading students of collective identity (1950). Yet, he more or less called the whole thing off in his inaugural lecture at Harvard in 1958. In this talk, and in a new introduction to the second edition of *The Lonely Crowd* (1961), he drew attention to the methodological deficiencies inherent in the wartime attempts of Benedict, Mead, and Gorer:

When anthropology was poor, anthropologists were autocratic and aristocratic; by this I mean that, like the early psychoanalysts, they were prepared to generalize on the basis of scanty evidence. They practiced an art requiring imagination and confidence in themselves, as well as ability to observe and record. Such brave adventurers as Margaret Mead, Ruth Benedict, and Geoffrey Gorer were willing under the impact of the war to attempt holistic or configurational interpretations of the United States, Japan, or the Soviet Union. ... The younger anthropologists seemed to steer clear of so controversial an area (Riesman 1961, XXIV-XXV).

Disguised as self-criticism, this was in fact meant as a devastating critique of the work done by Margaret Mead's project group on "Research in Contemporary Cultures". In 1942 Gregory Bateson, the then husband of Margaret Mead, delivered a talk on "Morale and national character" to explain to the American OSS (precursor of CIA) what sort of people the Nazis were and how misunderstandings among nations arose. The section on "Differences Which We May Expect Between National Groups" ends like this:

Differences of this order, which may be expected in all European nations, are probably the basis of many of our naive and often unkind international comments. They may, indeed, be of considerable importance in the mechanics of international relations, in as much as an understanding of them might dispel some of our misunderstandings. ... It is probable, however, that these differences are not so complex in their nature as to be beyond the reach of investigation. (Bateson 1942, 102-03).

Margaret Mead's main contribution to the war effort was the book *And Keep your Powder Dry*. Written in three weeks during the summer of 1942 in New Hampshire, it was as she put it, a "pioneer venture". She attempted what "no anthropologist had attempted before, to write about a major complex culture using the model of the whole culture that had been developed through the study of small primitive societies" (quoted from Howard 1984, 236). She asked questions such as "When will and when won't an American fight?"; "Where lies the American strength and the American weakness?" and "Why is it so important for us to think we're right?". The most urgent task in Mead's opinion was to build "from a hundred cultures, one culture which does what no culture has ever done before — gives a place to every human gift." (Howard 1984, 236).

In 1946 Mead's friend and mentor Ruth Benedict published an anthropological analysis of Japan, *The Chrysantemum and the Sword*, that won wider acclaim than any of her previous work, even the famous *Patterns of Culture* (1934). Without ever having set foot in Japan she wrote the book using information gathered from informants during her work for the Office of War Information. Benedict distinguished between cultures which rely heavily on shame, such as the Japanese, and those that rely heavily on guilt. This approach was paradigmatic for their new project variously referred to as "Cultures at a Distance", "the Study of National Character", and "Research on Contemporary Cultures" (see Mead & Métraux 1953). In a brief summary of their common theoretical assumptions, Margaret Mead distinguished between three possible approaches.

First, there is the analysis of relationships between the basic learning common to children within a nation or culture and later characteristics witnessed in the behaviour of adults within the same society. Formative childhood experiences are the immediate focus of such studies. Second, there are societal studies of the pattern and structure of interpersonal relationships. There are cultural sanctions operating continually throughout the society to reinforce behavioural patterns, and thus there is an expected consistency in cultural configurations. Cultural constraints become fixed and internalized aspects of personality. Third, there are studies comprising simple comparative descriptions of those configurations which distinguish one national unit from another; different life styles and ways of looking at things are defined as part of national character. Studies of this last variety remain, from a psychological standpoint at least, surface descriptions of what seem to be consistent culturally, defined values, or behaviour patterns, without reference to possible underlying motivations or personality mechanisms. In contrast, studies included in the first two categories mentioned by Mead seek to push beyond the descriptive level to trace out certain underlying structurally consistent aspects of personality that are manifested in the overt behaviour peculiar to members of a given society (Mead 1953).

Throughout her life Mead had a weakness for one-line generalizations about nationalities, and about practically everything else, so she was particularly well equipped for research at this level of generalization. Her main collaborator was Geoffrey Gorer. As early as 1941, at the Institute of Human Relations at Yale University, this scholar of English origin and indetermined specialization had studied the national characteristics of the Japanese. During the war Gorer's reports had recommended that neither the Mikado himself nor the abstract Throne should ever be attacked; indeed they should never be mentioned other than respectfully. Attacking the Mikado would be like attacking the Pope for medieval Catholics; it would merely excite anger against foolish sacrilege. Japanese society is inconceivable for the Japanese without a ritual head.

Gorer also recommended that the United States should adopt a "firm fatherly tone toward the Japanese". His suggestion was misinterpreted by the Office of the Coordinator of Information, which in a broadcast to Japan stated that "The United States is your father". The error, Mead later recalled,

was ours. There is no 'firm, fatherly tone' in the United States such as Gorer, an Englishman, had wished to evoke. The best we could have done to carry out Gorer's intent would have been to say "Talk to the Japanese as if they are fourth graders and you are fifth". (Quoted from Howard 1984, 275-76).

Ever the great organizer and tireless fund raiser, Mead succeeded in assembling a team of 120 people from 14 different disciplines and 16 nationalities. They should not get too smitten with quantifying, Mead had warned. But they soon ran into difficulties. Gorer's 1948 book *The American People* struck reviewers as an attempt to psychoanalyse a whole community. In the *Manchester Guardian* the renowned Alistair Cooke considered this "as perilous as brain surgery" and concluded

Mr. Gorer is a disciple of Malinowsky and a colleague of Margaret Mead. It makes you wonder if it's true what they say about the Trobriand Islanders. (Quoted from Howard 1984, 277).

This challenge has certainly been taken up, if only after the death of Margaret Mead (I am, of course, referring to the notorious attack on her studies of Samoa by the New Zealand anthropologist Derek Freeman, 1983).

Gorer's most celebrated but also most ridiculed idea, was his "swaddling hypothesis", which he developed after repeated interviews with representatives of pre-Soviet Russia (Gorer & Rickman 1949). He attempted to explain the "Russian character" on the basis of the Russian practice of swaddling their babies in order to make them stop kicking and go to sleep. This habit, he suggested, made adults suspicious and despotic: it leads to the idea that any restraint is unbearable; and yet, one is enormously strong and must therefore be swaddled in order to keep one from breaking things. Because of this profound childhood experience, Russians

tend to oscillate suddenly and unpredictably from one attitude to its contrary, especially from violence to gentleness, from excessive activity to passivity, from orgiastic indulgence to ascetic abstemiousness. They endure physical suffering with great stoicism and are indifferent about the physical sufferings of others. They also tend to oscillate between unconscious fears of isolation and loneliness, and an absence of feelings of individuality so that the self is, as it were, merged with its peers in a "soul-collective". They have deep warmth and sympathy for all whom (at a given time) they consider as "the same as" themselves; they direct their vague and unconscious hostility on all whom they consider "different to" themselves, paying little attention to which figure is momentarily the focus for their hostility. They seem to expect hostility from all who are "different". (Gorer & Rickham 1949, 189).

The "swaddling hypothesis" effectively killed the anthropological and behavioural study of national character. Maybe such overambitious explanations hold some truth at some level of abstraction or other but enemies soon nicknamed national character studies "diaperology" as a shorthand for the vogue of describing cultures in terms of psychoanalysis. Much the same happened to the studies of the "authoritarian personality" by the refugee critical social scientists of the Frankfurt School headed by Theodor W. Adorno. The point of departure for Adorno's study had been anti-Semitism, but he soon reached the conclusion that this was only one aspect of a certain kind of personality structure and not a separable quality itself. According to Adorno the result was a

demonstration of close correspondence in the type of approach and outlook [which] a subject is likely to have in a great variety of areas, ranging from the most intimate features of family and sex adjustment through relationships to other people in general, to religion and to social and political philosophy. Thus a basically hierarchical, authoritarian exploitive parent-child relationship is apt to carry over into a power-oriented, exploitively dependent attitude toward one's sex partner and one's God and may well culminate in a political philosophy and social outlook which has no room for anything but a desperate clinging to whatever appears to be strong and a disdainful rejection of whatever is relegated to the bottom. (Adorno *et al.* 1950, 43).

The implications of this could be very far reaching indeed if they were true or rather specific. The problem, unfortunately, was that the empirical research based on randomly chosen persons in New York turned out a disproportionate number of "authoritarian personalities" among Jews. As they were supposed to be the victims of the politics of "authoritarian personalities" the results were soon discarded. The approach simply explained too much and thus nothing which, is why we have not heard much of it for a long time.

The approach was still loved by Potter in 1954, but he was a late-comer, not a new beginner. Mead still defended the approach in 1961 in her contribution to an evaluation of the psycho-sociological work of Riesman on the changing American character (Mead 1961). Elaborated equivalents of Riesman's attempt to describe the American character have recently come back in force but in the late 1950's when Riesman called the whole thing off it already seemed completely outdated. In the above mentioned inaugural lecture he happily endorsed the tendency of the younger social scientists to get away from the grand questions about national character and suggested it be left to the historians because:

the differences among men that will increasingly matter will not arise from geographical location and will hence be more within the reach of the individual ... I can envisage a world in which we shall become more different from each other than ever before, and in which, as a result, national character will be an even more elusive concept than it is at present. (Riesman 1958, 603).

This was an early prophecy of what turned out to become the predominant theme of the 60's and 70's, differences in race, class, and gender. This new sociological approach of investigating differences instead of similarities was proclaimed in 1963 by Nathan Glazer (a former collaborator of Riesman) and Daniel Patrick Moynihan (a colleague from Harvard, now a long-serving senator for the State of New York) in a book with the programmatic title *Beyond the Melting Pot*. As they write in the preface:

It is an effort to trace the role of ethnicity in the tumultuous, varied, endlessly complex life of New York City. It is time, we believe, that such an effort be made, albeit doomed inevitably to approximation and to inaccuracy, and although it cannot but on occasion give offense to those very persons for whom we have the strongest feeling of fellowship and common purpose. The notion that the intense and unprecedented mixture of ethnic and religious groups in American life was soon to blend into a homogenous end product has outlived its usefulness, and also its credibility ... *The point about the melting pot, as we say later, is that it did not happen* (Glazer & Moynihan 1963, V, emphases added).

Cautious and suspicious by nature and upbringing, the historians never accepted the invitation (or challenge?) from the sociologist David Riesman. Instead, the torch was handed over to some brave and foolhardy representatives of the relatively young discipline of political science. Historicizing political scientists such as Seymour Martin Lipset ventured into the field. He approached the dangerous subject soberly, well prepared as he was from previous historical sociological studies of areas as different as contemporary Canada (Lipset 1950) and Nazi Germany (Lipset 1960). As a political scientist he was inclined to contrast a so-called historical with a so-called comparative approach. Yet the merits of his investigation of the revolutionary elements of the American political culture are due to the fact that he did not overemphasize the difference between the two:

The analyst of societies must choose between a primarily historical or a primarily comparative approach for a given piece of research. He must choose simply because each of these requires a different mode of generalization. But even if he chooses one approach, he cannot ignore the other. Without examining social relations in *different* countries, it is impossible to know to what extent a given factor actually has the effect attributed to it in a *single* country. For example, if it is true that the German *Ständestaat* (rigid status system) has contributed to the authoritarian pattern of German politics, why is it that similar status systems in Sweden and Switzerland are associated with very different political patterns? ... On the other hand the analyst obviously cannot ignore specific historical events in attempting to assess what is common to the evolution of different nations ... In the end the choice between a primarily historical or a primarily comparative approach is a matter of relative emphasis. (Lipset 1963, 9-10).

This and similar approaches opened up a whole field of comparative studies under the heading "political culture" (Almond & Verba 1963). Unfortunately they did not follow Lipset's sound advice regarding the historical specificity of their investigations. Interesting descriptions of differing political behaviour and values in various countries were presented but very often the explanations only amounted to sheer platitudes. This was due to the fact that, as is so often the case in comparative studies, they worked from an underlying assumption which was never made explicit either to the readers or to themselves. In this case it was the idea that a two-party system of the Anglo-Saxon type constitutes the only "normal" and viable form of democracy.

All these attempts came to an end in the sixties under the combined onslaught of the student rebellion and the demand for quantitative methodological refinements. Out went any talk of "national identity", and in came race, class, and gender. The socio-linguists dropped the very notion of "national language", as they were only able to define it as a dialect (sociolect) equipped with an army and a navy. Each person has his or her own linguistic "identity". The onslaught of the numbers turned out even more devastating. Very few people seemed to be able to remember the original questions as they went on refining the tools in order to come up with more precise answers. The grand old man of quantitative social history, Charles Tilly, would not agree, I am sure, but he seems to me one of the few who has kept trying to apply the numbers game to the grand questions (Tilly 1975). For the rest we have ended up knowing more and more about less and less. Hence the popularity among historians of the *Annales* School. Somehow they never got caught as much in numbers for the sake of numbers. An influential segment of the group even returned to the grand old questions of nineteenth century historians under the label *histoire des mentalités*. Interestingly, they rarely, if ever, addressed questions of national identity. The reason could be that the school after all is French! And French national identity never seems to produce the kind of doubt involved in most other national discourses. It is French and that's it.

In the last decade or so, interest in nationalism and national entities has resurfaced. Old books are being reissued (Kedourie 1960/85), and many new have been added. The American sociologist Robert Bellah recently led a team of pcychologists and sociologists in a venture to return to the kind of questions rejected by Riesman in 1958. He even dared to break down the rigid fence between is and ought and staked out some guidelines for a better America. In search of theoretical and methodological help, he went back to the French social philosopher Alexis de Tocqueville as the person who has offered the most pene-trating and comprehensive analysis of the relation between character and society ever written. In *De la démocratie en Amérique* (1835-40) Tocqueville defined his use of the classical concept *mores* (in French *moeurs*) in a paragraph entitled *Influence of Mores upon the Maintenance of a Democratic Republic in the United States*. It runs like this:

I have said earlier that I considered mores to be one of the great general causes responsible for the maintenance of a democratic republic in the United States. I here mean the term "mores" (*moeurs*) to have its original Latin meaning; I mean it to apply not only to "moeurs" in the strict sense, which might be called the habits of the heart, but also to the different notions possessed by men, the various opinions current among them, and the sum of ideas that shape mental habits. So I use the word to cover the whole moral and intellectual state of a people. It is not my aim to describe American mores; just now I am looking for the elements in them which help to support political institutions. (Tocqueville 1835-40, 287).[1]

Tocqueville's "habits of the heart" are very close to what later scholars have called national political culture or mentality and that is why Robert Bellah and his group have taken this phrase as the title of their book. They situate their own study in the tradition of Robert and Helen Lynd (1929 and 1937), David Riesman (1950), Hervé Varenne (1977), and David Potter (1954) though the latter is strangely omitted from their overview of research in the field. Through in-depth interviews they identify four dominant social characters and correlate them with four main political traditions and thus come up with a convincing description of the main ingredients in the political culture and mentality of the white middle class majority of the USA today.

Yet, the methodologically most cogent and convincing explanation of national identity is the functionalist position most forcefully represented by the Czech-British anthropologist and philosopher Ernest Gellner. For him, pre-modern "agro-literate" societies had no place for nations or nationalism. The élites and the food producing masses were always separated along cultural lines and no ideology able to overcome this divide was generated. For Gellner nations and nationalism are the exclusive outcomes of and preconditions for industrial society. Modern industry requires a mobile, literate, technologically equipped population and the modern state is the only agency capable of providing such a work force through its support for a mass, public, compulsory and standardized education system. The required cultural homogeneity of modern society has been generated through the ideology of nationalism. The nationalisms in their turn have invented nations that did not previously exist though they did according to the nationalistic mythology. Nations and nationalisms are basically contingent and arbitrary phenomena.

Whereas traditional society was determined by structure, modernity on the contrary relies on culture. This is why the boundaries of a nation-state are determined by the area in which its degrees are able to exercise a monopoly. In a lecture commemorating the anthropologist A.R. Radcliffe-Brown, Gellner analyses modern society as follows:

A society that lives by growth must needs pay a certain price. The price of growth is eternal innovation. Innovation in turn presupposes unceasing occupational mobility, certainly as between generations, and often within single life-spans ... The consequence of all this is the necessity of universal literacy and education, and a cultural homogeneity or at least continuity ... So culture, which had once resembled the air men breathed, and of which they were seldom properly aware, suddenly becomes perceptible and significant ... So at the very same time that men become fully and nervously aware of their culture and its vital relevance to their vital interests, they also lose much of the capacity to revere their society through the mystical symbolism of a religion. So there is both a push and a pull towards revering a shared culture *directly*, unmediated in its own terms: culture is now clearly visible, and access to it has become man's most precious asset. Yet the religious symbols through which, if Durkheim is to be believed, it was worshipped, cease to be serviceable. So — let culture be worshipped directly in its own name. *That is nationalism.* (Gellner 1983b, 15-16, emphases added).

An admirably clear and concise explanation of the ideology of nationalism! But this modernistic functionalist and instrumentalist approach does not explain why certain national identities have been chosen and others not; it has nothing to say about how the present national entities came about and why precisely these. This failure has given rise to a different line of thinking, which concentrates on the *ethnies* preceding the modern nation-states. The best known protagonists of this kind of thinking are the British sociologist Anthony Smith and the American political scientist John Armstrong. In a discussion of the other positions Anthony Smith presents them as follows:

In this enquiry, we shall have to depart from the assumptions of both the main schools of thought on the origin and formation of nations. While we can no longer regard the nation as a given of social existence, a "primordial" and natural unit of human association outside time, neither can we accept that it is a wholly modern phenomenon, be it the "nervous tic of capitalism", or the necessary form and culture of an industrial society. While the revolutions of industrial capitalism, the bureaucratic state and secular mass-education represent a watershed in human history comparable to the Neolithic transition, they have not obliterated or rendered obsolete many of the cultures and identities formed in pre-modern eras. They have certainly transformed many of them; others they have destroyed, yet others, amalgamated and revived. The fate of these cultures and identities has depended as much upon their internal properties as upon the uneven incidence of the modern revolutions. *This is because the constituents of these identities and cultures — the myths, memories, symbols and values — can often be adapted to new circumstances by being accorded new meanings and new functions.* Hence it becomes important to enquire into the "state of cultural identity" of a given community on the eve of its exposure to the new revolutionary forces, in order to locate the bases of its subsequent evolution into a fully-fledged "nation". (Smith 1986, 3, emphases added).

After a brief summary of the three dominant positions, Smith continues:

In a sense the "modernists" are right. Nationalism, as an ideology and movement, is a phenomenon that dates from the later eighteenth century, while a specifically "national" sentiment can be discerned a little earlier than the late fifteenth or sixteenth centuries in Western Europe. The "nation-state", too, as a political norm is quite modern. ... Even the "nation" and its "national character" would appear to be modern. ... Yet there are also difficulties with this view. *For we find in pre-modern eras, even in the ancient world, striking parallels to the "modern" idea of national identity and character, in the way Greeks and Romans looked on people who did not share their cultures or come from their city-states*; in the way in which ancient Egyptians looked upon Nubians and Asiatics; and in Mesopotamian and Biblical distinctions drawn between different "peoples". (Smith 1986, 11, emphases added).

Neither of the existing positions satisfies his requirements. Instead Smith attempts to formulate an alternative as-well-as position rejecting the claims of the modernists on the one side, who claim a radical break between pre-modern units and sentiments and modern nations and nationalism, and the perennialists on the other, who see nations as simply larger, updated versions of pre-modern ties and sentiments. In order to distance his analysis from the sweeping claims of both sides he introduces the concept of the *ethnie* or ethnic community and its symbols attaching crucial importance to the concepts of form, identity, myth, symbols and codes of communication. In contrast to John Armstrong he wants to uphold the distinction between ethnic community and nation, between ethnic identity and nationalism. His aim throughout the book is to trace the ethnic foundations and roots of modern nations thus modifying the modernist positions. For Smith the core of ethnic identity, "ethnicity", has been transmitted in historical records and individual experiences in "the quartet of myths, memories, values and symbols and in the characteristic forms or styles and genres of certain historical configurations of populations." (1986, 15). He lays special emphasis on the myth-symbol complex and the so-called *mythomoteur* or constitutive myth of the ethnic polity (the concept of *mythomoteur* has been developed by Armstrong who borrowed it from a Spanish study of the Visigoths). Both indicate the vital role of myths and symbols as embodying the corpus of beliefs and sentiments which the guardians of ethnicity preserve, diffuse and transmit to future generations. According to Smith, the special qualities and durability of the *ethnies* are to be found, not in their ecological locations, nor in their class configurations, nor yet in their military and political relationships but in their complexes of myths and symbols.

The problem, of course, is how to define *ethnos* in terms more precisely and coherently than did our Greek predecessors. According to Liddell and Scott's *Greek-English Lexicon* of 1869, the Greek term *ethnos* covers a variety of senses. In the *Iliad* we hear of *ethnos etairôn*, a band of comrades, of *ethnos laôn*, a host of men, as well as of *ethnos Achaiôn* or *Lykiôn*, the tribe of Achaeans or Lycians along with *klyta ethnea nekrôn*, glorious hosts of the dead in the Odyssey; of *ethnea melissôn* or *ornithôn*, a swarm of bees or flocks of birds again in the *Iliad*; *ethnos anerôn* or *gynaikôn*, the race of men or women, in Pindar; and the *Mêdikon ethnos*, the Median people or nation in Herodotus (1,101), as well as in the Attic orators. We also find the term used of a particular caste or tribe, as the caste of heralds (*ethnos kêrykikon*) in Plato's *Republic*, or of sex, as *to thêly ethnos*, in Xenophon. Finally, the word came to be applied to the Gentiles (*ta ethnê*) by the New Testament writers and Church Fathers, that is, all other peoples than the Christians and the Jews. (cf. Smith 1986, 21).

In all these usages, the common factor appears to be a number of people or animals living and acting together. Herodotus in his account of the early Medes (1,101,55) and later on of the Persians (1,125,66) suggests that tribes (*genos*) are sub-divisions of an *ethnos*. But he is never consistent nor systematic in his use of the words, which indicates that it was of no great importance to him nor to his audience. *Ethnos* seems to be more suited to cultural than biological or kinship differences. Like the Enlightenment philosophers Holberg and Montesquieu, he deduced the "national" character of a people from the nature of their political regime:

Thus Athens went from strength to strength, and proved, if proof were needed, how noble a thing freedom is, not in one respect only, but in all; for while they were oppressed under a despotic government, they had no better success in war than any of their neighbours, yet once the yoke was flung off, they proved the finest fighters in the world. This clearly shows that, so long as they were held down by authority, they deliberately shirked their duty in the field, as slaves shirk working for their masters; but when freedom was won, then every man amongst them longed to distinguish himself. (Herodotus 5,78,339).

Aristotle subscribed to a more deterministic and less cultural theory of national character. In chapter 7 of his *Politics* he wrote:

The races that live in cold regions and those of Europe are full of courage and passion but somewhat lacking in skill and brain-power; for this reason, while remaining generally independent, they lack political cohesion and the ability to rule over others. On the other hand the Asiatic races have both brains and skill but are lacking in courage and will-power; so they have remained enslaved and subject. The Hellenic race, occupying a mid-position geographically, has a measure of both. Hence it continues to be free, to have the best political institutions, and to be capable of ruling all others, given a single constitution. (Aristotle *Politics* 1327b 23-34, transl. Sinclair, 269).

One or the other of these two theories is probably the way most ordinary people think about the subject even today. Just like Herodotus, Plato, and Aristotle they have no qualms in discussing the subject in terms of "primitive ethnography". But modern scholars have. Some of us have come to believe that identity is only what we say it is, no more no less, however difficult that may be to accept from a Freudian point of view. In other and more complicated words sociologists and historians have learned to understand identity primarily as a discourse and not as the result of an "essence". The content is the form as some would put it, and not vice versa. National myths are real to the degree people believe in them and act accordingly. This, of course, does not imply that they are true. The crucial distinction between reality and truth is lost in Anthony Smith's otherwise laudable and methodologically refined approach.

A sociologist specializing in Indonesia, Benedict Anderson, has tried to moderate between the two antagonistic positions, functionalism and primordialism respectively, by introducing the term "imagined communities" (1983). He defines the nation as:

an imagined political community — and imagined as both inherently limited and sovereign. It is *imagined* because the members of even the smallest nation will never know most of their fellow-members, meet them, or even hear of them, yet in the minds of each lives the image of their communion. (Anderson 1983, 15).

The rise of these new imagined communities he explains by the rise of the new printing technologies, "print-capitalism" as he calls it. With the decline of religion and the rise of the printed word it became possible to "imagine" communities, at once sovereign and limited, through which a sense of immortality for the individual could be evoked and with which otherwise anonymous individuals could identify. Through the printed word, individuals who did not know each other, were able to inhabit the same homogeneous and empty time and space dimensions and believe they belonged to the same community as people who were already dead, not yet born or whom they would never meet. These "imagined communities", nations, came to serve a crucial psychological as well as economic need under the peculiar modern conditions of secular capitalism.

The other important factor in Anderson's approach is his definition of the precise meaning of the "invention" of national and ethnic identity. He criticizes Gellner's radical reversal of the relation between nationalism and national identity:

Nationalism is not the awakening of nations to self-consciousness: it *invents* nations where they do not exist — but it does need some pre-existing differentiating marks to work on, even if, as indicated, these are purely negative. (Gellner 1964, 168).

Gellner has softened this formulation somewhat in his latest book on the subject but not changed the thrust of the argument:

Critics of nationalism who denounce the political movement but tacitly accept the existence of nations, do not go far enough. Nations as a natural, God-given way of classifying men, as an inherent though long-delayed political destiny, are a myth; nationalism, which sometimes takes pre-existing cultures and turns them into nations, sometimes invents, and often obliterates pre-existing cultures: *that* is a reality, for better or worse, and in general an inescapable one. (Gellner 1983a, 48-49).

According to Anderson, the drawback to these formulations is that Gellner is so anxious to show that nationalism masquerades under false pretences that he assimilates "invention" to "fabrication" and "falsity", rather than to "imagining" and "creation". He therefore replaces this approach with another, inspired by the British historian E.J. Hobsbawm. In 1983 Hobsbawm together with Terence Ranger edited an influential collection of essays with the provocative title, *The Invention of Tradition*. In the introduction Hobsbawm explains the apparent paradox of the title as follows:

The term "invented tradition" is used in a broad, but not imprecise sense. It includes both "traditions" actually invented, constructed and formally instituted and those emerging in a less easily traceable manner within a brief and dateable period ... "Invented tradition" is taken to mean a set of practices, normally governed by overtly or tacitly accepted rules and of a ritual or symbolic nature, which seek to inculcate certain values and norms of behaviour by repetition, which automatically implies continuity with the past. In fact, where possible, they normally attempt to establish continuity with a suitable historic past. (Hobsbawm in Hobsbawm & Ranger 1983, 1).

The detailed examples in the book are much more telling — and fun — than these definitions. It is, however, of the utmost importance to be precise when using a terminology the implications of which differ so much from those of everyday language. "Construction" might be a better metaphor had it not already been destroyed by the "deconstructionist" philosophers and literary critics, and were it not for the element of arbitrariness implied in it. Therefore, historians have decided to stick to the term "invention", regardless of the dangers.

   Anderson's definition of national identity implies a less crudely functionalist explanation than Gellner's. Furthermore, it seeks to integrate social psychological factors, but explains these through specific social and technological developments

instead of arguing from vague assumptions of psychological needs among individuals. But it is possible to go even further. In a highly original analysis of
Danish national characteristics the anthropologist Michael Harbsmeier has
developed Benedict Anderson's framework further by arguing that national identity, unlike many other forms of social identity, is totally dependent upon the
imagined or real acknowledgment of this identity as national otherness by others,
i.e. other nations (Harbsmeier 1986, 52). This is a significant step forward. In
national discourse nations do not understand themselves as universal phenomena
as some religions do; and they do not not take their legitimacy from instances
outside of this world, as do many empires. Yet, in fact there is a universal element
in the modern national discourse which sets it fundamentally apart from ancient
usage.

When the Greeks called other peoples Barbarians, when the Christians classified
non-Christians as Gentiles and when "civilized" Chinese or 18th century Europeans
called other peoples "uncivilized" they did this in order to make them recognize
their inferior status. A basically asymmetrical relation was at stake. Modern
national identities are different. When people call themselves Danish, German,
English or French they implicitly recognize other nationalitities as belonging to
comparable categories. As is often the case, they may assume that theirs is the
better national identity, but they normally do not deny to others the right to belong
to a different national group. As a matter of fact, discrimination between people
is the whole point of modern nationalism. The positive definition of one national
identity always turns out to rely on exclusion and negative characteristics; Danish
is not-German, French is not-German and not-English and so on and so forth. (For
a recent study of such a national discourse, see Østergård 1991b on the Danish
conception of the Germans.) One's own nation may be thought superior but though
the reciprocity often is reverse it follows logically that they belong to the same
set of categories. This is the gulf that separates the concept of modern national
identity from that of antiquity.

This brings us to the world of national stereotypes. We do keep talking as if
national stereotypes somehow do exist out there in the "real" world. Even the most
refined scholar who would never dare enter such a word in his or her professional
work lapses in or back to "primitive ethnography" when going abroad and
attending learned conferences. Everybody knows "French" rhetoric, "American"
aggressiveness, or "Scandinavian" moodiness regardless of the number of times
one has been proven wrong. So, why not take as a point of departure these very

stereotypes and see where they lead us? Such an approach might be entitled the discursive approach. In delineating such an approach we can find help in the writings of today's leading functionalist anthropologist, the Norwegian Fredrik Barth. He has proposed a social interaction model of ethnic identity that does not posit a fixed "character" or "essence" for the group, but examines the perceptions of its members which distinguish them from other groups (Barth 1969, 9-10). Concentration on these attitudinal boundary mechanisms has three major advantages:

1. Because ethnicity is defined by boundaries, both the cultural and the biological content of the group can alter as long as the boundary mechanisms are maintained. 2. Although Barth points out that his boundaries may have territorial counterparts, he emphasizes that ethnic groups are "not merely or necessarily based on the occupation of exclusive territories." 3. His boundary approach facilitates consideration of other ethnic phenomena, exotic from the
modern European standpoint, such as the use of languages as alternative codes rather than ethnic identifying symbols or prescriptive communication media.

Primitive man, according to this interpretation, was disturbed by the uncanny experience of confronting others who, perforce, remained mute in response to his attempts at communication, whether oral or through symbolic gestures. Terms like *goyim*, *barbaroi*, and *nemtsi* all imply such perceptions of the human incompleteness of persons who could not communicate with the in-group, which constituted the only "real men". Usually, in their original application such terms singled out one or two alien neighbours, and by reference to such aliens large ethnic groups came to recognize their own relatively close relationship. Thus the extensive Germanic groups defined themselves as the peoples "between Wend and Walsche", never using either term to refer to any group that spoke a Germanic tongue. Just as the real referent for Wend shifted, probably from Finnic reindeer nomads located northeast of the Germanic elements to the Slavs who later occupied the Eastern limits of the Germanic sphere, the referent for "Walsche" changed from Celt alone to Celt, Latinized Celt, and Roman alike, on the southwest confines of the Germanic world.

Shifting the focus of the investigation from the internal characteristics of the group to its self-perceived boundaries is, of course, only a start toward an examination of ethnicity in history. The boundary approach implies that ethnicity is a bundle of shifting interactions rather than a nuclear component of social organization. It is precisely this complex and shifting quality that has repelled many social scientists from analyzing ethnic identity. Most of those who have tried have been attracted by the simplifying assumption that each ethnic group occupies an exclusive territory. Once one abandons the principle of territorial exclusivity, one must recognize that the phenomenon of ethnicity is part of a continuum of social collectives, including notably, classes and religious bodies. Over a sufficiently long time each may change into one of the others.

The primary characteristic of ethnic boundaries is attitudinal. In their origins and in their most fundamental effects, ethnic boundary mechanisms exist in the minds of people. Most often symbolic boundary mechanisms are words. Such words are traffic lights warning a group member when he or she is approaching a barrier separating their group from another. This intense power of language may be illustrated by early Yiddish. It was basically an Old High German dialect, but rigorously excluded certain words in the German environment that had specifically Christian connotations. For example, *sëganón*, "to bless", was rejected because it derived from Latin *signare*, "to make the sign of the Cross", in favour of retaining the neutral form *bentshn* from latin *benedicere*, "to speak well", which earlier Jewish communities had incorporated in Southern Laaz, their Romance dialect (Armstrong 1982, 8). Such verbal symbolic devices safeguarded group identity against penetration of Christian concepts. But, as the psychoanalyst Suzanne K. Langer once pointed out in a commentary on Ernst Cassirer's theory of language and myth, significant symbols also include gestures, drawings, musical sounds, etc. (Langer 1949, 386). To an extraordinary degree, ethnic symbolic communication is communication over time, sometimes over very long periods. Hence, the persistence of the symbol is more significant than its precise origins in the past. Persistence is closely related to the incorporation of individual symbols, verbal and nonverbal, in a mythic structure (Lévi-Strauss 1962). Over long periods of time, the legitimizing power of individual mythic structures tends to be enhanced by fusion with other myths in a *mythomoteur* (Armstrong 1982, 8-9, 129-67, 293), defining identity in relation to a specific polity. Identification of these complex structures as mythic does not imply that they are false, any more than references to religious myths call into question their theological validity. The philosopher Eric Dardel claims that demonstrable historical validity is not the critical aspect of the *mythomoteur*:

The mythic past cannot be dated, it is a part of "before time" or, better, outside time ... Primordial actions are lost "in the night of time", what happened "once" (nobody knows when) goes in a floating and many-layered time without temporal location ... [The myth narrator or epic poet] draws the audience of the story away, but only to make them set themselves at the desired distance. (Dardel 1954, 38).

A most significant effect of the myth recital is to arouse an intense awareness among the group members of their "common fate". From the perspective of myth-symbol theory, common fate is simply the extent to which an episode, whether historical or "purely mythical", arouses intense affect by stressing individual's solidarity against an alien force, that is, by enhancing the salience of boundary perceptions. Consequently, the symbolic rather than the material aspects of common fate are decisive for the establishing of the collective identity — and probably the individual identity as well but that is not my primary concern here.

In short, the discourse of national identity is at the same time the vehicle *and* the content of national identity. In this case as in so many others "the medium is the message" as Marshall McLuhan put it in 1962. The ancient Greeks did not believe this to be the case nor do the majority of today's nation states. Yet, the discourse of national identity has changed to such a degree that it has become impossible for us today to understand what was implied in the language of the ancients or for them to understand the real universality of the discriminating discourse of modern national and ethnic identity.

1. I have discussed the further implications of this definition in an essay on "Tocqueville and the contemporary study of American political culture and national character", Østergård 1988a, 153-54)

LANGUAGE AND LITERACY
IN EARLY HELLENISTIC EGYPT

Dorothy J. Thompson

In ancient Egypt, even the gods communicated in writing. That at least is the conclusion to be drawn from the New Kingdom tale of the contest between Horus and Seth for the kingship of Egypt, vacant through the death of Osiris (Lichtheim 1976, 214-23). In an attempt to establish the rightful succession, first Neith and later Osiris himself are written to by the Ennead, the Nine Gods of Heliopolis. In this exchange of divine letters it is the god Thoth, Thoth in his ibis-manifestation, who both writes and, when a reply is received, reads this out aloud before the court of the gods. It was not only gods, however, who communicated in written form. Princes too might read and write, like Prince Naneferkaptah in the demotic story of Setne Khamwas, whose practice of reading the hieroglyphs he found inscribed on tombs and holy shrines led him to the more dangerous book of magic, written by Thoth himself (Lichtheim 1980, 127-38).[1] In both these traditional tales Thoth reflects in the divine sphere the mundane role of the literate scribe. The profession of scribe in Egypt was a standard one and, if we may believe the writings of those who practised it, a highly-respected profession. So a father exhorts his son in the Middle Kingdom text known as the *Satire of the Trades* (Lichtheim 1975, 185):

> Read the end of the Kemit-Book,
> You'll find this saying there:
> A scribe at whatever post in town,
> He will not suffer in it;
> As he fills another's need
> He will not lack rewards.
> I don't see a calling like it
> Of which this saying could be said.
> ---

It's the greatest of callings,
There's none like it in the land.

In Egypt, the profession of scribe served as the standard paradigm of occupational security, and the value of education was reckoned in the rewards such a job might bring.[2] Scribes were regularly connected with the temples and it was here that sacred hieroglyphs and the hieratic script were taught; many priests were also scribes.[3] Whether those trained primarily in the demotic script, whose main concerns were with legal documents and the demands of the royal administration, learnt their skills in the same schools is uncertain; whilst a general temple context seems likely, some form of more secular schooling is possible.[4] So when Alexander of Macedon conquered Egypt in 332 BC, he took over from Persian domination a country with an established tradition both of writing and of the scribal education needed to impart such skills. For the Greeks, Egypt had long been viewed as the source of wisdom, of civilisation and indeed, for Plato, of writing itself.[5] And, as the importance of writing was valued, so those who could write held influence and, not surprisingly, employed their skills and control of the written word to reinforce their position in society.[6] The uses of writing were many; those who wrote were few, and even some of these might delegate the skills they had. The gods used Thoth, others the more lowly scribe.

The Macedonian conquest of Egypt brought some major changes to the country. When, on the Conqueror's death in 323, Ptolemy son of Lagos seized control in the name of Alexander's son, a new dynasty of Pharaohs was now in place, their rule legitimised by the Conqueror's corpse. Besides a change of capital (to Alexandria), came a change in language — to Greek. And with the language came the Greek tradition of literacy, which differed from that of Egypt. For in classical Greece, following the adoption from Phoenicia of an alphabetical script in the eighth century BC, literacy had become reasonably widespread through society. Here, in a very different social context, writing served a wider range of purposes. In Greece it was used for public records, for city laws and accounts, as well as for personal dedications, private communications and for other secular purposes.[7] Indeed, some of the differences in the two societies, Egyptian and Greek, may be seen reflected in the differing uses of writing within them.

This is the background to my present enquiry. What I am interested in considering, in the context of these two different traditions of literacy, is the effect on Egypt of Alexander's conquest and the subsequent establishment of Ptolemaic power in the country.[8] How did the Egyptians react to the new situation, and what effect did the Graeco-Macedonian conquest have on Egyptian literacy and, through this, the structure of Egyptian society? What were the implications of this change of ruler, the imposition of a foreign pharaoh, for the inhabitants of Egypt, and how far and how quickly did the language and culture of the minority immigrant group affect the majority? What, if anything, may the uses of writing, both Greek and Egyptian, tell of the relative positions of power within this new society? Through focusing on language and literacy, what insight may we gain into the development and the problems of the new immigrant administration? Can such an approach help answer the more general question of the personnel and of the problems involved in the setting up of the new regime? Finally, it would be interesting to consider how far the Egyptian picture might be relevant to the other Hellenistic kingdoms that followed Alexander, but that is outside my present scope. My two main concerns here may be quite simply stated as the nature of the new regime and the rôle of literacy within it.

I should start by defining what I understand by literacy. What I am talking about is the basic ability to read and write. Sometimes reading exists without writing, but here I encompass both in the term. In Greek documents we meet those who describe themselves as "writing slowly" — these I am prepared to include. We also frequently meet those described, in official contexts, as either "not knowing letters" or "without letters". Such a term is more difficult to assess since sometimes such "illiterates" may be literate in another language, generally Egyptian (Youtie 1966, 1971a, 1971b). For Egypt was a bilingual society, and in such a society the picture is inevitably complex; the process of integration, involving both language and literacy, forms a fascinating, though sometimes daunting, subject of study. The case of Paraguay may be adduced. For in twentieth-century Paraguay both Spanish and the native Indian Guarani have continued to play important rôles. Each language apparently enjoys its separate sphere or area of usage and this division of functions has been maintained both by the fact that a single Indian language has been predominant and by the country's isolation, producing a very different picture from elsewhere in South America. In Paraguay Spanish is used as the language of the courts (or at least for legal records and laws), for public documents, and for official use in all government departments and the legislature; it is the language of schooling and the official language of the military (though all basic military instruction is given in Guarani). Advertising is in Spanish (though sometimes Guarani on radio) and Spanish is the language of the seminaries and of churches in the capital, though not the countryside. Guarani in contrast is never formally taught but has persisted as the main language of the countryside despite 300 years of Spanish contact. Some plays and entertainments are in Guarani, as are many songs. On the popular level Guarani is the language of the workplace and, regularly, of the countryside. In 1968, 92% of the population spoke Guarani and 52% were bilingual in Guarani and Spanish, with a higher proportion of bilingualism existing among the men (Rubin 1968).

Whilst this sort of comparative picture if obviously of interest in helping pose questions for Egypt, it can never be of direct relevance.[9] Egypt was already a highly developed society when the Greeks arrived and the continuation, until the Roman conquest, of an Egyptian legal system is likely to have played an important part in the survival of Egyptian literacy. Bilingualism, too, is a question only of spoken language and not of literate skills. My interest in this sort of comparative material is as an indication of how complex a bilingual society may be (Grosjean 1972). Given the nature of the evidence, trying to estimate how many could read or write in one or other language, in Egyptian or in Greek, is not in itself a particularly useful exercise, since any estimate is likely to be so uncertain as to be open to question. More profitable perhaps is the attempt to establish the areas of society in which literacy in either language may be found, and to identify the activities for which literacy may or may not be required, or even desirable. We need also to consider the role of dual literacy. Were there areas in which not just bilingualism but also dual literacy was necessary and how does the picture change over time? These are the sorts of questions I want to look at, but what follows is only a preliminary consideration of the early years of the new regime.

Before further investigation of the experience of these years, two factors should be stressed. First, we should remember that others from outside had ruled Egypt before. Most recently, from 525-404 and again from 341/40-332 BC, Persia had controlled the country, with Aramaic as the language of the administration. Persian kings however were absentee pharaohs, ruling through satraps with military backing and a well-tried system of provincial rule. How deep into Egyptian culture the Persians penetrated is hard to gauge (Ray 1988), and the Egyptian reaction to Persian rule is rarely known. There were those who, through collaboration, would benefit from the occupation, men like Udjahorresne who passed a successful and varied career, first under the Egyptian pharaoh Amasis and later at the Persian court, and who finally returned to Egypt from Persia with grants to help his fellow Saites recover from the effects of the Persian invasion (Lichtheim 1980, 36-41).

Secondly to be noted is the fact that for the Egyptians this was not their first contact with Greeks. A Greek presence in Egypt dates back to Psammetichus I, who in the seventh century had established his rule with the help of Ionian (and Carian) mercenaries whom he later settled in the Delta at Stratopeda (Herodotus 2,152.5; 154). Herodotus indeed records (2,154.2) that he took the children of these troops to instruct his interpreters in the Greek language. Then there was Naukratis with its mixed Greek community and Memphis with its Helleno-memphites, descendants of the Ionian mercenaries moved there by Amasis in the sixth century (Herodotus 2,178-9; 154.3). Greek language and literacy had continued in use in these two cities, and their communities were to form an important source of personnel and information for the new Macedonian rulers. From the conquest of 332 BC, however, Greek was the language of those who controlled Egypt, and from 304 BC, when the Macedonian general Ptolemy son of Lagos was recognised as king, it was the language both of the new pharaoh's court and of his friends.

In the long-term, the impact of the new rulers' language on Egypt was to be considerable. Under the Ptolemies there is a notable increase in the volume of surviving documentation, especially in Greek. How far this is the result of the simpler alphabetical Greek script leading, in turn, to a more literate population cannot be measured; it seems a possible explanation. Even after the fall of the last Ptolemy, Cleopatra VII, Greek was to remain the language of administration under the Romans. It was in this period that the Greek alphabet, in modified form, was adopted for writing the Egyptian language in Coptic. The consequent growth in Egyptian literacy facilitated the spread through Egyptian society of a new religion — Christianity, a religion based on a sacred (written) text. The administration however continued in Greek and, even after the Arab conquest of 642 AD, Greek was in use for the next half century (Butler 1978, 490). My interest here, however, is in the first hundred years of Ptolemaic rule and what we can discover about the ways in which Greeks came to be part of Egyptian life, with the effects of this upon the society and the relation of these two peoples within it.

The administrative structure left in place by Alexander on his conquest is recorded by Arrian (3,5.2-6) and those involved are named. Kleomenes, Alexander's satrap from Naukratis, and later Ptolemy son of Lagos now faced the task of organising Egypt, a country freed from Persian control, and of setting up an administration in the name of their Macedonian masters. The process cannot be traced in detail, though we may assume from the surviving documentation (to be discussed below) that to a significant extent they relied on the expertise of those already on the job, the scribes and minor officials in post. But they also relied on the literate classes of the Egyptian elite. In the new capital of Alexandria they were, it seems, fairly intensively instructed by upper-class Egyptians.

The priest Manetho is probably the best known of these. Of priestly background from Sebennytos, the home of the last Egyptian dynasty, under Ptolemy I or II he wrote, in Greek, a history of the pharaohs said to be translated from Egyptian sacred sources. The fragments that survive suggest the form of a chronological listing, going back to the time of gods and heroes who preceded the first dynastic period, before 3,000 BC. The pharaohs were listed by name with the length of each reign and their order established. The antiquity of Egypt was now there for the Greeks to read, and the far greater detail of Manetho's history (which still serves as the chief base for the canon of pharaohs) was to supersede the sometimes fanciful tales of Herodotus. He also wrote on Egyptian religion, on rituals and festivals, providing the newcomers with a guide to Egyptian manners and customs.[10] The Ptolemies were quick to learn and may soon be found performing the rôle of pharaoh in the cults of their kingdom (Diodorus Siculus 1,84).

The earlier Egyptian attitude to foreigners had been expressed in the New Kingdom instructions of the scribe Any (Lichtheim 1976, 144):

One teaches the Nubian to speak Egyptian,
The Syrian and other strangers too.

But now the Egyptian Manetho was writing in the strangers' language. He was not alone in realising the new rulers' need for access to information on the ways of their new kingdom. There were other Egyptians too, many of them from important provincial priestly families, who became involved with the new regime. The Ptolemaic sarcophagus lid from Saqqâra, now in the Cairo museum, of one Wennofer has the following boast: "I spent life on earth in the King's favour, I was beloved by his courtiers" (Lichtheim 1980, 55), and it may be the same man's statue, now in Vienna, which claims: "at the time of the Greeks I was consulted by the ruler of Egypt, for he loved me and knew my intentions" (Quaegebeur 1980, 78). Similarly, a funerary stele from Vienna of one Tathot describes her grandson who "was in the king's service and transmitted the reports to the magistrates; the king preferred him to his courtiers for each secret counsel in the palace" (Quaegebeur 1980, 78-9). The old priestly nobility from the former Egyptian capital of Memphis could thus help the new king, and, together with the high priests of Memphis, they worked with the Ptolemies in what was generally a friendly collaboration to their mutual benefit. There are other examples from elsewhere,[11] and when we find a Nectanebo, from the same family as the last dynasty of Egyptian pharaohs, holding high military and administrative positions under Ptolemy I (or so he claims on his tombstone), the extent of interdependence in these early years is clear (de Meulenaere 1963, 90-3).

Greeks and Egyptians needed each other's cooperation. For Greeks, limited as they were in number, the need was for personnel and instruction on how to manage an economy based on irrigation agriculture. The borders of Egypt were good ones and the country better integrated to start with than many other of the Hellenistic kingdoms but, if Ptolemy was to hold on to his new realm, peace and prosperity at home were essential. Stability for the Greeks involved law and order within their new home; the preservation of this required local cooperation. For the Egyptians, the stability of the country and the preservation of order depended on the acceptance by the new ruler of the traditional role of pharaoh, together with respect for the temples and gods of Egypt. It was only thus that Egypt could prosper; but the temples and their priests had an added interest in the preservation of their lands and wealth. As earlier under the Persians, once again collaboration came from the Egyptian priestly and upper classes; the Greeks would need to recognize this help. Both had the incentives for adaptation and change.

Already as satrap, Ptolemy son of Lagos renewed endowments to temples in the Delta. At Sais, the Delta home of the twenty-sixth and twenty-eighth dynasties, the local cults were again allowed to receive the income from land that had been theirs before the Persians removed it; we know this from the so-called Satrap Stele.[12] As king, Ptolemy continued this policy, and a stele from Tel Balamun in the northern Delta (now in the collection of Sigmund Freud) dated 301 BC portrays Ptolemy making a religious endowment of land to four local deities; the gift is recorded in the accompanying inscription (Freud Museum Catalogue, forthcoming, no. 14). A papyrus too records an earlier royal decree of 304 BC prohibiting the disposal of temple enclosures; priestly control over temple property was, it would seem, to be guaranteed (*SB* XVI 12519.1-10 with Hagedorn 1986). Such a decree is reminiscent of the early orders of one of Alexander's two commanders left in post which, to judge from the nail holes in the papyrus, were posted up at Saqqâra where the papyrus was found (Turner 1974):

Orders of Peukestas. Out-of-bounds. Priest's property.

Ptolemy therefore followed such precedents, and as always mutual advantage was central. The king needed a literate class to run his new country, whilst the priests hoped to protect their temples and temple lands. The involvement of this group in the early administration is perhaps suggested by the find spot of one of the earliest pieces of evidence for the elaborate system of administrative control which was to develop under Ptolemy II Philadelphus, an ostrakon dated 258 BC referring to a full land survey and census of the country. Written in demotic, the ostrakon comes from Karnak, from the area of priests' houses near to the Sacred Lake (Bresciani 1978). The system which, still at an early stage of development, we know from the Greek documents of the Zenon archive or from the Petrie papyri, is here found recorded in demotic in a priestly context. Similarly the only record I know of a Ptolemaic land survey before the third century Greek material from the Fayum is a demotic plot-measurement from a temple context at Akoris in Middle Egypt (*P. Loeb dem.* 36; cf. 4-6; 22; 24). Priests, it seems, continued in key positions, often masking their Egyptian priestly rôle under Greek names and functions. For in Egypt to serve as priest in no way formed a bar to holding more secular administrative office.

The rôle of language in this interchange of services is a complex one, and as always in the ancient world we remain victims of the hazard of the survival of our sources. Whereas we know from the later copy of the royal order on temples quoted above (*SB* XVI 12519.1-10 (mid-second century BC)) that in some contexts Greek was in use, most documents to survive from the first fifty years of the new regime are written in demotic. An analysis of this early demotic documentation in general terms reveals several characteristics.[13] First, the material divides almost half and half into official and private documents; the demands of the administration were not yet overriding and many of the features of pre-Ptolemaic demotic documentation (Thissen 1980) continued in this period. And yet, over time, the material both increases and changes, with more papyri of an administrative nature. Next, in terms of content, many are demotic legal texts, property contracts and other family documents, providing perhaps some indication of the crucial role of an independent Egyptian legal system in the continuation both of the Egyptian language and a sense of national identity. Finally, the distribution of the texts is of interest, with a third from the Fayum and two thirds from Thebes and the rest of the Nile valley. We should consider further the effect of the regional variation of our documentation.

That Egyptian was used in the early years within the administration where later Greek would be the rule is certain, as after the Arab conquest Greek continued, to be replaced in turn by Arabic. We cannot however be so sure of the rate of change from demotic to Greek in these early years. The reason for this lies partly in the geographical bias of our texts. Whereas most of the documentation that survives from the first hundred years comes from the Arsinoite nome, it was some time before this area—the fertile Fayum basin—was fully developed, with further drainage and a more extensive system of irrigation. The majority therefore of papyri from the first fifty years of Ptolemaic rule are not from the Fayum but rather from the Nile valley—from the Thebaid and Middle Egypt—from areas that were to remain more Egyptian in both population and traditional structures. Some of the apparent predominance of demotic in the first two generations of Ptolemaic administration may thus simply reflect the preponderance of texts from the Nile valley where demotic continued in use, though not exclusively so, throughout the Ptolemaic period. On the other hand, the lack of early Fayum documentation is in itself an indication of the gradual rate of Greek and Macedonian penetration outside Alexandria.

Once the Fayum was settled from the early third century BC, demotic texts are joined there by the beginnings of an administration in Greek. Sometimes it is possible to see the change actually taking place, with scribes using the demotic rush pen and not the reed for writing documents now in Greek. Such is the case in the scribal office of the Themistos division of the Arsinoite nome from the reign of Ptolemy III Euergetes, where Greek tax lists are penned with a rush (*CPR* 13). The adoption in Greek documentation of various Egyptian abbreviations will have taken place in a similar environment (Pestman 1980, 8). Soon there is more in Greek than in demotic,[14] and this pattern is reflected in other areas. Given the nature of our evidence, only generalisations are possible. The further away from the capital, not surprisingly, the slower it seems was the penetration of Greek literacy. Our overall picture of the adoption of Greek for most administrative purposes is probably skewed by the predominance of Arsinoite Greek material, but over the three hundred years of Ptolemaic rule Greek did become the language in which the administration functioned.

The next problem therefore is that of personnel. Given that Greek immigration on any significant scale was confined to the early years of the new dynasty (Bagnall 1984), a necessary preliminary to an administration eventually functioning in Greek was a widespread programme of education in that language. Hellenizing priests alone could not provide sufficient personnel; a broader section of the population literate in Greek was needed. Greek schools and libraries in the countryside will have played an important part in spreading knowledge of the language amongst all sections of the population. The education in Greek literacy and culture of Egyptians for the army probably started under Alexander (Hammond 1990, 276), but it is only from the mid third century BC that evidence survives for widespread Greek schooling in the Egyptian countryside.

Under Ptolemy II Philadelphus the spread of Greek education was encouraged with a series of inducements in what appears to be a central, perhaps royal, initiative. Alongside gymnastic teachers, priests of Dionysus and those who won at Alexandrian games, school-teachers were now exempted from the salt-tax, the Ptolemaic equivalent of the poll-tax, to which others were liable (*P. Halle* 1.260-65). The application of this decree in practice is to be found in both Greek and demotic tax lists from the reign of Ptolemy III Euergetes. From the detailed listings of village and area populations in the West Fayum we may gain some sense of the scale and emphasis on schooling in this area. Thus, in a tax area covering a total adult (tax-paying) population of 10,876 (men: 5,245; women: 5,631) in 229/28 BC, 24 teachers are recorded, 15 of them men and, on the normal pattern of these lists, the other 9 their wives (*P. Lille dem.* 3,99 verso col. iv a.1-7). The density here is 1:725 adults or 1:350 taxable adult males. Other figures survive. In the small village of Trikomia with a total adult population of 331 (men: 171; women: 160), Greek tax lists record 3 teachers, all male, giving a ratio of 1:110 adults or 1:57 adult males (*CPR* 13,1,10, 12 (254-244 BC)). Similar figures are recorded for neighbouring Lagis, with a ratio of 1:161 overall (*CPR* 13,2.30 (254-244 BC)) or the hamlet of Per-Hemer with 1:398 overall (*P. Lille dem.* 3,99 verso col. ii.15 (229/228 BC)). Some villages, however, such as Lysimachis (total adult population: 80) or Athenas Kome (total: 153) had no teachers at all recorded (*CPR* XIII 2.4; 11.11), so the ratio of 1:350 adult males from the larger tax district should perhaps be adopted as giving a more representative figure. What these figures may mean in terms of actual staff:pupil ratios is unknowable, given our lack of information on life expectancy rates, the length of elementary schooling, the ages between which this took place, and other such relevant data. What is clear however is that the tax-breaks for teachers recorded in these lists went hand-in-hand with a concentration on schooling in the countryside.

What these Greek teachers taught may perhaps be seen from a third century BC papyrus roll preserving what appears to be a teacher's handbook (Guéraud & Jouguet 1938). In the one long roll is preserved a synopsis of Ptolemaic elementary education. Reading Greek was central to this. Starting with simple sounds in which the different vowels were paired with particular consonants — cha, che, chê, chi, cho, chu, chô, psa, pse, psê, psi, pso, psu, psô — the work progressed to three letter words in which all the consonants were added in turn to an, en, ên, in, on, un, and ôn — ban, ben, bên, bin, bon, bun, bôn; gan, gen, gên, gin, gon, gun, gôn, and so on through the alphabet. To my generation at least the technique is very familiar. Next numbers were learnt before real words of three and four letters were introduced. There followed lists to be learnt, a list of Greek gods, then one of rivers, an interesting list with rivers named both from Macedon and more distant parts. The Homeric Scamander of the plain of Troy is there besides the Macedonian Strymon and the river Indos. It is lists like this which give some sense of the world from which this school text came — the world of Alexander's Macedonian conquests.[15] The pupil would then graduate to proper names, two-syllable, then three- and four-syllable names, with the syllables carefully divided up and dots between to aid the beginning reader. Soon we move on to two extracts from Euripides, but then the syllable divisions end. With an extract from Homer — Odysseus is with Calypso — the text becomes continuous without division. By now our young scholar may be expected to have mastered the elements of reading. Other poetic extracts follow — an epigram on the subject of a fountain in Alexandria, a further one perhaps on a monument to Homer erected by a Ptolemaic king and finally some comic extracts to round off what has been a wide introduction to literature. The roll concludes with some mathematical tables and the fractions of a drachma. The three 'r's — 'reading, (w)riting and (a)rithmetic' — were all important elements of a well-rounded education; the papyrus roll would seem to contain the teacher's handbook for several years' work at school. Whilst numeracy in Greek (in both arithmetical functions and the currency system) and knowledge of the Macedonian calendar were also among the basic skills of literacy covered in the manual, the emphasis on old Greek culture combined with contemporary Alexandrian poetry gives a broader aspect to this education.

The effect of this wider study of literature may be illustrated from the somewhat later (mid second century BC) example of the two brothers Ptolemaios and Apollonios, sons of the Macedonian soldier Glaukias, from the village of Psichis in the Herakleopolite nome. Detained in the Serapeum at Memphis, where they lived in a bilingual world, in their spare time these brothers copied out the literature they must have learnt at school — Greek tragedy and comedy, and two epigrams of Poseidippos on Ptolemaic monuments, the lighthouse of Alexandria and the temple of Aphrodite Zephyritis (Thompson 1987). In the villages of Egypt it was more than simply the basics of Greek education that were taught. Those who went through this system had an important rôle to play in the Ptolemaic system of government, and, whatever their original background, the culture that they learnt was the conquerors' culture.

The tax lists recording the salt-tax exemption for Greek teachers and their families provide some illustration of the scale of the literacy drive of the early Ptolemies. The effects of all this on the native Egyptian population is where the problem of ethnicity must enter the discussion. So far I have seen the spread of Greek education and literate culture simply as a response to the needs of the administration. But what did it now mean to be "Greek", to be a "Hellene", and thus, along with the "Persians", to be exempt from the obol tax which others had to pay? This status was clearly of value for although individually the exemption was smaller than for the salt-tax exemption, the numbers affected were greater: 72 Hellenes from Trikomia, 29 from Athenas Kome and 17 each from Lagis and Lysimachis (*CPR* 13,1; 2; 11), with 1,756 or 16% of the total population from the tax-area covered by *P. Lille dem.* 3,99 *verso* (229/28 BC)). It is clear from these exemptions that the administration was discriminating not only in favour of teachers but also of "Hellenes". I have argued elsewhere that a detailed consideration of those so described suggests that these "Hellenes" may include those from Egyptian backgrounds who had been educated in Greek and adopted Greek culture and names.[16] Such men were needed to run the system, both the army and the bureaucracy. On this hypothesis, the label "Hellene" tells nothing of ethnic background, but forms a measure rather of the extent of Hellenisation within Ptolemaic society.

The tax-lists on which this suggestion is based, together with the teaching manual and other evidence for the spread of schooling in the countryside, all come from the mid or later third century BC. Earlier things seem to have been different. For the success of the establishment of Ptolemaic control depended in many respects on the continuity of personnel in key positions in the country. Through collaboration and Hellenisation, including the eventual acceptance of Greek for administrative purposes, the Egyptian literate classes adapted themselves to a change of regime. The first generation of Ptolemaic administrators, those of the later fourth and early third centuries, would seem to have functioned predominantly in demotic. Then came the spread of schooling, the teaching of Greek and an energetic literacy drive. A new generation of scribes and administrators was now prepared to function in Greek.

The picture presented here is somewhat schematic. Much work remains to be done. The different levels of the bureaucracy will be worth careful investigation, together with regional differences; for changes in language and style are unlikely to have taken place at an even rate throughout society. What the evidence for Egypt seems to be indicating is a gradual deepening of Ptolemaic rule, illustrated most clearly by the increasing use of Greek as the language of the administration. What takes place however is not so much a process of Hellenisation as one of integration. For hand in hand with this change in language went the increasing adoption, especially by the king, of traditional Egyptian rituals and ways. Ptolemy II, whose only home was Egypt, was in a different situation from Ptolemy I, a military adventurer concerned to secure the prize he had seized. As Greek became established, with an extensive programme of schooling in the capital and countryside, the administration itself was developed and organised to maximise revenues for its ruler, who used them on imperial ventures, especially against the Seleucids. But whether the nature of the integration which took place in Egypt between the literate Egyptians and the new Greek invaders made Egypt a different sort of state from Asia under the Seleucids, remains an open question.

Notes

1. Cf. 130-31: his sister/wife Ahwere is semi-literate, reading the spells without apparent difficulty but less proficient at writing than her brother.
2. Lichtheim 1976, 168-78, repeats this theme for the New Kingdom.
3. For the House of Life as temple scriptorium, see Gardiner 1938; Quaegebeur 1980/81, 233-4; Thompson 1988, 114, for priests as scribes.
4. *BGU* 8,1214.3-8 (second century BC) suggests a distinction, and those who wrote literary texts may not (so W. J. Tait) be the same as those who wrote documents. In the Setne story (Lichtheim 1980, 135) the local schoolteacher draws up the contract for Tabubu; cf. *UPZ* 1, 78.9 (159 BC), the school of Tothes (attended by the Serapeum twin-girls) in a Memphite dream text. For demotic teaching methods, see Kaplony-Heckel, 1974; Bresciani 1984; Devauchelle 1984.
5. See *Phaedrus* 274c-275b and *Philebus* 18b, where Thoth would seem to serve as the prototype for Theuth, the inventor of writing.

6. For Egypt as typifying a priestly scribal society, see Baines 1983, 584; 1988, 192-214; Finnegan 1988, 42; Goody 1986, 32-5, 64-5; 1987, 30-44.

7. Murray 1980, 91-9; Harris 1989, 45-64.

8. See my contributions to the forthcoming *Proceedings of the nineteenth international congress of papyrology (Cairo, September 1989)* and Thompson 1992 for two related studies.

9. Compare Will 1985, on the potential interest of colonial societies. The Ptolemies however were a resident dynasty and not a colonial regime.

10. Jacoby, *FGrH* III C no. 609; Mendels 1990; Fowden 1986, 52-6, on Manetho's *Sacred book* and other writings which treated Egyptian religion.

11. Kaplony 1971, 257-58, for Sebennytite and Herakleopolite support; Lichtheim 1980, 44-54, for Petosiris of Hermopolis.

12. Sethe 1904, 11-22, no. 9; Bevan 1927, 28-32, for a translation; Goedicke 1984.

13. See the table and preliminary discussion in *Proceedings of the nineteenth international congress (Cairo 1989)*, forthcoming. The figures there are provisional, providing only a rough guide.

14. From the mid third century Zenon archive, for instance, from Philadelphia in the Arsinoite nome, there is only a handful of demotic texts out of a total of around 1700 texts, *P.L.Bat.* 21 and Orrieux 1985, 47.

15. Hammond 1990, 288, argues that this, or similar texts, was used in the young adult education instituted by Alexander for Egyptian (and other Asian) youths trained for military (and administrative) purposes. Guéraud & Jouguet 1938, assume the text is that of a schoolboy, "un livre d'écolier".

16. In Thompson 1992, 338. The identity of the Medes (in demotic) or Persians (in Greek) is equally puzzling. They may have been the earlier Greek-speakers in Egypt, the Ionians and others already settled in Egypt when Alexander defeated the Persians, or else perhaps those Egyptians already trained by Alexander; see Hammond 1990, 278-79, for this usage.

ALEXANDRIAN SCIENCE:
THE CASE OF ERATOSTHENES

Jerker Blomqvist

An appraisal of Eratosthenes of Cyrene[1] as a scientist and scholar in his Alexandrian and, generally, Hellenistic environment conveniently starts from the entry *Eratosthenes* in the *Suda* lexicon. The text runs (cf. text 1, p. 70):

Eratosthenes, son of Aglaos or, according to some, Ambrosios, of Cyrene, disciple of the philosopher Ariston of Chios and of the grammarians Lysanias of Cyrene and Callimachus the Poet. He was sent for from Athens by Ptolemy III and dwelt (with the Ptolemies) until (Ptolemy) V. Since he came second in every branch of learning in comparison to those who reached the summit, he was nicknamed "Beta".[2] Some called him a second or new Plato, others "Pentathlos".[3] He was born in the 126th Olympiad (276/5—273/2 BC) and died at the age of eighty, starving himself to death since his eye-sight failed, leaving behind his distinguished disciple Aristophanes of Byzantium, whose disciple was Aristarchus. His disciples were Mnaseas, Menandros and Aristis.[4] He wrote philosophical treatises, poems, historical works, *Astronomy* (or *Katastêrigmoi*),[5] *On the Philosophical Schools*, *On Freedom from Pain*, several dialogues and much on grammar.

As the biographical articles in the *Suda* are generally problematic, none of its information on Eratosthenes should be accepted unless it is confirmed by other sources. The birth date given by the *Suda* is wrong. An anti-Eratosthenian pamphlet by Polemon,[6] quoted by Strabo, shows that Eratosthenes had attended the Stoic school already during Zeno's life-time. Since Zeno died in 262/1 BC,[7] Eratosthenes is likely to have been at least twenty years old at that time, but not much older. He is unlikely to have been born as early as in Ol. 121 (296/5—293/2 BC), as supposed among others by Jacoby (who corrects *Suda*'s "126th" into "121th"). A birth-date in the mid-eighties seems reasonable.

The same passage in Strabo shows, with quotations from Eratosthenes' own works, that he was acquainted with the Stoic Ariston of Chios, with Arcesilaus of Pitane, who was head of the Academy in the mid-third century, and his disciple

Apelles of Chios, and with the Cynic Bion of Borysthenes.[8] This dates Eratosthenes' stay in Athens to the sixties and fifties.

That Eratosthenes reached old age is confirmed by Lucianus, who gives his life-time as eighty-two years.[9] "Gentle old age" is given as the cause of Eratosthenes' death in an epigram of probably Hellenistic date. Its author expressly denies that Eratosthenes died from a disease (and, implicitly, rejects the allegation that his death was self-inflicted).[10]

Eratosthenes lived long enough to write some sort of biography or encomium on Arsinoe III Philopator. She was murdered shortly after the death of her husband in 205 BC. The frank judgment on the religious practices of Philopator that is contained in the only preserved fragment of the work[11] also indicates that it was written after his death.

Thus, Eratosthenes' life fell during the third century BC. If he was between, say, twenty and twenty-five when Zeno died and himself died at the age of eighty or eighty-two, his death occurred in the last years of the century. The evidence shows that, before arriving in Alexandria, he had spent some time in the philosophical circles of Athens.[12] The *Suda* may be right in stating that he was invited to Alexandria by Ptolemy III.[13] In that case, he came there perhaps in the forties and may have spent as much as forty years in Egypt. No evidence suggests that he ever visited Cyrene or Athens again, and his grave was certainly located in Alexandria, "on the fringe of Proteus' sea-shore", according to the epigram of Dionysius (above, note 10).

A discussion of the dating of Eratosthenes may seem irrelevant in this context. It is not. The foundation of the scholarly institutions of Alexandria had taken place already in the reign of Ptolemy I, in the first decades of the third century. When Eratosthenes arrived there almost half a century later, he could enter into a milieu that had been created by his predecessors. The collections of the Library and the Mouseion were already there, there was a staff of able scholars engaged in the different branches of science and scholarship, they had at their disposal the material amenities necessary for their work, and the organisation of the institutions had presumably been tested and brought to perfection in the preceding decades.

These were resources never before accumulated on one spot and liberally put at the disposal of the leading scientists of the day. The institutionalization of scientific studies, the engagement of political power in what had previously been a private enterprise, the enormous amount of resources spent by an ambitious government, these are characteristics of Alexandrian science at its hey-day that differentiate it from the pursuit of scientific activities in almost all other periods throughout history. It is only in the last century that comparable institutions have been created by nations belonging to the sphere of Western civilisation or influenced by it.

Eratosthenes was to spend a considerable portion of his active life in such surroundings, and his accomplishment as a scientist is to be viewed against that background. He did not stand alone. He could use the results of his predecessors, whether they had worked in Alexandria or in other places, for their writings were available in the Library. He had access to information, e.g., on geographical matters that had been amassed there and could profit from the collections of the Mouseion. There were colleagues he could discuss with or be inspired by. Such colleagues are traditionally called either teachers or disciples in the ancient sources, but there is little doubt that, in many cases, professor and student were on an equal footing and worked together for a common purpose.

After Alexander's death, great portions of the royal archives had been brought to Alexandria. They included among other things the *Ephêmerides*, the field diary of the Macedonian army, with information on routes and distances, peoples subjugated and cities captured. Alexander's army had been accompanied by a number of men with philosophical training, imposed with the task of recording geographical and ethnographical information on the countries of the East. The annotations they had made were also kept in the archives and brought to Alexandria.

The result was clearly visible in Eratosthenes' *Geography*. The great work is lost, but the main lines of its content can be reconstructed from the writings of later geographers who used it as a source, especially from Strabo. It appears that it offered a great amount of new, mostly correct information on Mesopotamia and Iran, even on India and Ceylon. The information on Italy, Africa and the western Mediterranean, on the other hand, was incomplete, vague or even faulty,[14] and Eratosthenes was criticized by Polybius for his ignorance, though excusable in a man who had only literary sources at his disposal, of western and northern Europe.[15] Thus, when Eratosthenes could exploit the original reports from Alexander's archives that were stored in the Mouseion or the Library, his *Geography* surpassed others, but when he had to rely on literary or obsolete sources only, the result was less happy. This is one example of how Alexandrian science was influenced by the institutions created by the Ptolemies.

That Callimachus was the teacher of Eratosthenes in Alexandria and

Aristophanes his disciple, as the *Suda* article states, may be mere guess-work; the names of Callimachus and Aristophanes were well-known enough to insinuate themselves into contexts where they did not belong. But there is more reliable evidence to show that Eratosthenes belonged to a community of scientists and scholars who influenced and inspired each other mutually; as might be expected in an independent mind, the inspiration sometimes resulted in criticism rather than imitation.

In the mid-century, his alleged teacher Callimachus had settled the standards for poetic production in Alexandria. In his own poems Eratosthenes appears as a follower of Callimachus' ideals. His *Erigone*, "an altogether faultless little poem" according to one of the most perspicacious literary critics of antiquity,[16] was a miniature epic of the same type as Callimachus' *Hecale*, and in his *Hermes* he presented astronomical and cosmological knowledge in poetic form, as, e.g., Callimachus' favourite among contemporary poets, Aratus, had done. But when it came to geography and related matters, his independence becomes clear. Contrary to the grammarians and learned poets who were his colleagues in the Library and the Mouseion, he denied that poetry, be it by reverend Homer or by contemporary Apollonius, could be used as a reliable source of geographic information. While other scholars of Alexandria amassed what they regarded as true knowledge from myth and poetry and passed it on to an admiring audience in their own literary masterpieces or in learned commentaries on those of others, Eratosthenes' methodological principles excluded the use of such source material. Poetry was for entertainment, not teaching, he declared according to Strabo,[17] and, when in his *Hermes* he himself produced a didactic poem, we may assume that its contents were based on what he regarded as sound and proper scientific research and that he used the poetic form as a convenient vehicle for disseminating the truth in a way that would gratify the audience.

One of Callimachus' works had, according to the *Suda*, the title *Collection of wonders from the whole world, geographically distributed*.[18] Some idea of its contents may be gathered from Antigonus of Carystus, who quotes from the work in sections 129–173 of his *Mirabilia*. Paradoxography was a popular genre in Hellenistic times. Works of that genre had some superficial resemblance to science. Also scientists collected facts from the whole world and from all domains of nature; naturally, in their reports they gave some preponderance to what was unusual and remarkable rather than well-known and trivial. The paradoxographers collected material in the same way. But the paradoxographers were content with merely doing collections of wonders and presenting them in an aesthetically acceptable form to their readers. For a true scientist like Eratosthenes it was also necessary to assess the veracity of the reports, to analyse the facts reported, to integrate them into a totality with previous knowledge. Consequently, paradoxography, as practised by Callimachus and others, was not a favourite of Eratosthenes'. We have no evidence for a direct reaction on Callimachus' *Synagôgê* but a sarcastic remark where Eratosthenes compares unreliable geographers to another representative of the paradoxographical genre, Euhemerus, and his equally irresponsible colleagues, has been preserved.[19] In the lively intellectual milieu of Alexandria it was probably realized that such a statement had a general bearing.

There is indisputable evidence that at least one other great scientist among Eratosthenes' contemporaries found reason to discuss mathematical problems of a high order with him: Archimedes of Syracuse, who had spent some time in Alexandria but returned to his native island, dedicated his *Methodus* to him, and the preface testifies to earlier contacts between the two and to Archimedes' high appreciation of the addressee.[20] If the evidence is to be trusted, there existed also a letter from Archimedes to Eratosthenes in which he presented the problem of calculating the number of cattle in the Sun-god's herds; the addressee was supposed to act as an intermediary between Archimedes and the Alexandrian mathematicians.[21] These are but glimpses of the discussions that went on between the scientists of Alexandria and their colleagues in other parts of the Greek world.

Eratosthenes originally came from Cyrene. Before settling in Alexandria, he had spent a considerable time, perhaps two decades, in the philosophical schools of Athens. When he "was sent for" by the Ptolemies he was a mature man and must have been a philosopher of some standing; otherwise he would not have been selected for a task that included not only the ordinary work at the Mouseion but also would make him chief librarian and tutor of the future Ptolemy IV Philopator. Seen from Eratosthenes' point of view, the position in Alexandria must have offered better opportunities than a philosophical career in Athens: the Ptolemies were evidently able to make him an offer he could not resist. Eratosthenes was only one among many learned men who answered to the summons from Alexandria. In fact, we may speak of brain-drain effect on the rest of Greece when the Egyptian flesh-pots were opened to the philosophers and scientists of the day. Few of the scholars who created the fame of Alexandria in the third century were born in Egypt,[22] and many of them had received their education elsewhere.

There were institutions that competed with those of Alexandria: in Athens, of course, but also in new centres such as Pergamon, Antioch, Rhodes, and Syracuse. But Egypt was spared the wars that ravaged Greece, Asia Minor and Syria in the third century, and its economy prospered. The scholars of Alexandria were protected from the vicissitudes of political upheaval, and its kings could assign to them the financial resources that they needed.

The relative dominance of Alexandria becomes more pronounced in the following centuries. Not all Hellenistic centres underwent the same violent fate as Syracuse at the Roman sack in 212 BC, but they all suffered when the political power shifted from the Macedonian kings to the Romans. Athens, in view of its ancient traditions, still had its attractions, but, as for science, its hey-day was over. Already in the decade 270–260 BC, after the death of the Peripatetic Strato of Lampsacus and the contemporary leaders of the other philosophical schools, independent speculation in the field of theoretical physics and science practically came to an end there. The philosophers tended to confine themselves to barren polemics, merely defending the teachings of the founders of their respective schools, and their main interest became ethics or the theory of knowledge.[23] It is typical that Aristarchus of Samos received his education in Athens under Strato but, by all probability, did his own work in astronomy in Alexandria.

Rhodes could, in the second century, still boast of an astronomer like Hipparchus, and in the first century Posidonius, a philosopher with scientific interests, taught there. But it was the rhetorical school that attracted students to Rhodes, even if it could also serve as a meeting-place between Romans and learned Greeks of other professions. Rhetorical studies also continued in Antioch. Pergamon ceased to be a centre of learning after 133 BC.

In Alexandria scientific studies survived. Neither the attraction that Rome exerted on the learned men of the time nor the partial destruction of the learned institutions in the first century BC could put an end to that. We find astronomers educated in Alexandria in the service of the early emperors, e.g., Sosigenes and others, who inspired Caesar's reform of the Roman calendar,[24] and Thrasyllus in the time of Tiberius.[25] Later on in the Roman period science and mathematics still flourished in Alexandria, with names like Menelaus, Claudius Ptolemy, Theo, and, at the close of antiquity, John Philoponus — to mention just a few.

The name Eratosthenes is not a common one in the ancient texts, i.e., bearers of that name only rarely left an imprint in the historical records. Presumably, it was not a name ordinarily given to members of nobility families. This applies to an even higher degree to Aglaos, his father's name.[26] We know practically only one more historical — if he really is that — personality from the Greek area with that name, viz., the poor farmer of Psophis in Arcadia whose happiness was made proverbial by the Pythia when Gyges (or Croesus) of Lydia asked her for the name of the most fortunate man of the world.[27] The appearance of these undistinguished names in two successive generations indicates that the family did not belong to the nobility of Cyrene. By contrast, his compatriot Callimachus bore a more aristocratic name, and the name of his father, Battos, even had a regal ring in Cyrene.[28]

Thus, it seems probable that Eratosthenes descended from a rather inconspicuous family, even if they possessed the financial means for sending a son to philosophical schooling in Athens. It has been pointed out that the philosophers of Classical Greece mostly came from the old aristocracy.[29] When the developing democracy ousted them from the positions of power that traditionally had belonged to the aristocracy, they tried to assert their influence by means of the newly invented intellectual activity of philosophy. Beginning in the fourth century, the situation had changed. Of the founders of the four philosophical schools in Athens, Zeno of Citium and Epicurus certainly were of humble origin;[30] among secondary figures the same applies to Diogenes of Sinope, Bion of Borysthenes and Pyrrhon of Elis.

In Eratosthenes' times it was possible for a man of his origin to become an educator of princes, an intimate friend of the Egyptian queen and chief librarian in the most prestigious learned institution of the Greek world. He had not risen to his position because he could refer to a royal or aristocratic ancestry. That may have played some role in the case of Callimachus, but Eratosthenes had no such merits. When he was summoned to Alexandria, it was for his personal qualities and his accomplishments as a philosopher and, possibly, a poet. Callimachus and other Cyrenaeans already present at the court may have been aware of those merits in their compatriot and brought them to the attention of the king, as Fraser suggests.[31]

If this interpretation of the facts is correct, the career of Eratosthenes illustrates the new possibilities that opened themselves for able individuals of all classes during the Hellenistic period. Monarchical rule did not put an end to the opportunities that democracy is supposed to have offered to the man in the street. Instead, when the distance, in social terms, between the king and the rest of the population became wider, the opportunities of the citizens — or subjects — for individual careers in the king's service tended to become more equal, in the sense that personal merit mattered more than inherited distinction, endowed wealth or political versatility. The phenomenon is visible not only in the learned professions, as is well known, but the change probably meant more to them than to, e.g., political careers. A politician could always expect his activity, risky though it may be, to pay off in terms of fame or gold, but democracy offered little hope of that for an astronomer, a geographer or a mathematician. The royal institutions of Alexandria and elsewhere opened better prospects for ambitious scientists.

In the Hellenistic period, it has been said, ancient science reached its culmination. What followed meant a decline in almost all branches of science, and the achievements of Hellenistic science were surpassed only in the sixteenth century of our era. What preceded was a period when science had not yet freed itself from the grip of that all-embracing phenomenon *philosophia*. It was only in the Hellenistic period that science — or rather: *the* sciences — emerged as independent, self-contained entities and the scientists of different branches could effectively pursue their work, applying the proper methods without being hemmed by the demands of one philosophical system or another that was striving for extra-scientific goals, such as human happiness, and did not pay due respect to the ideal of pure knowledge. It has been stated by one of the most influential Swedish classicists that in the Hellenistic period "science became the principal domain of Greek civilisation and the main interest of educated people" and "science becomes the particular characteristic of the Hellenistic epoch in the history of Greek civilisation."[32]

As all generalizations, such statements need modification. A scientific ideal, such as the one described, somewhat pointedly, in the preceding paragraph, belongs to the twentieth century (will it survive into the twenty-first?). The belief that science is respectable and beneficial to mankind only when it is allowed to pursue its own goals unguided by morals, philosophy, religion, democratic ideology or whatever is a phenomenon of our time. There is no evidence to show that it was subscribed to in the Hellenistic or any other period of antiquity. The Danish cultural historian Grønbech, whose spiritual presence perhaps may be felt at the seminar, has, in his inimitable way, retraced the opinions of the Hellenistic thinkers on the position of sciences in relation to philosophy, as they appear in Philo of Alexandria, Plutarch and Pliny the Elder.[33] It appears that the specialized branches of science, *ta mathêmata*, were always regarded as subordinated to philosophy. If they contributed to the objective of philosophy, they were to be pursued; if not, they were useless.

Nor were the learned men of Alexandria and other Hellenistic centres normally pure scientists in the sense that they directed their activities towards science only or towards only one science. Eratosthenes, the Pentathlos, is a good instance. He attained distinction within several branches of both science and scholarship. Archimedes, not a despicable witness, respected him for his achievements in the field of mathematics. Among other things, he could pride himself on having constructed an instrument by which two mean proportionals in successive proportion to two given straight lines could be found, i.e., a mechanically tractable solution to the Delian problem of doubling the cube along the lines indicated by Hippocrates of Chios.[34]

To us, Eratosthenes' fame mainly rests on his geographical works. With good reason he is regarded as the founder of mathematical geography. Although criticized on some points by Hipparchus, Strabo and others, he gave scientific geography a new direction, and his influence, by the intermediary of Claudius Ptolemy, lasted into modern times.[35] Also as regards descriptive geography, his *Geographia* meant an advance. A most conspicuous feat was his calculation of the circumference of the earth, accomplished with sound method and with a surprisingly small error.[36] He was also active as an astronomer, but his accomplishments in this field cannot be properly evaluated, for the sources fail.[37]

Outside the domain of what is today called science in the narrow sense of this word, Eratosthenes did serious research in the fields of history and philology. With his *Olumpionikai* he created a chronological frame-work for Greek history, and his *Chronographia* contained chronological tables for the period from the sack of Troy at least to the death of Alexander. These two works make him the founder of another branch of learning, chronology. On what the ancients called grammar Eratosthenes wrote much according to the *Suda* (*grammatika suchna*), and he is repeatedly called *grammatikos* in the sources.[38] A more proper designation would be philologist, and he is said to have been the first to use the word *philologos* to designate his profession.[39] A work in two books with the title *Grammatika* is ascribed to him by Clement of Alexandria, and his *Peri tês archaias kômoidias* exerted a considerable influence on later literary criticism.

Although he preferred to call himself *philologos* rather than *philosophos*, Eratosthenes is credited by the ancient sources with a number of treatises with a philosophical content. Little is known about them, but one, the *Peri alupias*, which appears in the *Suda* catalogue, existed in a private library in Memphis at the beginning of the third century AD.[40]

Such multifarious activity in several fields of learning is typical of most Alexandrian scholars, especially in the third century. The "two cultures", as defined by C.P. Snow in our century, were certainly not differentiated in Hellenistic Alexandria. Many scholars were also poets. Today, certain representatives of the humanities, at least in Swedish universities, are criticized for not properly distinguishing between scholarly research and literary pursuits. The same criticism could be directed against the Alexandrians, as Eratosthenes was himself well aware.

There is also a danger in being a polyhistor, as the Alexandrians normally were. If it is not just malicious slander when the sources report that Eratosthenes was nicknamed Beta because he busied himself in *panti eidei paideias* but did not attain the highest standard in any branch of learning, he illustrates the precarious situation of the omniscient: versatility must often be bought at the price of superficiality, in our academic world as in Alexandria.

To sum up: Alexandrian scientists did not devote themselves to the ideal of pure science, as delineated at the beginning of this section, and science was not such a dominating interest of Hellenistic man as has been supposed. On the other hand, it can hardly be denied that Hellenistic science marks the apogee of ancient science and that its influence dominated scientific thought in Europe for more than 1500 years. We still stand in debt to Eratosthenes and other Alexandrians for the insights they left to posterity.

If Eratosthenes can be regarded as typical of his time, there was also in that period a tendency to assert the independence of science in relation to other learned pursuits. He was a polyhistor, no doubt, but saw at least some advantage in specialization. We have already noticed that Eratosthenes, presumably in opposition to Callimachus and Apollonius, drew a line of demarcation between poetry and science. He denied that the *Odyssey* or the *Argonautica*, *qua* poetry, offered reliable information on geographical matters. His pointed remark that the wanderings of Odysseus could be located in the real world only when one found the cobbler who had sewn the bag in which Aeolus locked up the winds, is preserved in a quotation from Polybius by Strabo.[41]

What is more important is that Eratosthenes also tried to establish the independence of science from philosophy. When he chose to call himself a *philologos*, it was a signal that he did not want to be mistaken for a philosopher, and there is evidence to show that he kept his distance to certain varieties of philosophy that he had become acquainted with in Athens. According to the criticism of Polemon of Ilium, which the Stoic Strabo is anxious to report, Eratosthenes had failed to pay due respect to the orthodox successors of Zeno and enhanced the reputation of heretics with no lasting influence like Ariston of Chios.[42] Ariston can be said to represent the opposition against the Athenian philosophical establishment, just as two other alleged cronies of Eratosthenes who are linked with Ariston in the same passage in Polemon/Strabo, viz. Arcesilaus, who gave the Middle Academy its sceptical inclination, and Bion of Borysthenes with his shocking Cynic habits and opinions. From our point of view, this can be seen as an attempt to establish the independence of Eratosthenes and his scientific endeavours from the current philosophical systems of the period, i.e., to define himself as a true scientist. The ancients took another view, and Eratosthenes was accused of not being a true philosopher but somebody who only goes half the way, and his own philosophical writings were maliciously adduced as evidence of his failure.[43] Evidently, Eratosthenes' strivings to free science from its associations with philosophy and poetry had not been successful.

Finally we shall touch upon the main theme of the seminar, the interaction between the Greek and other imported cultures and the indigenous civilisation of Egypt. There is little to be said about Alexandrian science in this particular context. None of the characteristics that distinguish Hellenistic science from the science of the Classical age is due to Egyptian influence. Rather, Alexandrian science may be seen as the continuation of a development that had started already in fourth-century Athens, especially in the school of Aristotle, the influence of which on Eratosthenes is clearly visible.

Egypt was a land of learning long before Greece, and the Greeks were well aware of the fact. The Egyptians are credited with the "invention" of a number of institutions that the Greeks regarded as indispensable in a human society. The inventions also included sciences, e.g., geometry and astronomy. The belief in the Egyptian priority in these fields, expressed already by Herodotus,[44] persisted into Hellenistic times, as witnessed by Strabo and Diodorus of Sicily.[45] These authors also speak of buildings erected for the convenience of priests who studied astronomy and philosophy and of astronomical records kept for an incredibly long period of time and eventually translated into Greek.[46] But the activities that had resulted in these records from time immemorial had ceased to exist in Strabo's own time.[47]

Among the names of scientists and scholars active in Alexandria, the Egyptian ones are a small minority.[48] Egyptians normally appear as astrologers, some of them only as authors of trivial horoscopes, not as astronomers. There are a number of doctors among them, even one *basilikos iatros*,[49] but nothing indicates that they contributed to or profited from the advance of anatomical studies in Alexandria under Herophilus and Erasistratus or, in general, that they took part in the debate between the different schools of Greek medicine. Among men of letters we may mention the hymnographer Isidorus, the historians Manetho and Ptolemy of Mendes, the paradoxographer Bolos from the same Egyptian city, and the philosopher Aithiops.[50] Thus, indigenous Egyptians seem to have contributed little to the scientific achievements of the Greek immigrants.

As for Eratosthenes' relations with the Egyptians, we should firstly note that he did not share the prejudices that many Greeks felt towards other nations, the so-called barbarians. Towards the end of the introductory book of his *Geography* he criticized Aristotle's advice to Alexander to treat Greeks as friends and barbarians as enemies and praised Alexander for ignoring it and bestowing his favours on men according to their talent but irrespective of their ethnic origin.[51]

Arriving in Egypt with that un-prejudiced attitude towards its non-Greek inhabitants, did Eratosthenes profit from their knowledge of the country when he wrote his geography? Did he exploit the annals kept in the Egyptian temples or Manetho's Egyptian history, that was certainly available in the Library, when he laid the chronological frame-work for historical research? Are there any other traces of Egyptian learning or experience in his scientific or literary works?

These questions must, on the whole, be answered in the negative. I have been able to detect only one item in the whole work of Eratosthenes that, with some degree of certainty, reveals an Egyptian influence.[52] In his *Hermes*, the god plays the role of an expounder of cosmological wisdom to mankind. This is a role that is, on the whole, alien to the Greek god. But it is characteristic of the Egyptian god of wisdom, Thoth, with whom Hermes was identified at an early stage. The *Hermes* of Eratosthenes may be said to fore-shadow the merging of Thot and Hermes that took place later on in the shape of Hermes Trismegistus.

For the rest, it seems clear that Eratosthenes, like his colleagues in Alexandria, was very little interested in the surrounding *chôra* and its inhabitants. The Egyptian temple records, that would have been a gold-mine of historical information, have left no trace in Hellenistic historiography, except in the Egyptian Manetho, who, writing in Greek, presented the past of his country to other nations. Eratosthenes did not use them for his chronology, it seems. In his *Geography*, as we know it through the intermediary of Strabo, Egypt was described on the same lines as the other parts of Alexander's kingdom, but it is not clear whether Eratosthenes' information came from records kept in Alexandria or from indigenous informants, consulted by him.

In one case, Eratosthenes must have used information on Egypt that was obtained by him for a particular purpose. His calculation of the circumference of earth is based on two items of information that were not readily available to an astronomer making observations in Alexandria, (i) that at Syene, on the day of the summer solstice, the sun-rays at noon reach the bottom of wells dug there (i.e., the sun stands directly above the spot) and (ii) that the distance from Syene to Alexandria was 5000 stades. How did Eratosthenes get hold of these two facts? According to the only ancient source that comments on this detail, viz., Martianus Capella, the information was obtained from the king's surveyors;[53] in modern times this has been interpreted in the sense that the royal bematists were sent out by the king with orders to measure the distance for the sole profit of the scientist, and the wording of Martianus points in that direction.[54] If the interpretation is correct, this means that, instead of consulting the Egyptians, who sailed and travelled between Syene and Alexandria, Eratosthenes used the resources put to his disposal for this very purpose by his royal employer. However, the interpretation is far from certain, and the information may have been obtained from people who had acquired it by practical experiences, as in a similar case reported by Strabo.[55]

Thus, the inhabitants of the learned institutions of Alexandria seem to have had little contact with the native Egyptians. We may add: with the Greeks of Egypt, too. The finds of papyri have given us ample insight into the life of the Greek population in Egypt, and the literary texts among them indicate their literary tastes. Among the papyri of the Hellenistic period the scientific writings of the Alexandrians do not appear at all. What there is of science — if the sense of the word is defined in a liberal way — mainly consists of medical prescriptions and horoscopes. In addition there is one elementary astronomical text-book, the so-called *Eudoxi Ars astronomica*, in a papyrus from c. 195 BC.[56] On the basis of the papyrus texts no one could imagine that scientific research on an advanced level had ever been going on in Hellenistic Alexandria. The same may be said of Alexandrian poetry. There are few specimens of it in the Hellenistic papyri and they are greatly outnumbered by the Classical texts of earlier periods. In comparison, the philological work of the Alexandrian grammarians has left more traces in contemporary papyri.

"An Athens among Assyrians" was the designation one Hellenistic poet used about his Graeco-Macedonian home-town in its barbarian environment.[57] Alexandria, in its capacity of a centre for science, may be described in similar words. The Athenian, and in the case of Eratosthenes especially the Aristotelian, tradition had been brought there by immigrants. They formed a closed circle, which opened itself when a new, preferably highly accomplished, colleague arrived from somewhere else in the Greek world. They were little interested in their Egyptian surroundings, Greek or indigenous, and the surroundings, on their part, went about their own business and ignored the scientists.

Notes

1. The fragments of Eratosthenes are cited from the sources. In addition the relevant numbers from the principal fragment collections are given (Berger 1880, Jacoby *FGrH*, Powell 1925, Parsons 1952). In addition to literature explicitly referred to in the foot-notes, the article is based on a number of works mentioned only in the bibliography (which, however, does not raise any claims to be exhaustive).
2. *Suda* s.v. *Eratosthenês*, T 1 Jacoby. The reading *bêta*, which we adopt here instead of Adler's *ta bêmata*, is found in pseudo-Hesychius *Peri tôn en paideiai dialampsantôn sophôn* 260, a compilation from the 9th or 10th century that used the *Suda* as one of its sources; it is confirmed by Marcianus of Heraclea and an anonymous geographical chrestomathy with excerpts from Strabo (cf. *Geographi Graeci minores* I.565 (text 2), and II.531 (text 3) (frg. 17–18 Berger)). It was introduced into the *Suda* text by Meursius.
3. I.e. a "jack of all trades".
4. Aristophanes and Aristarchus are the famous Alexandrian grammarians. Mnaseas of Patara in Lycia was a mythographer, Menandros is possibly identical with the historian Menandros of Ephesus. The name *Aristis* is perhaps corrupt.
5. *Katastêrigmoi* is probably identical with the *Katasterismoi* mentioned by other sources. The text of the *Suda* may be corrupt as, e.g., Jacoby supposes.
6. Polemon of Ilium, active as geographer and grammarian in Alexandria c. 200 BC. Cf. Strabo 1.2.2, frg. 11 Berger.
7. Dicks 1971, 388 argued that the date given by the *Suda* is correct and, consequently, that Zeno died in the mid-fifties. His argument has been accepted by Dragoni 1979, 13–15. However, Dicks mainly bases himself on information given by Diogenes Laertius. Diogenes is a late source, and conclusions based on the Herculaneum papyri are more likely to be correct.
8. Strabo 1.2.2, frg. 14 Berger (text 4).
9. Lucianus *Macrobii* 27, frg. 14 Berger, T 3 Jacoby (text 5).

10. *Anthologia Palatina* 7.78, T 6 Jacoby (text 6). The epigram is ascribed in the MS to a Dionysius of Cyzicus. He is elsewhere unknown and cannot be dated with certainty, but the epigram gives the impression of being intended for the grave of Eratosthenes and written by a contemporary of his. With due reservation for its literary character, the epigram may be regarded as a primary source to Eratosthenes' biography.

11. Athenaeus 276a—c, F 16 Jacoby.

12. There is no evidence to show that he had been educated in Alexandria before he went to Athens. Dragoni 1979, 17—20 thinks that Eratosthenes had been Callimachus' disciple in Alexandria in his very youth. This is hardly correct. Firstly, at that early period the Alexandrian grammarians had not acquired enough fame to attract disciples from other parts of the world. If a family of Cyrene sent their son to receive higher education abroad, that would be to the philosophers in Athens rather than the grammarians of Alexandria. Secondly, the information that Eratosthenes was Callimachus' disciple comes from the *Suda* and must be viewed with distrust, especially so since the names of the two famous Cyrenaeans would tend to gravitate towards each other in the biographical tradition.

13. This information is not confirmed by any other source, but the enthronement of Ptolemy III in 246 may be regarded as a *terminus post quem*. The *terminus ante* will be 236, the latest possible date for the death of Apollonius of Rhodes, who was Eratosthenes' predecessor as chief librarian. Eratosthenes had probably been in Alexandria for some years before he became chief librarian.

14. Knaack 1907, 372.

15. Strabo 2.4.2, III B 96 Berger (text 7). Cf. Strabo 2.1.41, III B 96 Berger (text 8).

16. Pseudo-Longinus, *Peri Hypsous* 33.5 (text 9).

17. Strabo 1.2.3 (I A 20 Berger) *poiêtên gar ephê panta stochazesthai psuchagôgias, ou didaskalias.* Cf. also the other passages collected by Berger under the heading *Homerfrage* and Fraser 1970, 190f, Fraser 1972, 759f. Gertrud Lindberg points out to me that *psuchagôgia*, although generally translated by "entertainment" in this passage, also may denote "persuasion" — especially on moral issues — as opposed to knowledge imparted by logical demonstration (*didaskalia*).

18. *Thaumatôn tôn eis hapasan tên gên kata topous ontôn sunagôgê.* Cf. Callimachus frg. 407—411 Pfeiffer.

19. Strabo 1.3.1, I B 6 Berger (text 10). *Bergaios* here means "romancer", after the notorious story-teller Antiphanes of Thracian Berge.

20. Archimedes *Peri tôn mêchanikôn theôrêmatôn pros Eratosthenên ephodos* II.426.4f, 428.16—20 Heiberg (text 11).

21. II.528.1—4 Heiberg (text 12).

22. Cf. the names listed in *Prosopographia Ptolemaica*, in the section "La vie culturelle" (nos. 16509—17250). Apollonius, whom we generally call a Rhodian, was, according to some sources, born in Naucratis. Among the early chief librarians also Apollonius *ho eidographos* was born in Egypt (Alexandria). In the second and first centuries the situation is different. At that time the Alexandrian scholars had their own families and followers; e.g., the homonymous son of Apollonius of Perge was presumably born in Egypt.

23. This development is described by Steinmetz 1969. Cf. also Blomqvist 1973-74.

24. Plutarchus *Caesar* 59.3, Plinius *Naturalis historia* 18.211f (Sosigenes mentioned), Dio Cassius 43.26.2 *touto de ek tês en Alexandreiai diatribês elabe*, Appianus *Bella civilia* 2.154.

25. Tiberius actually met Thrasyllus during his stay in Rhodes 6 BC—AD 2.

26. That his father was really called Aglaos is confirmed by Dionysius of Cyzicus and Lucianus. *Suda*'s alternative Ambrosios appears only in this late source. Stephanus of Byzantium, s.v. *Kurênê*, has provided Eratosthenes with a loftier patronymic, *Agaklês*.

27. Plinius *Naturalis historia* 7.151, Valerius Maximus 7.1.2, Pausanias 8.24.7. Another historical Aglaos (or Aglaus) appears in an imperial prescript of 222 AD (*Codex Justinianus* 5.51.4; cf. *RE* s.v. Aglaos).
28. On the Cyrenaeans' pride of their Dorian ancestry cf. Fraser 1970, 177f. It was still strong in the time of Synesius.
29. Vatai 1984, 31 (with n. 12; on philosophers in general), 84 (on Plato's disciples).
30. The case of Aristotle is a little different. He was the son of a doctor, but the family had contacts with princely and royal families long before Aristotle became Alexander's tutor. Plato, of course, was an Athenian aristocrat.
31. Fraser 1970, 183f.
32. Wifstrand 1950, 23, 25.
33. Grønbech 1939 (I), 312-322.
34. Eratosthenes erected in Alexandria a stele with a specimen of the instrument attached to it and a metrical inscription that described its use. The poem is quoted and the instrument described in a possibly fictitious letter to King Ptolemy, preserved by Eutocius in his commentary on Archimedes' *De sphaera et cylindro* (III.89.3—97.27 Heiberg). On Eratosthenes as a mathematician in general, cf. Wolfer 1954. On his *Peri mesotêtôn*, Muwafi & Philippou 1981.
35. On Eratosthenes' *Geographia*, cf. Knaack 1907, 364—377, Aujac 1966, 49—64.
36. How small — or great — the error was continues to be a matter of contention; cf. Cimino 1982, Engels 1985, Firsov 1972, Goldstein 1984, Gulbekian 1987, Newton 1980, Rawlings 1982a and b.
37. *POxy.* 2521 (of the second century AD with fragments of a Hellenistic hexameter poem) has been thought to contain an astronomical fragment of Eratosthenes. Cf. Treu 1967.
38. Strabo 17.3.22 (frg. 13 Berger, T 2 Jacoby), Lucianus *Macrobii* 27 (frg. 16 Berger, T 3 Jacoby), Clemens Alexandrinus *Stromateis* 1.79.3 (T 8 Jacoby).
39. Suetonius *Grammatici* 10 (frg. 15 Berger) *philologi appellationem assumpsisse videtur* [sc. Ateius], *quia, sicut Eratosthenes, qui primus hoc cognomen sibi vindicavit, multiplici variaque doctrina censebatur.*
40. Mitteis & Wilcken 1912, I:2, 182—184 (*Pap. Petersburg* 13). On Eratosthenes as a philosopher, cf. Solmsen 1942, Wolfer 1954, 55—64.
41. Strabo 1.2.15 (I A 16 Berger, Polybius 34.2.11) (text 13). Cf. Eustathius on *Odyssey* 11.19.
42. Strabo 1.2.2 (frg. 11 Berger)(text 14).
43. Strabo *ib.* (text 15). Cf. also Marcianus of Heraclea, quoted above n. 2 (text 2).
44. Herodotus 2.109.3 *dokeei de moi entheuten geômetriê heuretheisa es tên Hellada epanelthein.*
45. Strabo 16.2.24, Diodorus 1.9.6; 1.50.1—2.
46. Strabo 17.1.29 (buildings in Heliopolis; translation of astronomical texts into Greek), Diodorus 1.81.4 (records of astronomical observations).
47. Strabo 17.1.29. Cf. Plinius *Naturalis historia* 2.46 on the decline of Oriental science in general.
48. I refer once again to *Prosopographia Ptolemaica*, where the Egyptian scientists and doctors are listed under their own headings (nos. 16564-16570, 16652-16667) and totally outnumbered by their Greek colleagues (nos. 16522-16563, 16571-16651).
49. *Prosopographia Ptolemaica* no. 16661.
50. *Prosopographia Ptolemaica* nos. 16697, 16934, 16946, 16740, 16865, 16727. The list is made up on the basis of a superficial perusal of the prosopography, but I doubt that further research will reveal many more names. The name of the grammarian Komanos of Naucratis is Greek, as Dorothy Thompson points out to me, and he came from a Greek city.
51. Strabo 1.4.9 (text 16). Contrast Aristotle's view on the inborn abilities of barbarians, *Politica* 1252b5-9 (text) 17.

52. This is said with all reservations that are made necessary by the fact that the works of Eratosthenes, the *Hermes* in particular, are known only in fragments.

53. Martianus Capella 6.596 *Eratosthenes vero a Syene ad Meroen* [read *Alexandriam*] *per mensores regios Ptolemei certus de stadiorum numero redditus.*

54. Knaack 1907, 365, who also imagines that wells were dug at Syene for the same purpose.

55. Strabo 2.2.2 where it is stated that the distance from Meroe to the parallel of the Land of Cinnamon is known precisely because people sail or travel over it (*touto men oun to diastêma pan esti metrêton, pleitai te gar kai hodeuetai*).

56. Dorothy Thompson points out to me that one of the illustrations in the papyrus, for no intrinsic reason, shows an ibis. This is the only sign of Egyptian influence in it.

57. Meleagros of Gadara, *Anthologia Palatina* 7.417.2.

Texts

Ἐρατοσθένης· Ἀγλαοῦ, οἱ δὲ Ἀμβροσίου· Κυρηναῖος, μαθητὴς φιλοσόφου Ἀρίστωνος Χίου, γραμματικοῦ δὲ Λυσανίου τοῦ Κυρηναίου καὶ Καλλιμάχου τοῦ ποιητοῦ. μετεπέμφθη δὲ ἐξ Ἀθηνῶν ὑπὸ τοῦ τρίτου Πτολεμαίου καὶ διέτριψε μέχρι τοῦ πέμπτου. διὰ δὲ τὸ δευτερεύειν ἐν παντὶ εἴδει παιδείας τοῖς ἄκροις ἐγγίσασι τὰ βήματα ἐπεκλήθη. οἱ δὲ καὶ δεύτερον ἢ νέον Πλάτωνα, ἄλλοι Πένταθλον ἐκάλεσαν. ἐτέχθη δὲ ρκϛ΄ ὀλυμπιάδι καὶ ἐτελεύτησεν π΄ ἐτῶν γεγονώς, ἀποσχόμενος τροφῆς διὰ τὸ ἀμβλυώττειν, μαθητὴν ἐπίσημον καταλιπὼν Ἀριστοφάνην τὸν Βυζάντιον, οὗ πάλιν Ἀρίσταρχος μαθητής. μαθηταὶ δὲ αὐτοῦ Μνασέας καὶ Μένανδρος καὶ Ἄριστις. ἔγραψε δὲ φιλόσοφα καὶ ποιήματα καὶ ἱστορίας, Ἀστρονομίαν ἢ Καταστηριγμούς, Περὶ τῶν κατὰ φιλοσοφίαν αἱρέσεων, Περὶ ἀλυπίας, διαλόγους πολλοὺς καὶ γραμματικὰ συχνά.

1.   *Suda* s.v. *Eratosthenes*, T 1 Jacoby.

... Ἐρατοσθένης, ὃν βῆτα ἐκάλεσαν οἱ τοῦ Μουσείου προστάντες ...

2.   Marcianus of Heraclea (*Geographi Graeci minores* I.565), frg. 17 Berger.

ὅτι Ἐρατοσθένης οὔτε τῶν ἀπαιδεύτων ἦν οὔτε τῶν γνησίως φιλοσοφούντων· διὸ καὶ βῆτα ἐκαλεῖτο, ὡς τὰ δευτερεῖα φέρειν δοκῶν ἐπὶ πάσῃ παιδείᾳ.

3.   *Chrestomathia geographica* (*Geographi Graeci minores* II.531), frg. 18 Berger.

ἐντυχών, ὡς εἴρηκεν αὐτός, ἀγαθοῖς ἀνδράσιν. "ἐγένοντο γάρ" φησίν "ὡς οὐδέποτε, κατὰ τοῦτον τὸν καιρὸν ὑφ᾽ ἕνα περίβολον καὶ μίαν πόλιν οἱ κατ᾽ Ἀρίστωνα καὶ Ἀρκεσίλαον ἀνθήσαντες φιλόσοφοι." οὐχ ἱκανὸν δ᾽ οἶμαι τοῦτο, ἀλλὰ τὸ κρίνειν καλῶς οἷς μᾶλλον προσιτέον. ὁ δὲ Ἀρκεσίλαον καὶ Ἀρίστωνα τῶν καθ᾽ αὑτὸν ἀνθησάντων κορυφαίους τίθησιν· Ἀπελλῆς τε αὐτῷ πολύς ἐστι καὶ Βίων, ὅν φησι πρῶτον ἀνθινὰ περιβαλεῖν φιλοσοφίαν· ἀλλ᾽ ὅμως πολλάκις εἰπεῖν ἄν τινα ἐπ᾽ αὐτοῦ τοῦτο "οἵην ἐκ ρακέων ὁ Βίων."

4.   Strabo 1.2.2, frg. 14 Berger.

γραμματικῶν δὲ Ἐρατοσθένης μὲν ὁ Ἀγλαοῦ Κυρηναῖος, ὃν οὐ μόνον γραμματικόν, ἀλλὰ καὶ ποιητὴν ἄν τις ὀνομάσειεν καὶ φιλόσοφον καὶ γεωμέτρην, δύο καὶ ὀγδοήκοντα οὗτος ἔζησεν.

5. Lucianus *Macrobii* 27, frg. 14 Berger, T 3 Jacoby.

πρηΰτερον γῆράς σε καὶ οὐ κατὰ νοῦσος ἀμαυρὴ
ἔσβεσεν· εὐνήθης δ᾽ ὕπνον ὀφειλόμενον
ἄκρα μεριμνήσας, Ἐρατόσθενες· οὐδὲ Κυρήνη
μαῖά σε πατρῴων ἐντὸς ἔδεκτο τάφων,
Ἀγλαοῦ υἱέ, φίλος δὲ καὶ ἐν ξείνῃ κεκάλυψαι
πὰρ τόδε Πρωτῆος κράσπεδον αἰγιαλοῦ.

6. *Anthologia Palatina* 7.78, T 6 Jacoby.

Ἐρατοσθένους δὲ εἴρηται ἡ περὶ τὰ ἑσπέρια καὶ τὰ ἀρκτικὰ τῆς Εὐρώπης ἄγνοια. ἀλλ᾽ ἐκείνῳ μὲν καὶ Διακαιάρχῳ συγγνώμη, τοῖς μὴ κατιδοῦσι τοὺς τόπους ἐκείνους.

7. Strabo 2.4.2, III B 96 Berger.

καὶ νῦν δ᾽ εἰρήσθω, ὅτι καὶ Τιμοσθένης καὶ Ἐρατοσθένης καὶ οἱ ἔτι τούτων πρότεροι τελέως ἠγνόουν τά τε Ἰβηρικὰ καὶ τὰ Κελτικά, μυρίῳ δὲ μᾶλλον τὰ Γερμανικὰ καὶ τὰ Βρεττανικά, ὡς δ᾽ αὔτως τὰ τῶν Γετῶν καὶ Βασταρνῶν. ἐπὶ πολὺ δ᾽ ἀγνοίας ἐτύγχανον ἀφιγμένοι καὶ τῶν κατ᾽ Ἰταλίαν καὶ τὸν Ἀδρίαν καὶ τὸν Πόντον καὶ τῶν ἐφεξῆς προσαρκτίων μερῶν.

8. Strabo 2.1.41, III B 96 Berger

Ἐρατοσθένης ἐν τῇ Ἠριγόνῃ (διὰ πάντων γὰρ ἀμώμητον τὸ ποιημάτιον) Ἀρχιλόχου πολλὰ καὶ ἀνοικονόμητα παρασύροντος, κἀκείνης τῆς ἐκβολῆς τοῦ δαιμονίου πνεύματος ἣν ὑπὸ νόμον τάξαι δύσκολον, ἆρα δὴ μείζων ποιητής;

9. Pseudo-Longinus, *Peri Hypsous* 33.5.

ὁ δὲ Δαμάστη χρώμενος μάρτυρι οὐδὲν διαφέρει τοῦ καλοῦντος μάρτυρα τὸν
Βεργαῖον [ἢ τὸν Μεσσήνιον] Εὐήμερον καὶ τοὺς ἄλλους, οὓς αὐτὸς εἴρηκε διαβάλ-
λων τὴν φλυαρίαν.

10.   Strabo 1.3.1, I B 6 Berger.

ἀπέστειλά σοι πρότερον τῶν εὑρημένων θεωρημάτων ἀναγράψας αὐτῶν τὰς προτά-
σεις ... τούτων δὴ τῶν θεωρημάτων τὰς ἀποδείξεις ἐν τῷδε τῷ βιβλίῳ γράψας ἀ-
ποστελῶ σοι. ὁρῶν δέ σε, καθάπερ λέγω, σπουδαῖον καὶ φιλοσοφίας προεστηκότα
ἀξιολόγως καὶ τὴν ἐν τοῖς μαθήμασιν κατὰ τὸ ὑποπῖπτον θεωρίαν τετιμηκότα.

11.   Archimedes II.426.4f., 428.16-20 Heiberg.

Πρόβλημα, ὅπερ Ἀρχιμήδης ἐν ἐπιγράμμασιν εὑρὼν τοῖς ἐν Ἀλεξανδρείᾳ περὶ
ταῦτα πραγματευομένοις ζητεῖν ἀπέστειλεν ἐν τῇ πρὸς Ἐρατοσθένην τὸν Κυρη-
ναῖον ἐπιστολῇ.

12.   Archimedes II.528.1-4 Heiberg.

φησὶ τότ' ἂν εὑρεῖν τινα ποῦ Ὀδυσσεὺς πεπλάνηται ὅταν εὕρῃ τὸν σκυτέα τὸν
συρράψαντα τὸν τῶν ἀνέμων ἀσκόν.

13.   Strabo 1.2.15, I A Berger, Polybius 34.2.11.

τοῦ Ζήνωνος τοῦ Κιτιέως γνώριμος γενόμενος Ἀθήνησι τῶν μὲν ἐκεῖνον διαδε-
ξαμένων οὐδενὸς μέμνηται, τοὺς δ' ἐκείνῳ διενεχθέντας καὶ ὧν διαδοξὴ οὐδεμία
σῴζεται, τούτους ἀνθῆσαί φησι κατὰ τὸν καιρὸν ἐκεῖνον.

δηλοῖ δὲ καὶ ἡ περὶ τῶν ἀγαθῶν ἐκδοθεῖσα ὑπ' αὐτοῦ πραγματεία καὶ μελέται καὶ
εἴ τι ἄλλο τοιοῦτο τὴν ἀγωγὴν αὐτοῦ, διότι μέσος ἦν τοῦ τε βουλομένου φιλοσο-
φεῖν καὶ τοῦ μὴ θαρροῦντος ἐγχειρίζειν ἑαυτὸν εἰς τὴν ὑπόθεσιν ταύτην ἀλλὰ
μόνον μέχρι τοῦ δοκεῖν προϊόντος, ἢ καὶ παράβασίν τινα ταύτην ἀπὸ τῶν ἄλλων
τῶν ἐγκυκλίων πεπορισμένου πρὸς διαγωγὴν ἢ καὶ παιδιάν.

14-15.   Strabo 1.2.2, frg. 11 Berger.

οὐκ ἐπαινέσας τοὺς δίχα διαιροῦντας ἅπαν τὸ τῶν ἀνθρώπων πλῆθος εἴς τε
Ἕλληνας καὶ βαρβάρους καὶ τοὺς Ἀλεξάνδρῳ παραινοῦντας τοῖς μὲν Ἕλλησιν ὡς
φίλοις χρῆσθαι, τοῖς δὲ βαρβάροις ὡς πολεμίοις, βέλτιον εἶναί φησιν ἀρετῇ καὶ
κακίᾳ διαιρεῖν ταῦτα· πολλοὺς γὰρ καὶ τῶν Ἑλλήνων εἶναι κακοὺς καὶ τῶν βαρβάρων ἀστείους, καθάπερ Ἰνδοὺς καὶ Ἀριανούς, ἔτι δὲ Ῥωμαίους καὶ Καρχηδονίους
οὕτω θαυμαστῶς πολιτευομένους. διόπερ τὸν Ἀλέξανδρον ἀμελήσαντα τῶν παραι-
νούντων ὅσους οἷόν τ' ἦν ἀποδέχεσθαι τῶν εὐδοκίμων ἀνδρῶν καὶ εὐεργετεῖν.

16. Strabo 1.4.9

ἐν δὲ τοῖς βαρβάροις τὸ θῆλυ καὶ τὸ δοῦλον τὴν αὐτὴν ἔχει τάξιν. αἴτιον δ' ὅτι
τὸ φύσει ἄρχον οὐκ ἔχουσιν, ἀλλὰ γίνεται ἡ κοινωνία αὐτῶν δούλης καὶ δούλου.
διό φασιν οἱ ποιηταὶ "βαρβάρων δ' Ἕλληνας ἄρχειν εἰκός", ὡς ταὐτὸ φύσει βάρβα-
ρον καὶ δοῦλον ὄν.

17. Aristotle, *Politica* 1252b5-9.

ETHNICAL STRATEGIES
IN GRAECO-ROMAN EGYPT

Koen Goudriaan

In 113 BC Menchês, the village clerk of Kerkeosiris, reported to his superior a case of transgression of the royal oil-monopoly. A complaint about this trespass had been lodged by the oil seller Apollodôros, whose letter was included in the report. Apollodôros writes that the smuggling is the work of "a certain Thracian, whose name I do not know and who lives in Kerkesêphis".[1] He has been caught *in flagranti* in the house of the cobbler Petesouchos (l. 18). We cannot tell why Apollodôros was unable to produce the smuggler's name. Perhaps the name was Thracian and sounded too barbarous to be remembered, but this is pure speculation. The characteristics on account of which Apollodôros identified the transgressor as a Thracian also remain in the dark. Was it his name? Or the language he spoke? His dress? Manners? Or did Apollodôros recognize him as a member of a well-known group of Thracian settlers at Kerkesêphis? The only thing we may be sure about is that Apollodôros applied an ethnic label for the purpose of identification. It is also a fair guess that the ethnic traits selected by Apollodôros for identification purposes were exhibited by the Thracian involuntarily: It was not in his interest to be recognized.

Half a century earlier a votive inscription on behalf of the royal family was dedicated to Zeus Sôtêr by Lysimachos the son of Bastakilas together with his sons Bastakilas and (Eurô)mos;[2] Lysimachos expressly called himself "Thracian". The inscription is in Greek and the names are partly Greek (or Macedonian), partly Thracian. So Lysimachos had undergone hellenization to a considerable degree. Yet he seemed not to be ashamed of his Thracian ethnic identity; rather he considered it important enough to have it carved on the stone.

These cases illustrate the working of ethnicity in two ordinary situations. A smuggler originating from a neighbouring village is recognized by indications of his Thracian ethnical identity, a (presumably rather well-to-do) family immortalizes its Thracian descent by having it included in an inscription. In neither case is there any trace of ethnic tension, yet ethnicity plays a definite rôle.

Ethnic conflict may have been present in an incident of the year 218 BC reported from the Fayum. The Egyptian woman Senobastis molested the Greek Hêrakleidês by emptying the chamber pot on his body. In the ensuing wrangle she also tore Hêrakleidês' cloak to pieces and spat him in the face. Hêrakleidês thereupon wrote a petition to the king requesting him "not to overlook the insult done without reason to him as a Hellene and a stranger by an Egyptian woman".[3] As to his claim to his being a Hellene, the purport of this is not easy to grasp. Did Hêrakleidês mention the ethnic identities of the two parties with a view to the court to which the case should be relegated? Was the case aggravated by the fact that the wrong was done by an Egyptian to a Hellene, and not, for example, vice versa? Perhaps Hêrakleidês only thought this to be so and tried to present his case in as favourable a light as possible?

In any case, the misfortune that befell Hêrakleidês is somewhat similar to the troubles into which Ptolemaios the son of Glaukias got in the 160's and 150's BC. This recluse in the Serapis temple at Memphis repeatedly complained about attacks made on him and his relatives by other inhabitants of the temple area on account of his being a Hellene. Ptolemaios connected this violence with a rebellion that had taken place some years earlier and that apparently had had ethnic implications. Of course we need not take Ptolemaios on his word. Maybe the violence was ethnically coloured in his perception only. We may even doubt his sincerity and suspect that he hid his real motives beneath an ethnic pretention. What we cannot deny, however, is that Ptolemaios, just like Hêrakleidês and the Thracians mentioned earlier, did apply ethnic categories and believed them to have at least some relevance to the situation.[4]

Ethnicity is a type of social organization based on ascription. According to the Norwegian anthropologist Fredrik Barth, ascription to a certain category is ethnic "when it classifies a person in terms of his basic, most general identity, presumptively determined by his origin and background. To the extent that actors use ethnic identities to categorize themselves and others for purposes of interaction, they form ethnic groups".[5]

The implications of this approach to ethnicity can be summed up as follows:

1. Ethnicity is looked at from the inside. Central to it are the categories used by participants in social interaction in order to classify themselves and the "others". Ethnic groups are not considered to be fixed entities with an objective

existence based on inherent qualities of the people belonging to them, but as projections of the minds of those participating in ethnically coloured interaction.

2. Ethnicity, as a way of organizing cultural differences, implies that specific features of culture (in the broad sense) are singled out as ethnically significant, whilst others are neutral. On the basis of these traits the participants in a given society are divided in a "we" and a "they". The features that serve as boundary marks between the ethnic groups may vary greatly in time. For the maintenance of ethnicity it is necessary, however, that the boundaries themselves are kept intact.

3. Ethnicity is an independent dimension of social life. Though it may borrow features of culture such as religion, occupation, mode of life and especially language, to serve as boundary marks, it cannot be reduced to any one of these aspects of life in society. Moreover, in itself it is not connected with juridical status; neither is ethnicity identical with "nationality", *Staatszugehörigkeit*, or with naturalization, which are anachronistic concepts if applied to Hellenistic Egypt.

4. Survival of an ethnic identity group, in this view, is not the result of its biological reproduction, but the outcome of a continued interest on the part of its members in maintaining the boundaries. Each generation must decide for itself whether or not to adopt the transmitted ethnic identity. As soon as the maintenance of ethnic identity is considered irrelevant, the ethnic group disappears; many minor immigrant identities did so in Ptolemaic Egypt. One might describe the history of an ethnic group as the outcome of the combined ethnical strategies of its members and of those with whom they are in contact. An *ethnical strategy* can be defined as the policy adopted by an individual or a group for applying ethnical categories to themselves and to "others" in a range of different circumstances. People may prefer, e.g., to stick to a fixed set of categories, no matter on which occasion they use it. Alternatively, they may manipulate the ethnical labels at their disposal in such a way as to serve their immediate interests or to express their varying loyalties on a series of moments.

5. Ethnicity is a *normal* feature of social life. It does not automatically entail tension between the ethnic groups: so long as these are in agreement on the roles they have to play in society they may live peacefully together. So some of the examples given at the start of this paper are somewhat misleading. The case of Menchês, the village clerk of Kerkeosiris, who enumerates a score of Hellenic farmers as part of his administration, is much more normal. The *degree* of ethnic tension and of ethnic exclusivism are aspects of ethnicity that must be considered

for themselves. In the present paper this will be done in connection with the Alexandrian pogrom.

6. In projecting the concept of "ethnicity" back to Antiquity I start from the premise that, fundamentally, this marking off of boundaries is a universal trait of human experience. The way in which it manifests itself may, of course, vary greatly through the ages.

It is important to realize the nature of the connection between ethnicity and culture. An image might be helpful. The ethnic groups of a given society can be compared to a couple of vessels communicating through a filter. Though the filter will block the percolating of certain elements from one vessel into another, osmosis will cause the chemical composition of the liquids in all vessels to be much alike and the levels to be even. The vessels are the ethnic groups, their content is the culture of the society they share, the filter is the ethnic boundary. It can be seen that for the working of ethnicity the content of the shared culture is largely irrelevant so long as a filter is blocking certain elements from filtering through: these are the cultural traits that serve as boundary marks. Over the times both the content of the vessels and the filters used may change, but if the installation of the vessels remains unchanged the game of ethnic oppositions is continued with the same set of categories. This amounts to saying that, to a large degree, ethnicity is a formal affair. To those applying ethnic categories it does not appear so, however. They usually think that the cultural traits singled out by them as ethnically relevant reveal the very nature of the groups concerned.

Returning once more to ethnic strategies, they can be said to be generally directed at the aim of attaining certain "resources" (cultural as well as material). In this respect they may be influenced considerably by the degree to which government policy takes ethnicity into account for distributing (material and/or legal) "resources". It seems probable that the Ptolemaic government, at least during the first two centuries of its existence, did not use ethnicity as a factor in governing the country otherwise than for identification purposes (the reasons for this I have given in my *Ethnicity in Ptolemaic Egypt*).[6] Conditions prevailing in early Roman Alexandria were different, however, as we shall see in a moment.

The present paper will study some aspects of the dynamics of ethnicity, by focusing first briefly on the Thracians, then in more detail on the Jews.

The Thracians

The papyri allow us to observe the gradual merging of the Thracians of Egypt

with the other ethnic groups (presumably mainly with the Greeks, though we cannot be sure of that). The majority of Greek papyri mentioning Thracians (52 out
of 87, amounting to a percentage of 59,8) date from the third century. Then the
numbers decline: 21 documents (24,1%) date from the second and 4 (4,6%) from
the first century BC; 10 documents (11,5%) are undated but probably Ptolemaic.
In the Imperial period, Thracians only occur in connection with specific Roman
cohorts: that is quite different from ethnicity as studied here. As to individual
Thracians known, statistics are as follows: 71 Thracians in the third century, 31
in the second, 5 in the first and 10 undated (60,7%; 26,5%; 4,3% and 8,5%
respectively out of a total of 117).

    I am aware that indications such as "Thracian" might be considered as *pseudo-
ethnic*: instead of real "ethnic" Thracians only members of a Thracian army corps
were meant. In fact, most Thracians handed down to us are military settlers and
the papyri often, in addition to their name and the Ethnikon *Thraix*, mention the
regiment to which they belong or the military status "of the *epigonê*" which they
possess. A hipparchy "of the Thracians" is known to have existed in the early
Ptolemaic period.[7] One might easily get the impression that the situation was the
same as in the Roman period. Yet against this interpretation several objections
must be made:

    1. In a number of cases Thracians are mentioned without any connection with
the military; we had occasion already to study two of them.[8] Even some Thracian
women are known.[9] 2. Army divisions are normally indicated by the name of
the officer in command.[10] 3. Often soldiers belonging to the same army corps
have different Ethnika.[11] 4. Apart from an occasional mustering of cavalry horses
(*PPetrie* 3,35) most documents mentioning Thracians deal with thoroughly civilian
affairs, such as payments, loans, contracts and testaments. Several are of a
religious nature.[12] Often Thracians, along with persons belonging to other ethnic
groups, are mentioned among the witnesses of a *syggrafê hexamartyros* (a six-
witnesses-contract). *PPetrie* 3,10, for instance, starts a list of witnesses with
"Artemidôros, a Thracian, possessor of 100 *arourai*, belonging to the men of
Nautas (?), about 55 years old, tall, with black skin and a scar on the nose". For
particular types of documents a *Nomenklaturregel*[13] was in force, obliging
individuals to mention their *patris* as one of the elements of a person's description.
For non-Hellenic groups Ethnika such as "Thracian", "Libyan", "Mysian" were
the equivalent of *patrides* of the type "Athenian", "Cyrenaean" etc. This obligation
may have strengthened ethnic consciousness, but it has nothing to do with the

military. 5. Persons labelled "Thracian" but exhibiting Greek nomenclature are Hellenized Thracians rather than Thracized Hellenes. And how are we to interpret cases of individuals with a Greek proper name in combination with a Thracian patronymic?[14] 6. The theory of pseudo-ethnicity presupposes biological descent as the criterium for real ethnicity; this must be rejected.[15]

So the Thracians mentioned in the papyri were really "Thracian" in the ethnic sense: they looked at themselves as Thracian and were considered to be so by others. Once this is established, we may observe the early and thorough Hellenization of the Thracians as shown by their personal names (notice that this involves *culture*, not *ethnicity*!). From the third century 59 sufficiently legible names of Thracians came to my notice; 40 of them (67,8%) were Greek (including Macedonian), 19 only (32,2%) Thracian. In the second century the share of Greek names mounts to 22 out of 26 (84,6%); from the first century we have four Thracians with Greek names and one with a Thracian name; the undated documents yield 6 Greek names and one Thracian name. For the patronymics the outcome is paramount.[16] Very interesting is the case of a Thracian with an Egyptian name, Orsenouphis (*OMich.* 734; 1st century BC). He parallels the two dozen Hellenes of Kerkeosiris with Egyptian names mentioned by Menchês.[17]

The Thracians of Egypt adopted Greek names, they used the Greek language, the army made them familiar with the Greek way of life. They worshipped the same Gods as the Greeks (Zeus Sôtêr, Euodos, Sarapis). In the end, there was no cultural feature left by which they could (or, for that matter, would) distinguish themselves from the Greeks. At that moment they vanished from history.

The Jews: Philo of Alexandria

The hellenization of the Jews was thorough, too. In contrast with the Thracians, however, the Jews did not disappear. The situation of the Jews in the Diaspora including Egypt has been characterized as a "spectrum of attempts to strike a balance between" two "competing factors", the "constraints of the Jewish tradition" on the one hand and the "values of the Hellenistic world" on the other.[18] Despite hellenization, both the Jews themselves and the non-Jews continued to perceive an ethnic boundary. The features selected to mark that boundary were, no doubt, religious and not, for instance, linguistic: Egyptian Jews ceased to speak Hebrew.

Studying the ethnic position of the Jews may contribute to the solution of a difficulty that confronts us in connection with the Greeks and the Egyptians of Ptolemaic Egypt. Continuation of ethnic identity groups — we stated above —

might be explained as the result of a large number of individual ethnic strategies. Can we observe such strategies in Ptolemaic Egypt? It would require us to be able to trace the ethnic behaviour of some individuals or of a neatly defined group in a range of circumstances. Papyrological evidence hardly meets this requirement. The material collected in my *Ethnicity in Ptolemaic Egypt* presents only a very limited number of persons figuring in ethnically defined situations more than once.[19] The use of ethnic categories alone is not sufficient. We must be sure that this use reflects the way in which the persons mentioned in a document perceived their own ethnic identities as well as of those of the other individuals mentioned. An administrative record enumerating "Greek" tax-payers is no indication of the ethnic strategy of these Greeks, but discloses only the outlook of the clerk that drew up the list.[20] The case that comes nearest to it is that of Ptolemaios the son of Glaukias who complained that, as a Greek, he was wronged by a couple of Egyptians.[21] His strategy, so far as we can tell, was rather simple. As to Dionysios the son of Kephalas, it is conceivable that his career[22] contained a shift in ethnic identity. The papyri, however, are silent about it.

It is here that a side leap to the case of the Jews offers relief. The writings of Philo Judaeus contain numerous indications of the ethnical strategy adopted by this Jewish philosopher in his dealings with Jews, Greeks, and Egyptians. And the pogrom of 38 AD in Alexandria, an ethnic conflict, is well enough documented to allow a glimpse of both Philo's attitude and that of his opponents.

Of course, basing oneself on the works of Philo has several disadvantages. Philo lived half a century after the close of the Ptolemaic era. He resided in Alexandria, not in the *chôra*. He was a Jew living under Roman rule, and so his situation was *ipso facto* more complicated than that of the Greeks and the Egyptians confronting each other under the Ptolemies. Above all, we catch sight of his ethnic strategy for a large part through writings of a philosophical or exegetical nature, not as it was operating in real life. Philo starts from the Scriptures and so is obliged to use the ethnic categories mentioned by his source in addition to those current in his own age. These difficulties are serious, indeed; yet I suggest that we take the risk. The prize offered to our experiment is the uncovering of an ethnical strategy that is both firm and subtle.[23]

We start by passing in review the ethnical categories applied by Philo.[24] In order to indicate the Jewish people and the Jewish inheritance he has several terms at his disposal. The first one, *Hebraioi*, obviously is derived from the Septuagint. It is applied only to the historical people of Israel. Neither Philo nor the papyri ever use this term to indicate the contemporary Jews.[25] Often the terms *Hebraioi* and *Hebraisti* refer to the Hebrew language. Usually in those cases Hebrew is opposed to Greek.[26] In the remaining instances the use of this term is connected with the exegesis of Biblical passages.[27] Often the Hebrews are confronted with the *Aigyptioi*, and this is exactly what the Biblical context suggests. Moses himself is called a Hebrew (*Mutat.* 117). Hagar was of Egyptian extraction, but she became a Hebrew according to her choice of life (*Abr.* 251). When the Israelites left Egypt they were followed by "a mixed and fused crowd, descendants from Egyptian women and Hebrew men" (*Mos.* 1,147). Sometimes the name *Hebraioi* receives a spiritual explanation — the Hebrew is the one who "crosses over" from the world of the senses to the spiritual, noetic sphere (*Migr.* 20; cp. 141; *Her.* 128; *Fug.* 168) — but there is no discontinuity between the allegorical and the historical meaning. The most recent "Hebrews" figuring in Philo's work are the translators of the *Tora* sent by the High Priest to Ptolemy Philadelphus (*Mos.* 2,32). Of course Philo is aware of the historical connection between the Hebrews and the Jews of his times. Joseph, in conversation with Potiphar's wife, defends the Jewish laws on chastity in a way that is more apt to first century Alexandria. Here he speaks of "we descendants of the Hebrews"(*Ios.* 42).[28]

The term *Ioudaios* (or *Ioudaikos*) is used sparingly in the exegetical works. It is reserved mainly for the treatises *In Flaccum* and *Legatio ad Gaium*, thus indicating contemporary Jewry. Philo avoids calling the ancestors of the Jews prior to Moses' time *Ioudaioi*. Moses himself, however, is repeatedly styled "lawgiver of the Jews" (*Mos.* 1,1; *Prob.* 29; 43). In sum, in his explanation of the Biblical writings Philo displays awareness both of the continuity between the ancient Hebrews and the Jews of his days and of the distance, caused mainly by linguistic diversity.

Rather peculiar is Philo's use of the synonyms *to ethnos* and *ho laos / leôs*. In the Septuagint the word pair *laos* — *ethnê* (plural) sometimes occurs as the Greek equivalent for the Hebrew *âm* (Israel) and *goyim* (the gentiles). This idiom does not recur in Philo. Moreover, the term *laos* is found rather infrequently in his writings, mostly in a quotation (*laos*) or explanation (*leôs*) of a scriptural passage. Elsewhere we usually find the expression *to ethnos*, "the people", *tout court*, as a designation of the Jewish people.[29] The Jews are called *hoi apo tou ethnous*, "those of the people".[30] *Ethnos* in this sense sometimes is set in mild opposition to "the whole human race", "the whole inhabited world".[31]

The gentile peoples figuring most prominently in Philo's works are the Egyptians and the Greeks. In contrast with the Greeks, the Egyptians are consistently given a bad press by Philo, whether he has to deal with them as a philosopher and biblical exegete or as a politician in the reality of contemporary Alexandria.[32] Both in the exegetical works and in the *Legatio* he censures them for their *atheotês* (ungodliness), meaning their zoolatry.[33] When the children of Israel worship the golden calf they imitate the manners of the Egyptians (*Mos.* 2,161). In *Legatio* 80 Philo describes Gaius taking on the shape of various gods, in the manner of "Egyptian" Proteus: the Egyptians prefer the manifold to the One. Moreover, the Egyptians are envious, rebellious, lacking in discipline, scurrilous and inhospitable.[34] Seldom Philo has anything friendly to say about the Egyptians. According to *Spec.* 1,2, Egyptians and Jews share the rite of circumcision. And in *Ios* 20,3 Joseph's brothers discover that in the ordering of a banquet the Egyptians apply the seniority principle adopted by themselves, too.[35] In the exegetical works Egypt, is the symbol for a life spent in the passions and desires of the flesh.[36] In this allegory the connection between the real, historical Egyptians and the spiritual Egypt is maintained, as is made clear by *Mos.* 2,193ff, where Philo discusses the veneration of the Nile divinity and explains it in philosophical terms as a choice for the earthly things against the heavenly ones, for the Changeable rather than for the Unchangeable.[37] In sum, there is a sharp opposition between the Egyptians and the Jews, on two levels: the implacable enmity between Egypt and Israel on the spiritual plane is reflected in the historical antithesis between the Egyptians (both of Moses' and of Philo's days) and the Jews, and/or vice versa.

The *Hellênes*, on the other hand, are mostly treated in a neutral way. Often Philo refers to the Greek language,[38] or to other aspects of Greek culture.[39] Sometimes he keeps some distance from the Hellenes, e.g. in connection with their myths. Oedipus is an instance of incest "among the Hellenes" (*Spec.* 3,15f; also *Praem.* 8). Elsewhere he is distinctly positive, i.a. in his praise for Augustus as the hellenizer of the barbarian countries (*Legat.* 147). His interest in Greek *paideia* is well known.

Philo also adopts the Greek term *barbaroi* to indicate the non-Greeks. Often the dual expression "Greeks and barbarians" is used to indicate the *oikoumenê*. In these cases the two terms are more complementary than antithetic.[40] Here, too, often a linguistic context is present (*Confus.* 6; 90). According to another passage, the large diversity in political constitutions is brought about by the lack of contact between Greeks and barbarians, but also within both these categories

(*Ios.* 30). Once Philo adduces the instance of a barbarian sage, Kalanos, who contrasts favourably with the Hellenes: a familiar theme of Greek culture criticism (*Prob.* 94-96). More usual is the rejection of barbarism, i.e. the lack of Greek culture (*Spec.* 3,163), or the branding of objectionable customs, such as ritual child murder or *proskynêsis*, as "barbarian".[41] In the last resort Philo sides with the Hellenes against the barbarians.

So far the main ethnic categories used by Philo. In order to understand his "ethnical strategy", however, it is also necessary to study the way in which he organizes these labels into pairs of opposites, to analyse how the Jews fit in, and to estimate the degree in which he identifies himself with the Jews. As we saw, Philo lacks an equivalent for the Hebrew word pair *âm — goyim*. Attempts to recognize in his *barbaroi* the *goyim* of Scripture are mistaken.[42] Would this be true, one should expect to meet the word pair "Jews — barbarians", but that does not occur in Philo. Whenever we find "Greeks" and "barbarians" a Greek way of ethnical categorization is reflected.

This does not mean that the opposition between the Jews and the other peoples is unknown to Philo. In fact it is all-pervasive in his works. In *Numbers* 23,9 the people of Israel is described thus:

> Lo, a people dwelling alone,
> and not reckoning itself among the nations![43]

This text is explained by Philo thus: The isolation of the Jews is not caused by the remoteness of their dwelling place, but by the extraordinary nature of their laws and their refusal to give up the national mode of life and to assimilate with the neighbouring peoples.[44] No doubt Philo's exegesis of the biblical text has the contemporary *diaspora* in mind. As a consequence of their separation the Jews are wanting in good helpers, so that they become like an "orphan among the nations". Moreover, "necessarily they are solemn (*semnos*), because they exercise the highest virtue, and this solemnity becomes severity (*to de semnon austêron*); but the masses loathe severity, due to their propensity to pleasure" (*Spec.* 4,179). On the other hand, in his exegetical and philosophical works Philo tries to mitigate the opposition between the "Jews" and the "others". According to *Spec.* 2,163 the Jews have a priestly function on behalf of the human race as a whole: the Jews as the choice part of a larger whole. Sometimes he parallels the sages who through their philosophy have a perception of the Almighty with the Jews who honour Him thanks to the excellence of their Law (*Virt.* 65). Unlike some other Jewish writers Philo, when speaking in his own name, never characterizes the non-Jewish population as *echthros* (inimical).[45] When the children of Israel leave Egypt a large crowd of proselytes (*epêlytai*) is following them out of admiration for their piety (*Mos.* 1,147). Hagar, though of Egyptian descent, has adopted Hebrew identity (*Abr.* 251).[46] Moses is in high esteem as a lawgiver not only with the Jews, but with Greeks and barbarians as well. So it was right for the excellent king Ptolemy Philadelphus to invite Hebrew scholars and have them translate the *Tora* into Greek. Even in Philo's days the labour of the Seventy (two) translators is commemorated every year by a celebration on the island of Pharos to which not only the Jews but also the other inhabitants of Alexandria flock (*Mos.* 2,17-44).

Apologetic and missionary passages like the last one reflect the universalist trend in Philo's thought. Universalism is the very opposite of ethnocentrism, so this trait mitigates all that might be said about his ethnic strategy. The opposition between the Jews and the rest of mankind, however, is equally present in his works. Declaring that the Law of the Jews should be made available to Greeks and barbarians by having it translated implies this fundamental opposition. In several passages and with varying terms Philo deals with the "Jews versus the others" theme. Moses, as a lawgiver, contrasts favourably with Greeks and barbarians alike.[47] Other expressions found are "the descendants of the Hebrews and the others" (*Ios.* 42), "the Jews and the rest" (*Spec.* 1,97; 2,166), "the Jewish people ... some cities" (in connection with the sabbath, *Decal.* 96), "the Jewish people ... all other peoples" (*Spec.* 4,179). "Moses venerates the number seven more than Hellenes and barbarians do" (*Opif.* 128). Throughout, Philo underscores the excellency of the Jewish Law and the incompatibility of the Jewish way of life with those of the other nations.

Saying that the Jews keep aloof from the rest of mankind does not imply that they are at equal distance from all non-Jewish peoples. The principal difficulty confronting Philo was the problem how to reconcile the two dichotomies, Greeks versus barbarians and Jews versus the rest. At first sight, Philo seems to rank the Jews among the barbarians. In *Mos.* 2,27 the *Tora* is said to have been translated into Greek because otherwise its propagation would be restricted to one half of mankind, viz. the barbarians. Here the Jews, on account of their language, are reckoned among the barbarians. In *Prob.* 73ff Philo lists some groups of wise men: the Hellenes can boast of the Seven Sages; the barbarians have the Persian *magoi*, the Indian gymnosophists, and among the Jews the Essenes. Here, too, the Jews are ranked with the barbarians. But in *Legat.* 215 Philo combats the slander against the inhabitants of Judaea which suggests that they gave proof of a barbarian frame of mind.

That Philo is not indifferent to the question whether the Jews are more akin to the barbarians or to the Greeks is made especially clear by the way he treats their relation to the Egyptians. The native inhabitants of Egypt symbolize in his eyes all that is contrary to a life of virtue and piety. His handling of the opposed pair of ethnic labels "Jew" (or "Hebrew") and "Egyptian" is in accordance with this. In *Mutat.* 117, e.g., he exclaims: "They call Moses an Egyptian, he that is not only a Hebrew, but a Hebrew of the purest kind".[48] Jews and Egyptians are confronted in *Mos.* 2,193, where Philo treats the case of a "bastard" (the son of an Egyptian father and a Jewish mother) who "went over to the impiety of the Egyptians". The commandment of *Deuteronomy* 23,7, "the Egyptian thou shalt not loathe, for thou hast been a stranger in his country" gives Philo occasion to the remark that the Egyptians have done all kinds of wrong to the People (*Virt.* 106f). The enmity between Jews and Egyptians and the contrast between their modes of life is implicitly present on many pages of writings such as *Mos.*, *Decal.* and *Spec.*[49]

So far as the Greeks are concerned, Philo never formulates himself so as to contrast Jews and Greeks directly. He prefers to say covertly that Moses' law or doctrine are better than those of the Hellenes,[50] or calls attention to the difference between Greek priestesses and the Therapeutrides (*Contempl.* 68). Whenever Hebrews and Hellenes confront each other it is the linguistic difference that is at stake.[51]

So, Philo avoids directly opposing Jews and Greeks; his preference for Greek culture is well-known. The universalistic trend present in his work has already been commented upon. Yet there is no ground for doubting his profound loyalty to the Jewish ethnic identity. This is revealed additionally by an analysis of the ways in which he handles the categories "we" and "our" (Greek: *hêmeis* and *hêmeteros*) — words often used involuntarily and therefore betraying "subconscious" persuasions. Here, too, his language sometimes reflects his universalism, when by "we" "all mankind" is meant as opposed to God[52] or to the animals (*Spec.* 4,123), or when "we" designates "people of our time".[53] There are a few references to "our" language" as opposed to Hebrew, in which Philo ranges himself with the Greeks.[54] But these are counterbalanced by passages in which Philo refers to the *Tora* as to "our" Law or to the Jews as "we the followers of the Law".[55] So far the exegetical and philosophical works, but what holds true there is valid for the historical treatises *In Flaccum* and *Legatio ad Gaium*, too. It is evident that Philo takes the side of the Jews in connection with the disturbances at Alexandria and as an ambassador to Gaius. Nevertheless, the strong terms in which he formulates the opposition between "we, Jews" and the others deserve attention. Flaccus "knew that the city contained two kinds of population, *us and them*, and Egypt likewise", yet he took the risk of estranging the influential Jewish population group (*Flacc.* 43). He "edited a decree in which he proclaimed us to be strangers and immigrants" (*Flacc.* 54). During the pogrom even the women were driven together to undergo maltreatment; "whenever they were found to be of a different race, they were released ... but if they appeared to belong to *us*" they were compelled to eat pork (*Flacc.* 96). The "promiscuous and unruly Alexandrian mob attacked *us*" (*Legat.* 120). By Gaius' power, "*we*, prosperous though we had been in earlier times" were brought to ruin, "for it was only of the *Jews* that Gaius was suspicious" (*Legat.* 114f).

The Alexandrian pogrom

This brings us to the pogrom at Alexandria in 38 AD. A closer investigation of the manner in which Philo and some of his adversaries deal with that conflictuous period may reveal some remaining aspects of ethnicity.[56] If we are right in starting from the assumption that ethnicity should be viewed as a kind of reciprocal categorization by members of a given society this would imply the possibility that in particular situations people interacting with each other do *not* share the same set of ethnical categories, or apply them differently. The result would be, at best, a certain amount of friction, if ethnicity does not play a prominent role. If it does, a clash may ensue. Something of the sort happened at Alexandria in 38 AD and following years.

As we saw, Philo identified himself fully with the Jewish people, both in the years of tension under Caligula and in the more peaceful periods in which he wrote his philosophical and exegetical works. It was suggested also that the enmity with which he treated the Egyptians — as compared with the Greeks — is not confined to exegetical situations but affects his attitude towards them in real life. This is confirmed by the observation that, according to Philo, those responsible for the anti-Semitism that victimized the Alexandrian Jews belonged to the Egyptian part of the city population. In his account of the embassy to Gaius a particularly odious role is reserved for a member of the imperial household,

Helicon. "The scorpion-like slave Helicon injected his Egyptian poison into the Jews".[57] Exaggerating, Philo states that most members of the household "were Egyptians, a worthless breed, whose souls were infected with the poison and bad temper alike of the crocodiles and asps of their country. The leader of this whole Egyptian dance-band was one Helicon, a damnable and abominable slave who had wormed his way into the imperial household" (*Legat.* 205). Helicon himself and the members of the Alexandrian counter-embassy are hand in glove, the ambassadors having bribed the imperial servant.[58] Although he does not say so directly, Philo seems to imply that the representatives of Alexandria, too, belonged to the Egyptian part of the population. In connection with the situation at home he makes the statement that when the ruler wavers, rebellious elements will soon lift up their heads, "among which the Egyptian populace takes pride of place, wont as it is to kindle the fire of rebellion out of the slightest spark" (*Flacc.* 17). So when Flaccus receives the news of the accession of Gaius he becomes the puppet of "demagogues like Dionysius, paper-porers like Lampo and masters of rebellion like Isidorus, busybodies, mischief contrivers and agitators as they are"[59] (*Flacc.* 17-20). As soon as king Agrippa arrives at Alexandria the Egyptian element shows its envy (*baskanon gar fysei to Aigyptiakon*), manifesting the ancient and innate hatred which they bare against the Jews (*Flacc.* 29). The Alexandrians place portraits of Gaius in the synagogues, pretending to honour him, although they never did anything of the sort on behalf of previous monarchs, "those worshippers of dogs, wolves, lions, crocodiles and all kinds of animals on the land, in the air and in the sea".[60]

There can be no doubt that Philo regarded the anti-Semites and their leaders as Egyptians. But it is equally probable that the opponents of the Jews considered themselves to be "Hellenes". The Alexandrian anti-Jewish embassy to Gaius is called by Josephus the embassy of the Greeks[61] — this is particularly striking because elsewhere he brands Apion, one of the ambassadors, as "Egyptian" (*c.Ap.* 2,28). In the *Acta Alexandrinorum*, the earliest of which may be taken to represent the propaganda made by the anti-Semites of Philo's days, Isidorus is introduced calling himself a "Hellene".[62] Isidorus and Lampo were gymnasiarchs; so, they were associated with the institution that was most typical of Hellenism.[63] Moreover, as Josephus tells us, Apion tried to conceal his Egyptian descent and to pass for a genuine Alexandrian (*c.Ap.* 2,29); though Josephus must not be trusted on his word, he may very well be right. In the last part of the *Acta Isidori* the anti-Semites are seen connecting the *Jews* with the Egyptians: The Jews "are not of the same temperament as the Alexandrians, but live rather after the fashion of the Egyptians".[64] By implication they dissociate themselves from the Egyptians. A minor indication for the Greek consciousness of the Alexandrian enemies of the Jews may be contained in Tacitus' report on the visit Germanicus paid to Alexandria in 19 AD. From Josephus we know that on this occasion the Jews were excluded from a corn dole granted by Germanicus to alleviate a famine (*c.Ap.* 2,63). Tacitus represents Germanicus as ingratiating himself on this occasion with the Alexandrian populace by parading "barefoot and in Greek dress" (*Ann.* 2,59).

The version given by Apion of traditional anti-Semitic themes is remarkable for its emphasis on the enmity between Jews and Greeks and on the closeness between Jews and Egyptians. This is revealed by a comparison between Apion and Manetho.[65] For Manetho (frg. 21), only Moses is an Egyptian priest, but Apion calls the Jews generally *Aigyptioi to genos* ("Egyptians by descent"; frg. 164 § 8). The theme of the Jewish worship of Typhon, the donkey-god and the enemy of Osiris, which made them particularly odious to the Egyptians (Manetho frg. 21), is not found in Apion, who compensates for it by telling the story of the Greek fattened in order to be immolated to the Jewish God (frg. 171). The tale that the Temple of Jerusalem was the place of worship for a donkey, a rumour that originated probably in Egyptian circles,[66] is repeated by Apion (frg. 172) but with the emphasis shifted to Jewish credulousness. Apion ridicules circumcision, a custom shared by Jews and Egyptians (frg. 176). And Apion alone gives the story of the Jewish oath of hostility towards the Greeks (frg. 171 § 95; 173).

For Jews like Philo it is exceptionally painful to be put on a level with the Egyptians. During the pogrom a number of Jewish elders are dragged into the theatre and scourged with a whip before the eyes of the Alexandrian mob flocked together to watch the spectacle. This event strikes Philo as particularly shocking because hitherto Egyptians only had been deemed worthy of such a punishment.[67]

We would come to the conclusion, then, that Philo on the one hand, the anti-Semites on the other, mapped the ethnic composition of the society they were obliged to share in different and even incompatible ways. Both parties tried to associate themselves as much as possible with the Hellenic ethnic entity and claimed to be real Alexandrians, with the exclusion of the other; both parties kept the Egyptians at the largest possible distance and tried to push down the adversaries to that level. One might also put it thus: the position taken by the opponents of the Jews was the mirror of the one taken by the Jewish leaders. Both sides rivalled with each other in their contempt for the Egyptians. That such was the case is expressed by Josephus in a lucid though not impartial passage of his *Against Apion* (2,28-32): Apion accused the Jews of descending from the Egyptians, he who himself was of Egyptian extraction. By abjuring his Egyptian kinship he admitted its baseness, and by branding his Jewish adversaries as "Egyptians" he confirmed that he considered the Egyptians to be utterly worthless. "With regard to us" — Josephus adds sarcastically — "the Egyptians experience two different feelings; either they forge consanguinity with us, being proud of it, or they pull us down to share their bad reputation".[68]

Were Isidorus and his fellow anti-Semites right in claiming to belong to the Hellenes and in rejecting the Egyptian ethnic identity? One of the implications of our theory of ethnicity is that a definite answer to this question cannot be given, or rather, that the question has been put wrongly. An objective distribution of people across the two ethnic groups is impossible. The only thing that counts is the way ethnic labels are applied by the partners in social intercourse themselves. So, in a sense, the anti-Semites and Philo were both in their right. One gets the impression, however, that the adversaries of the Jews, or at least a significant number of them, were worried about their own ethnic status. With some hesitation one might explain their uneasiness by referring to the composition of the Alexandrian population at the beginning of the Christian era. The hesitation is due to the fact that we know next to nothing about that population.[69] Yet it is a fair guess that a considerable part of the inhabitants of the city were recent immigrants from Egypt. They must have spoken Greek and tried to imitate the Hellenic manners prevalent in the metropolis to the best of their ability; but inevitably a large part of them retained some cultural traits that linked them with the countryside from which they came. To indicate this layer of the Alexandrian population Fraser uses the expression "Greco-Egyptian class".[70] Braunert coined the term *Gräko-Ägypter*.[71] According to Braunert in the late Ptolemaic and early Roman period migration to Alexandria from the provincial capitals was strong, involving mainly the "Gräko-Ägypter". If Braunert was right, and provided that these movements did affect the ethnic composition of the population of Alexandria as Braunert suggested, what would this mean in ethnical terms for the *Gräko-Ägypter* migrating to Alexandria? The result would certainly *not* be that they came to constitute an ethnic identity of their own. No contemporary used the label "Graeco-Aegyptian": this is just a convenient but dangerous reification by modern scholarship. They had to be classified either as "Greeks" or as "Egyptians".[72]

In the provincial districts they had, as city-dwellers, been treated as Greeks, but from the point of view of a born Alexandrian an origin from the countryside or from a rural town did not make much difference. Because there was much in their behaviour reminiscent of the Egyptian *chôra*, they ran the risk of being labelled "Egyptians" once they moved into the capital. In both cases the qualities that distinguished them from the "others" were decisive. In the country towns speaking Greek and participating in the gymnasium set them apart from the Egyptians. In the capital, on account e.g., of their rural manners and of their peculiar religious cults, they were considered "different", non-Hellenic, i.e. "Egyptian", by many of the resident Alexandrians and by Hellenes visiting the city from abroad.[73] This must have been particularly embarrassing for the most ambitious among them. Josephus contends that Apion stemmed from the Oasis and consequently was an Egyptian, perhaps rightly (*c.Ap.* 2,29). Such people felt insecure about their own position, and in this situation it would have been perfectly understandable if they took recourse to the strategy of pointing out the "otherness" of the Jews in order to stress their own adherence to the Hellenic identity.

The argumentation up to this point may have suggested that the pogrom in 38 AD was the result of the incompatibility of two rival sets of ethnic categorization. Of course, this was an important factor, but for the violent outbreak of that year this explanation is insufficient. Generally, the adoption of ethnic policies is an attractive device in troubled times. And inherent in ethnicity is a certain *dynamism* that can be observed clearly in the case at hand.

The course of events leading to the pogrom was directed by the overwhelming importance attached to the opposition between Jews and non-Jews. Alexandrian society in the beginning of the Christian era was both intricate and full of tensions, intricate not only to us but also to contemporaries. In addition to the usual conflicts of a social and economic nature there were problems caused by the presence of the Romans. Uncertainty with respect to Alexandrian citizenship and the fiscal consequences entailed by possession or lack of it, and irritation caused by the compulsory cohabitation of people with different and even incompatible religious outlooks played their part, too. The decisive factor is that some people adopted the ethnicity principle to create order, first in their own minds and next in society as well. They reduced the manifold problems to a straightforward ethnic dichotomy. By giving a simplified and untrue but convenient explanation of their situation they created a manageable, though cruel, way out of their problems. From this point of view, ethnicity cannot be denied a peculiar rationality.

The advantage of this approach is that it enables us to integrate several explanations of the anti-Semitic outburst. Different parts of the population of Alexandria may have had widely divergent grievances directed against a plurality of enemies, but when the decisive moment came the alignment was made along the lines of the opposition "the others versus the Jews". The acquisition of Alexandrian citizenship as the fulfilment of political aspirations may have been relevant mainly to the upper strata of both the Jewish and the non-Jewish population. So was admission to the gymnasium (which appears to have been the necessary precondition for citizenship):[74] Participation required well-being, so that the lower strata of both Jewish and non-Jewish Alexandrians were automatically excluded. We have no indication that poorer Alexandrians tried to push their way into the gymnasium. Social climbers will have been welcomed, while gymnasiarchs like Isidorus and Lampo were in a particularly good position to thwart just the Jews. Insofar as political aspirations were concerned, both the Jewish and the non-Jewish part of the city population must have contained a segment for which not the *polis* but monarchy constituted the ideal. Philo's report on Agrippa's arrival at Alexandria shortly before the pogrom suggests that among the Jewish populace messianic hopes were smouldering.[75] Our concentration on Philo with his strong tendency to Hellenism must not blind us to the fact that he may have been representative of a minority only of his fellow Jews.[76] The presence of the Jewish king aroused the jealousy of the Alexandrians (*Flacc.* 29); apparently they looked back with nostalgia to the Ptolemies. In the background there was hatred against the oppressing Romans. Both Greeks and Jews resented the loss of military functions brought about by the arrival of the Romans.

One could imagine, in addition, that economic motives might have played a part, but on these we have no information. Boats owned by Jews were seized when entering the city from the countryside, and many houses of Jews were burnt, but this is no indication of purely economic grievances.[77] It has been established that the Jews were not concentrated in a small number of occupations, neither is there any evidence that they were considered to be powerful in some key branches of the economy. Of far greater importance was the religious aspect. The Jewish refusal to participate in pagan cults is well known, and the Alexandrian populace was particularly sensitive about their cults. Diodorus relates how a Roman who had killed a cat by accident was lynched by the Alexandrians.[78] Jewish *atheotês* irritated them, and it must have given them much satisfaction to get the opportunity of attacking the synagogues of these worshippers of Typhon the donkey-god.[79] Finally, for people like Isidorus and Lampo anti-Semitism may have presented an instrument to acquire a power which in more normal conditions they would never have had.

Decisive is the fact that the tensions present in Alexandrian society neither caused open rebellion against Rome, nor did they lead to civil war between the rich and the poor (or between citizens and non-citizens), nor to a clash between Greeks and Egyptians. All issues were organized along the ethnic demarcation line Jew versus non-Jew. Rich and poor, those of the gymnasium class and those below, and perhaps even Greek and Egyptian, cooperated in the battle against the common enemy-within-the walls, the Jews.

For this to come about, however, it was necessary that a process of *ethnic incorporation* had taken place. This expression has been borrowed from D. Handelman, [80] who indicates by it the degree to which members of an ethnic category have been organized "such that greater ethnic incorporation progressively strengthens the centrality of the ethnic factor in social organization while defining more clearly, and limiting, the modes of its expression in social life" (189). Handelman distinguishes four ideal types of ethnic incorporation, which may be seen as four points on a continuous line of progressively increasing incorporation. The greater the ethnic incorporation becomes, the smaller is the opportunity for individual ethnic strategies. The last two stages are those of "ethnic association" and "ethnic community". An *ethnic association* comes into being "when persons, who define themselves as belonging together in ethnic terms, also begin to maintain that they hold common interests which they can only express together" (196). The ethnic group chooses its place of reunion, and its members are required to spend a part of their time on ethnically coloured activities. Finally, on becoming an *ethnic community*, the ethnic group marks off an exclusive territory, within which it has the sole power of decision. This territory must be defended, and all persons residing within its confines must accommodate to the ethnic characteristics. The only personal ethnic strategy left is a choice between adaptation and expulsion.

It is evident that during the pogrom the ethnic situation in Alexandria had entered upon this last stage of ethnic incorporation. The categorization along ethnic lines had become overriding, pushing all other categories into the background. "The city had two species of inhabitants, *them and us*, and likewise the whole of Egypt", according to Philo (*Flacc.* 43). According to the decree preserved in Josephus, Claudius enjoins *both parties* to avoid in the future disturbances like those of the past few years.[81] (The tense situation of the years 163-156 BC, during which Ptolemaios the son of Glaukias was maltreated by Egyptians, may have been somewhat similar).[82]

This rise of ethnic temperature was not quite a natural event. It was, partly at least, the result of deliberate action by one or both of the parties concerned. Anti-Semitic propaganda made clear to the Alexandrians where the boundaries were. In this type of communication the content of the slander is less important than its function, the identification of the "self" and the "enemy" and the conveyance of the notion that this enemy is odious. A nucleus of organization of the "ethnic community" may also be identified. A group of leaders of the anti-Semites came to the fore and displayed activities in *hetaireiai, synodoi, thiasoi* and *klinai*[83] (perhaps the gymnasium should be added). A common ethnic cause was formulated, and people began to mark out a territory from which the Jews were to be driven into the ghetto. Sudden political instability — a Roman governor perplexed after Gaius' accession — did the rest.

This still does not explain why something of the sort happened exactly in the early Roman period. Of a number of possible causes I single out two. In the first place, the set of ethnic categories had become relatively simple now. Since most allochthonous ethnic entities had vanished only the Egyptians, the Greeks and the Jews were left (apart from the Romans, of course). Secondly, the Roman policy of introducing fiscal difference between various groups within the population (the *laographia*)[84] strengthened the ethnic boundaries and made them more rigorous. It was necessary, now, to devise operational criteria for deciding whether a person belonged to the privileged Hellenes or not.[85] Apparently, citizenship was the principal criterium, and this in its turn was dependent upon the ephebate, besides or in combination with descent. From the early Roman period date some elaborate genealogies handed down on papyri, like the one in the *epikrisis*-document *POxy.* 2,257 = *W.Chrest.* I,147, an application for admission among the *apo gymnasiou* of the boy Theogenes, dating from the year AD 94/5. The father of the boy traced back the ancestors of the family to his own great-great-grandfather, who had been a gymnasiarch nearly a century before, under Augustus.[86] Parallels from the Ptolemaic period are not known to me. But the Ptolemies, precisely, took no account of "descent" in their fiscal administration. By introducing the principle of "descent" for the distribution of important material resources and by favouring one "descent" group against another, the Romans involuntarily increased the impact ethnical relations made on Egyptian and Alexandrian society. They could not have foreseen that in the end the Jews, once their allies, would be among the principal victims.[87]

Conclusion

Hellenistic Egypt has been discussed as a plural society, in which a large number of ethnic groups lived together. The boundaries between these groups were fluid, and over the centuries the set of ethnic categories available changed considerably. Some ethnic entities ceased to exist, as was the case with the Thracians. This was only an illustration of what happened to the non-Hellenic and non-Egyptian parts of the population of Egypt generally; in order to get a more precise picture it would be necessary to study them all. The fate of the Macedonians, for instance, would be very interesting. The first century BC may have been of crucial importance, but unfortunately this is a dark period in the history of Egypt.

Some doubts keep surrounding the question whether the Ptolemaic government took ethnicity into account. Consequently, one hesitates to contrast the Ptolemies with the Romans in this respect. Is it possible to connect this issue with other aspects of the policies of Ptolemies and Romans? As to the Ptolemies, Préaux[88] denied any intention on their part to use the cult of Serapis for cementing the Greeks and the Egyptians together. If she is right, this absence of a policy of ethnic unification and the refrainment from applying ethnic distinctions to create a privileged class may have been the two sides of the same medal: The Ptolemies simply took no notice of ethnicity.

Ethnicity does not operate in isolation from other factors. The treatment of the 38 AD pogrom may have made this clear. Ethnicity even presupposes a variety of other features of culture because it singles out some of them as ethnically distinguishing. But ethnicity itself is an independent phenomenon of social life. So, for once, I wished to treat it separately.

The Jews have been studied both for their own sake and as a particularly well documented example of a general phenomenon, the application of (personal or collective) ethnic strategies to an intricate situation. This implies that the confrontation between the Jews and the anti-Semites is considered as a "normal" case of ethnicity. I feel this can be done so far as Antiquity is concerned, but do not imply that this approach is valid for latter day anti-Semitism, too. The dilemma whether the Jews are a religious or an ethnic group, in my opinion, is false. The Jews were and remained a distinct *ethnic* group just because they themselves as well as the non-Jews focused on Jewish loyalty, in whatever form, to the Law.

Finally, distinguishing between "culture" and "ethnicity" allows a new formulation of some central problems of Hellenism. It becomes possible again to speak of "hellenization" and "orientalization" as the adoption of features of Greek culture by non-Greeks, and of elements of oriental cultures by Greeks, respectively, provided it is not implied that these changes of culture automatically entailed changes of ethnic identity, and, of course, so long as we do not repeat Livy's verdict on the Macedonians who, by becoming orientalized, *in Aegyptios degenerarunt* ("degenerated into Egyptians": 38,17,11). Modifying an expression coined by Claire Préaux, who spoke of *étanchéité des cultures*[89] (separateness of cultures), we might characterize the situation as *étanchéité des ethnies*. The cultures of East and West did fuse to a large degree, but this did not bring the *unity of mankind*[90] significantly nearer.

Notes

   *   Papyrological sources are indicated according to the system adopted in Oates J. & Bagnall R.A. & Willis W.H. 1978.

       Philo's writings are cited in accordance with the conventions of the French edition by Arnaldez R. & Pouilloux J. & Mondésert Cl. 1961ff.

1. *PTebt.* 38; the quotation is from l. 13: *Thraika tina hou to{n} ono]ma agnoôi tôn ek Kerkesêpheôs.*
2. *OGIS* 734 = *SB* 8928, dated at 172-169 BC. The name of the younger son has been reconstructed.
3. *PEnteux.* 79. Hêrakleidês called himself a stranger because at the moment of the insult he was sojourning in a village not his own.
4. On Ptolemaios the Son of Glaukias: Lewis 1986, 69-87; Thompson 1988, 212-65; Goudriaan 1988, 42-57.
5. F.Barth, "Introduction", in Barth 1969, 11 and 13f. I repeat here summarily what I have said in my *Ethnicity in Ptolemaic Egypt*, 8-13.
6. It was the intention of my book on Ethnicity in Ptolemaic Egypt to explore some basic aspects of ethnicity by applying Barth's theory to Hellenistic Egypt. I considered it to be my task primarily to make an inventory of the ethnic labels used in the papyri, thus to provide an Archimedal point from which to start further investigation of the behaviour of ethnic groups in Ptolemaic Egypt. For convenience's sake, I restricted myself to Greeks and Egyptians. I did not wish to offer a new view on the relationship between these two groups. I still hold true, for example, with most scholars, that on the whole the Greeks were better off than the Egyptians socially. The conclusion that nomenclature is unreliable as a criterion of ethnic belonging — most clearly seen in the case of Menchês's Hellenic farmers bearing Egyptian names — was reached before, e.g. by Dorothy Crawford in her book on *Kerkeosiris* (p. 133). It was only with much hesitation that I formulated another finding, *viz.* that for the greatest part of its existence Ptolemaic government did not take ethnicity into account for fiscal purposes.
7. See the documents assembled by Lesquier 1911, 88f; Uebel 1968, 371-73.
8. More or less comparable to *PTebt.* 38 is *PCol.* 80,8 (246 BC), in which a person is vaguely indicated as *tou an[dros] Thrakos.*

9. *Chrest.* 2,301 = *PPetrie* 1,19 l. 26; *CPR* 13,14a47; *SB* 2031; 6679.
10. Uebel 1968, 355-84.
11. E.g. *PAmh.* 43; *PHamb.* 24; *SB* 8974.
12. Apart from *SB* 8928: *SB* 8562; and the graffiti *SB* 1057; 1062; 1873 and 3676. These texts are difficult to date, however. Cp. also the grave-stone *SB* 2115.
13. Uebel 1968, 11-13, on the basis of *PHamb.* 168.
14. *BGU* 1271: *-kratês Bithyos*; *Chrest.* 2,280: *Ptolemaios Amadokou*; *Chrest.* 2,301: *Axiothea Dizoulou*; *PPetrie* 3,21: *-oiniki* (probably *Foiniki*) *Bithuous*; and *SB* 8928: *Lysimachos Bastakilou.*
15. The "Persians of the *epigonê*" and the Jewish Macedonians (Josephus, *Ant.* 12,8) remain stumbling blocks, though. I consider them as thoroughly atypical. The (pseudo-)ethnical *politeumata* may be left out of account, because no Thracian *politeuma* has been handed down. See Lesquier 1911, 142-55; W.Ruppel, "*Politeuma.* Bedeutungsgeschichte eines staatsrechtlichen Terminus", *Philologus* 82 (1927) 268-312 and 432-54; Launey 1949/50 II, 1064-85; Thompson 1984. Dorothy Thompson does not seem to consider the *politeuma* of the Idumaeans as pseudo-ethnic.
16. Third century: 14 Greek, 8 Thracian (63,6 % and 36,4 %); second century: 8 and 4 resp.; first century: 3 and 1; undated: two Greek patronymics only.
17. *PTebt.* 1107 l. 279-344; Goudriaan 1988, 70ff.
18. Collins 1983, 244.
19. Strictly speaking only Ptolemaios the son of Glaukias (documents 8, 9 and 10) and Hôros the son of Nechoutês (documents 224, 225 and 226).
20. *PTebt.* 1107, l. 279-344; Goudriaan 1988, 70-87.
21. *UPZ* 1,7; 8; 15; Goudriaan 1988, 42-57.
22. Boswinkel 1982, 3ff; Lewis 1986, 123-39; Goudriaan 1988, 88f.
23. Analyses of the situation of the Jews in Ptolemaic Egypt and in Roman Alexandria are made by other contributors to the Conference; see the papers by Mr. Kasher and Mr. Borgen.
    Joel P. Weinberg, "'Wir' und 'sie' im Weltbild des Chronisten", *Klio* 66 (1984) 19-34 is an investigation with respect to Paralipomenon, similar to ours, though on a different theoretical footing.
24. For the following cp. Barraclough 1984, 476-86.
25. The term "Israel" is left out of account. The survey offered here is based on G. Mayer *Index Philoneus* Berlin/New York 1974. I discuss only the most significant cases.
    Absence of the name *Hebraioi* in Ptolemaic papyri: F.Preisigke *Wörterbuch der griechischen Papyrusurkunden aus Ägypten* III Berlin 1931, with *Supplement* by E.Kiessling Amsterdam 1971; Tcherikover 1957: Index.
26. *Plant.* 169; *Sobr.* 45; *Confus.* 68; 129f; *Migr.* 13; *Congr.* 37; 40; 42; *Mutat.* 71; *Somn.* 1,58; 2,250; *Abr.* 17; 27f; 57; *Ios.* 28; *Decal.* 159; *Spec.* 2,41; 86; 145.
27. *Her.* 128; *Fug.* 168; *Ios.* 50; 104; 203; *Mos.* 1 *passim*; *Virt.* 34f. *Hebraikos*: *Mos.* 1,16; 240; 285.
28. As a synonym for "Hebrew" in the linguistic sense Philo sometimes uses the term *Chaldaios*: *Abr.* 8; 12; 99; 201; *Mos.* 2,26; 31; 38; 40; 224; *Praem.* 14; 23; 31; 44; *Legat.* 4. This is explained by the fact that Abram, "the ancestor of the Jewish people, was a Chaldaean by descent, the son of an astronomer": *Virt.* 212. Abram gave up astrology, but passed the Chaldaean language on to his progeny; so even Moses can be called a Chaldaean: *Mos.* 1,5.
29. E.g. *Fug.* 185; *Mutat.* 191; *Somn.* 1,167; *Abr.* 276. Usually the context makes clear which people is meant.
30. E.g. *Spec.* 2,134; 3,159; *Virt.* 103; *Legat.* 161.

31. Resp. *Spec.* 1,190; 2,162; 167; and *Spec.* 2,263.
32. Cp. Barraclough 1984, 484.
33. *Atheotês*: *Poster.* 2; *Legat.* 163; cp. *Mos.* 2,193; 196. Zoolatry: material contained in the notes by Nikiprowetzky on *Decal.* 76 and by Starobinsky on *Fug.* 180. Philo likes to call this the Egyptian "arrogance" (*typhos*): *Migr.* 160; *Fug.* 90; *Mos.* 2,169; 270; *Spec.* 1,79; 3,125. See also A. Pelletier, in his edition of *In Flaccum*, p. 170-74, esp. 170f; Sevenster 1975, 97 n. 93; Smelik 1984, 1906ff.
34. Envy: *Flacc.* 29. Rebelliousness: *Flacc.* 17. Lack of discipline: *Abr.* 93 and 107; *Spec.* 3,23. Scurrility: *Agric.* 62. Inhospitality: *Abr.* 93 and 107.
35. In *De Iosepho* Egypt is treated slightly less unfriendly than elsewhere, due to the role Joseph plays in the country.
36. E.g. *Confus.* 70; *Her.* 203; *Congr.* 163; *Somn.* 2,281.
37. Same argument *Fug.* 180; cp. *Virt.* 65.
38. *Hellênes* and *hellênikos*: *Confus.* 68; *Congr.* 37; 42; *Mutat.* 71; *Abr.* 17; 27; *Ios.* 28; *Mos.* 2,97; *Spec.* 2,194; *Praem.* 23; 31; *Prob.* 75.
39. *Mutat.* 179; *Prob.* 140 (Athens the pick of the Hellenes); *Contempl.* 14; *Aet.* 57.
40. *Opif.* 128; *Cher.* 91; *Plant.* 67; *Ebr.* 193; *Mutat.* 35; *Abr.* 136; 180f.; 267; *Ios.* 134; *Mos.* 2,12; *Spec.* 1,211; 2,44; 165; 4,120; *Praem.* 165; *Prob.* 98; *Contempl.* 21; 48; *Legat.* 83; 102; 141; 145; 162; 292.
41. Resp. *Abr.* 184; *Legat.* 116 (here "barbarian" is opposed to "Roman").
42. One could think of it in *Spec.* 1,313 (cp. the commentary by S.Daniel). But I know of no other instance.
43. *Revised Standard Version.*
44. *Mos.* 1,278; *Spec.* 4,179.
45. An exception must be made for a few passages in *Flacc.* (58; 61f; 75; 89) and *Legat.* (371). Here, special circumstances prevail.
46. On Hagar see also the contribution by Peder Borgen, p. 132 (with a different emphasis).
47. *Abr.* 180f.; cp. *Mos.* 2,12; *Spec.* 4,120.
48. In the same vein *Migr.* 141; *Her.* 128; *Mos.* 1,143f and 147. Less antithetic *Abr.* 251; *Ios.* 203.
49. E.g. *Decal.* 76; *Spec.* 3,23ff.
50. *Leg.* 2,15; *Plant.* 14; *Her.* 214 (Moses' philosophy older than that of Heraclitus); *Mos.* 1,2; *Spec.* 4,61.
51. See before, page 82. There is one exception: the Hebrews invited to Egypt for the translation of the *Tora* are familiar with their own as well as with the Hellenic culture (*paideia*).
52. *Cher.* 91/2; *Confus.* 127; *Virt.* 188; *Legat.* 347. Mankind unqualified: *Fug.* 91; *Abr.* 28/9. Cp. Borgen 1984b, 118 on *Opif.* 170.
53. *Spec.* 1,95; 2,160; *Legat.* 49.
54. *Confus.* 129 and, less explicitly, *Congr.* 44. Philo probably did not know Hebrew: Nikiprowetzky 1977, 50-96; more cautious: Sandmel 1978, 107-112.
55. *Spec.* 1,314 (with notes by S.Daniel); also *Mos.* 2,31; *Spec.* 2,142. Though in general only passages in which Philo speaks on his own behalf have been taken into consideration, Joseph's words in *Ios.* 42/3 are relevant, too.
56. A recent discussion of some of the ethnic implications of this episode: Barraclough 1984, 426f.
57. *Legat.* 205; the translations from this treatise are Smallwood's.
58. *Legat.* 172 (he speaks of *tôn Alexandreôn hoi presbeis*).
59. *Flacc.* 20 (translation adapted from Colson's). In *Flacc.* 142, too, Isidorus receives the reproach of tumultuousness.

60. *Legat.* 139; cp. *Aigyptiakês atheotêtos* in *Legat.* 163. That Philo considered the Alexandrian opponents of the Jews as Egyptians has been observed repeatedly, e.g. Smallwood's and Pelletier's notes on *Legat.* 139; Smallwood on *Legat.* 106, and L.Troiani, "Gli Ebrei e lo stato pagano in Filone e in Giuseppe" *Ricerche di Storia Antica* II Pisa 1980, 210. Cp. also the contribution by Peder Borgen p. 122ff.

61. Josephus, *Ant.* 18,257; cp. *Ant.* 19,278: after Gaius's death civil strife begins "between the Greeks and the Jews".

62. *Acts of the Pagan Martyrs* 4 B l.35 *Hell[ên*; perhaps also III col. iii l.9: *Hel[lên*; but here the text is too mutilated to be of any value.

63. Isidorus: *Acts of the Pagan Martyrs* 4 passim; Philo, *Flacc.* 138. Lampo: Philo, *Flacc.* 130.

64. *Acts of the Pagan Martyrs* 4 C 25f.: *ouk eisin Al[exandreusin] homoiopatheis, tropô de Aigypt[iôn...]*; translation Musurillo. The fact that here the problem of the *laographia* is dealt with reinforces rather than impairs the implications of this passage with regard to ethnicity.

65. The fragments according to M.Stern *GLAJJ* 1976, 389-416 and p. 62-87 respectively. Since the main fragments of both Manetho and Apion have been transmitted in Josephus' *Contra Apionem*, possible distortions by Josephus are neutralized.

66. Stern, *GLAJJ*, 97f.

67. *Flacc.* 78-80.
     It was apparently a different device when the anti-Semites trapped Flaccus into declaring the Jews to be *xenous kai epêlydas*, 'foreigners and intruders' (*Flacc.* 54): in this case they implied that the Jews ought to be expelled from the city and sent back to Palestine, where they belonged. Agrippa was their "Marin" - *Aramaic* for "Lord" (*Flacc.* 39).

68. Josephus, *c.Ap.* 2,31. Subsequently, Josephus touches upon the subject of Alexandrian citizenship. That subject is beyond the scope of the present investigation; see Kasher 1985.

69. The "statistics" put forward by Fraser 1972 1, 91f on the basis of the Abusir el Meleq papyri are unconvincing: Fraser tries to add chalk and cheese. A new discussion of these papyri, replacing Schubart 1913 and Fraser 1972, would be necessary.

70. Fraser 1972 1, 80; 89f.

71. Braunert 1964. 79f; 102f. Cp. also Goudriaan 1988, 117f.

72. Polybius 24,14 eventually labels his *migades* "Hellenes".

73. Braunert 1964, 80: "...so dass sie namentlich Fremden eher als Ägypter denn als Griechen erscheinen mussten".

74. Tcherikover 1957, 38f and 59; El-Abbadi 1962, 112f and 118.

75. *Flacc.* 27-30.

76. The literature on this subject is abundant. See e.g. Tcherikover 1957, "Introduction" p. 66-69; Paul 1984, 92-94; Paul 1987, 317f.

77. *Legat.* 129. See Tcherikover 1957, 48ff.

78. Diodorus Siculus 1,83,8 (59 BC). But here were polical motives, too: the Alexandrians hated the Roman intruders.

79. Cp. Stern, *GLAJJ* 97f (on Mnaseas of Patara) and fr. 172 (Apion).

80. Handelman 1977, 187-200.

81. Josephus, *Ant.* 19,285. Cp. *BJ* 2,487, referring to the events of AD 66: "Between the Jewish communion and the indigenous always discord had reigned".

82. Cp. earlier in this paper, p. 75, 80.

83. Philo, *Flacc.* 4; 136f. These clubs have a prehistory of their own at Alexandria; in the late Ptolemaic period already anti-Roman *hetaireiai* existed: Dio Chrys. 32,70.

84. On the introduction of the *laographia* by the Romans, see Tcherikover 1950; Tcherikover 1957, 60-65; Kasher 1985, 200ff.

85. This was seen very clearly by Tcherikover 1957, 60f. These pages of the "Introduction" to the *CPJ* are, in my opinion, still the most perceptive treatment of the situation of the Alexandrian Jews in the early Roman period.
86. Cp. also W. *Chr.* 144-48.
87. Initially, the position of the Jews with regard to Alexandrian citizenship was not clear. This explains the hesitation perceptible in *CPJ* nr. 151 (the case of Helenos son of Tryphon). In the aftermath of the pogrom, however, and due to the propaganda made by the anti-Semites, Claudius decided that the Jews *as Jews* had no access to the gymnasium and the citizenship: *PLond.* 1912.
88. Préaux 1978 2, 650.
89. Préaux 1978 2, 588.
90. Cp. H.C. Baldry *The Unity of Mankind in Greek Thought* Cambridge 1965.

THE CIVIC STATUS OF THE JEWS
IN PTOLEMAIC EGYPT[1]

Aryeh Kasher

1. Introduction

Following its conquest by Alexander the Great, Egypt became the destination of many immigrants from all over the Greek world, and from Near Eastern countries as well. Jews were one of the most prominent groups among those immigrants, due to their relative large numbers and their well defined and organized communal life. Some Jews, in fact, had been present in Egypt long before the Hellenistic period, so that we will not err in stating that their immigration to that country during and after Alexander's time was but a continuation of a long established phenomenon.

This article will dwell mainly on questions related to the civic status of the Jews in Ptolemaic Egypt as reflected in literary, epigraphical and papyrological sources. Since I have already dealt more fully with this subject elsewhere (Kasher 1985), my intention here is to develop in more detail certain issues that arise from that treatment.

Greek law, which prevailed in Ptolemaic Egypt as in other ancient constitutions, made a clear distinction between two sectors of the population: slaves and free persons. It is commonly agreed that, in Hellenistic Egypt, the latter sector consisted of citizens of the Greek *poleis*; permanent residents without citizenship (*metoikoi* or *paroikoi*) who lived within the Greek *poleis*; people from abroad (*xenoi*) who settled in the *chora* and were employed in government service (army and civilian administration), and Egyptian "natives" (*laoi*).[2] The question of primary concern to us is how the Jews fitted into that picture.

2. Slaves

Let us start with Jewish slaves, a group mentioned in various sources of the Ptolemaic period. Astonishing as it might sound, slavery was not as rooted in the Egyptian economy as it was, for example, in Roman Italy. Agricultural work was done mainly by the free rural population of small peasants and tenants, and not by slaves.[3] The latter were mostly to be found in the service of rich people, as those who were in charge of housekeeping, entertainment, and so forth. The main source of slaves to Egypt was Syria, including Palestine; most of the slaves, in fact, were prisoners of war.

It is well known that from the beginning of the Hellenistic period, Palestine became (so to speak) a wrestling arena for the successors of Alexander the Great, and was conquered by Ptolemy I, son of Lagus, four times in succession (Tcherikover 1977, 50ff). *Letter of Aristeas* (12-27,37; cf. Josephus *Ant.* 12,12-33) states that that king took 100,000 Jewish captives with him into Egypt; of these, 30,000 men were enrolled into garrison service in his realm, and the remainder (mainly old men, women and children) were sold into slavery. Admittedly, the figures appear too round and too large to be credible; the authenticity of the evidence, however, is no longer in doubt.[4] The event apparently took place in 302/301 BCE and was probably referred to by Agatarchides of Cnidus and quoted by Josephus.[5] Josephus himself supplemented that testimony with the vague information that the captives were taken "from the hill country of Judaea and the district round Jerusalem and from Samaria and those on Gerizim".[6] He does not give the source of his information, which would in any event be difficult either to prove or to disprove. Nonetheless, he does not appear to have erred in his comment on the exile of captives from Samaria in the days of Ptolemy I, nor does he seem to have confused these captives with those transferred to Egypt in the reign of Alexander the Great (Josephus *Ant.* 11,345). As these two events were described in writing in such close connection, it is inconceivable that he could really have made so gross an error. The fact that he appended this matter to the report of the Jewish-Samaritan dispute concerning the sanctity of the temples in Jerusalem and on Mt. Gerizim (Josephus *Ant.* 12,10) means that he may possibly have had at his disposal an independent source, which did not rely either on *Letter of Aristeas* or on Agatharchides of Cnidus. Unfortunately, we have no possibility of shedding additional light on this report - although, as stated above, there is no real reason to doubt the historical credibility of the event itself.

The Greek terminology used by both *Letter of Aristeas* and Josephus for those slaves — *aichmalôtos, oiketês, sôma, doulos* — corresponds exactly to the terminology known from papyrological evidence.[7] As mentioned above, captivity was the principal procedure by which slaves were obtained for Egypt; the slaves were accordingly called *sômata doratoktêta* or *aichmalôtoi*. Legally, they were the King's property; yet many of them, if not the majority, were granted as booty to private owners, mostly soldiers.[8] Following the information of *Letter of Aristeas* (12,14), at least one group of those captives (described as "chosen men") had been freed by Ptolemy I and were settled as garrisons in forts (*phrouria*) throughout Egypt.[9] The rest were eventually freed by King Ptolemy II Philadelphus, as also related in *Letter of Aristeas* (22ff).

The authenticity of the story that appears in *Letter of Aristeas* withstands the test of criticism in light of similar cases attested to by papyrological and literary documentation. The most famous papyrological evidence is, of course, the royal *prostagma* (edict, decree) of King Ptolemy II Philadelphus, the so-called *Rainer Papyrus* (*SB*, no. 8008), which prohibited (*inter alia*) the enslavement of the free native population in Syria and Phoenicia,[10] and which will be referred to again later in this article. Another document, *P. Petrie* II, no. 29 (b) = III, no. 104 (p. 249) = *W. Chr.* no. 334 (dated 244/243 BCE), for example, contains a list of *klêroi aneilêmmenoi*, of which one belonged to a free *klêrouchos* called *Achoapis tou Alketou aichmalôtôn tôn apo tês Asias*, a man who was the son of one "of the prisoners of Asia" taken to Egypt during the Syrian Wars, either by Ptolemy II Philadelphus or by Ptolemy III (Euergetes I). Diodorus Siculus (19,85,3-4) also tells us about the settlement of 8.000 *aichmalôtoi*, captured in the Battle of Gaza (312 BCE) by Ptolemy I, as soldiers in Egypt. Rostovtzeff even maintained that "it was probably Syrian *aichmalôtoi* who formed in the third century BCE the population of a *Surôn kômê* in the Fayûm" (Rostovtzeff 1941, 1366); in our opinion, it is quite logical that many of these were Jews (see below).

It seems that the enslavement of Jews by Ptolemy I as narrated in *Letter of Aristeas* 22ff is indirectly hinted at in the royal decree promulgated by Ptolemy IV Philopator and cited in 3 *Maccabees* 2,28-30. The words of verse 28 ("All the Jews will be degraded to the rank of natives and condition of servitude") are paraphrased by those of verse 29 ("and be reduced to their former limited status"). I am inclined to accept Gutman's interpretation that the "former limited status" was the status that prevailed before the liberation decree of Ptolemy II Philadelphus (*Letter of Aristeas* 22ff), whereas the "degradation to the rank of natives and condition of servitude" in Philopator's time was aimed at abolishing the privileges granted in the reign of Philadelphus (*Letter of Aristeas* 14-16, 20).[11]

The Ptolemaic enslavement of the free "native" population of Palestine apparently did not cease after the conquest in 301 BCE. Indefinite numbers of Jews — most of them apparently belonging to circles in opposition to the

Ptolemaic rule — were probably taken into captivity during the Syrian Wars as well. Unfortunately, however, the evidence which has come down to us in this matter consists only of allusions rather than detailed testimony. For example, the bill of rights given by Antiochus III the Great contains a reference to "those who were carried off from the city [Jerusalem] and are now slaves" (Josephus *Ant.* 12,144). It may be assumed that this does not only refer to those who paid the price of the Fifth Syrian War (202-198 BCE), as Antiochus' order also related to the liberation of descendants born in slavery. The order may therefore be deemed to have referred to those descended from prisoners of the Fourth Syrian War which ended in the Battle of Raphia (217 BCE). Furthermore, as Antiochus III could not possibly have liberated Jewish slaves in Egypt, his order must refer to those who were present in conquered Palestine and Phoenicia only. There is no information in any source about those Jewish slaves who had been transported to Egypt, as we suppose had happened. Several scholars believe that the Demotic inscription of Ptolemy IV Philopator (praising his victory in Raphia) contains a reference to some sort of Jewish insurrection against him. This appears reasonable enough, if we take into account the hostility of the Jewish population in Judaea towards the Ptolemaic rule, as expressed, for example, in 3 *Maccabees*.[12] We may not err in believing that most of the Jewish captives brought to Egypt were eventually liberated with the help of their brethren, as redemption of prisoners was always considered a Jewish religious duty of great importance.[13]

Captivity was not the only cause of slavery; arbitrary acts of kidnapping, oppression and debt bondage were also quite common causes and are occasionally reflected as such in the papyri. The feeling of impermanence and insecurity surrounding the Ptolemaic rule in Palestine in the first half of the third century BCE apparently manifested itself, *inter alia*, in the abduction of "native free persons" who were subsequently enslaved in various unlawful ways. Clear evidence of this appears in the *Rainer Papyrus*, which, as mentioned above, includes a royal *prostagma* issued by Ptolemy II Philadelphus in 262/261 BCE (or rather 261/260 BCE), putting an end to the anarchy hitherto prevailing in that matter (see n. 11 above). There is no doubt that Jews might be included among those "enslaved free persons" (*sômata laika eleuthera*); unfortunately, though, we have no idea how many of them were involved. In any event, this royal decree falls into line with the one cited in *Letter of Aristeas* 22ff regarding the liberation of the enslaved Jews taken to Egypt as prisoners of war by Ptolemy I. In our opinion, some indirect echoes of the gloomy reality which prevailed in Ptolemaic Palestine, can also be found in Egypt. For example: *CPJ* I no. 126 dated 238/237 BCE from Arsinoë-Crocodilopolis in the Fayûm mentions a Jew as being a "debtor in bond" to a certain Cyrenean. The document takes the shape of a testament written by the latter, in which he left all his fortune to his wife and daughters including his slaves. The testator stated that "Apollonius was a resident alien (*parepidêmon*),[14] also known by the Syrian name of Jonathas" — a designation which implies, of course, that he was a Jew from Palestine. Since the testator had the ethnic designation of "Cyrenean" (lines 6-7) and was a permanent resident of the Fayûm, and as his witnesses were all "of the Epigone" (lines 21, 23, 25), he must have been a military settler who had formerly served in Palestine. Tcherikover's treatment of this document and his conclusions were correctly based on the *Rainer Papyrus*. He accordingly contended that Apollonius-Jonathas was an example of a free man who was enslaved for his debt, exactly as was the case in the *Rainer Papyrus* of "enslaved persons who are free". Furthermore, the enslavement of Apollonius-Jonathas is easily understood against the background of the relations between a military settler and his tenants. Legally speaking, that man was "a free person" whose enslavement was temporary pending the repayment of his debt. The fact that *CPJ* I no. 126 explicitly notes that the "debt bondage" of Apollonius-Jonathas was "in accordance with the sentence recorded in the public archives" (line 14) shows that the requirements of the royal decree cited in the *Rainer Papyrus* were indeed taken into account. Thus it is quite likely that Apollonius-Jonathas had previously been "a free native" (*laikon eleutheron*) like those mentioned in the *Rainer Papyrus*, and had been taken into slavery by his master because of some debt, during the latter's service in Palestine. It was only natural for the master to take his slaves,[15] including the Jewish "debtor in bond", along with him to Egypt. In his will he bequeathed them, along with his other property, to his wife and daughters, so that the Jewish "debtor in bond" was supposed to continue his service until his debt was repaid.

Quite a different case is that of a Jewish slave-girl mentioned in one of the Zenon papyri. She bore the Hebrew name Johanna, and worked in the household of Apollonius, the famous Dioicetes (namely, the finance minister in the service of Ptolemy II Philadelphus).[16] As this very papyrus also mentions "slaves sent from Syria by Nikanor" (a travelling agent of Apollonius), it may be concluded that Johanna was bought in Palestine as well. The reason for her servile status is unknown, but as the document is dated 257 BCE — that is to say later than the *Rainer Papyrus* — it may be suggested that she had indeed been born a slave (*oiketis*). Such a conclusion can find even greater support in the fact that she was bought by an official agent of Apollonius the Dioicetes, probably in a legal transaction of the sort mentioned in the *Rainer Papyrus*.

Another papyrus from the Zenon archive (also dated 257 BCE) mentions the consignment of four young slaves (*paidaria oiketika*) by Toubias to Apollonius, two of whom were circumcised.[17] The first impression is that they were of Jewish origin, but this is not necessarily true, since other nations in the neighbourhood of Palestine performed circumcision as well.[18]

The last papyrological evidence at our disposal, which probably refers to Jewish slaves, is also incorporated in the Zenon archive (*PCZ* no. 59710 = *CPJ* I no. 11). It mentions a certain Khanounaios, who might have been a Jewish slave in charge of the dogs on Apollonius' estate. From a legal point of view, this case is no different from the previous ones.

Summing up our knowledge about Jewish slaves in Ptolemaic Egypt, we may state that the meagre information can indirectly prove the historical authenticity of the narration by *Letter of Aristeas* regarding the liberation of Jewish enslaved captives in the days of Ptolemy II Philadelphus. If this were not really the case, we would expect to find an abundance of papyrological evidence recording the presence of Jewish slaves throughout Egypt. The lack of such records is telling; in other words, the famous story of *Letter of Aristeas* is indirectly proved by *argumentum ex silentio* as well.

3. Natives

From both the political and judicial points of view, the "natives" (*laoi*)—the vast majority of the "free" (*eleutheroi*) Egyptian population—were considered inferior to the Greeks. Socially too, they constituted a lower class, settled mainly in the *chora* as "royal peasants" (*geôrgoi basilikoi*), tenants and simple craftsmen. The exact proportion of Jews within this sector of the population remains unknown to us. We can only presume that the main bulk of such "native" Jews in the *chora* consisted of those liberated from slavery by Ptolemy II Philadelphus.[19] Others might be descendants of those who had settled in Egypt before the Hellenistic conquest. It is not impossible that the so-called "Syrian villages" located in different regions throughout Egypt had become populated by many liberated Jews since the days of Ptolemy II Philadelphus—the more so as that king is known to have been the initiator of the great settlement projects in the Fayûm region.[20] As Egyptian economy was mainly based on agriculture, most of the "natives", including the Jews, were small lease-holders, who cultivated the "royal land" (*gê basilikê*) and paid an annual rent, either to government officials at the regional banks and granaries, or to the military settlers who had obtained the lands by lease (or present) from the King (*gê en aphesei*). Not a few were simple workers and craftsmen: shepherds, fishermen, potters, weavers, tanners, dyers, and even unskilled day laborers.[21] Being "natives", they had no free hand in economic activities; moreover, they were even limited in their personal liberty (cf. *CPJ* I nos. 12, 13). Bound to their domicile, they were forbidden to move by free choice to other places. They were, in short, semi-serfs, subject to restrictions and tied strictly to their villages.[22] It is well known that one of the most conspicuous signs of their inferior status as "natives" during the Roman period was the payment of poll-tax. Whether or not such a tax was levied on "natives" under the Ptolemaic rule is not yet known for certain because of lack of evidence (Tcherikover 1950, 179ff). In actual fact, there is not even one example related to Jews who paid this tax during the Ptolemaic period, but as there are no traces of other instances either, we should not be misled into thinking that Jews were not counted among the "natives".

The Ptolemies' dual policy as regards their Hellenic and native subjects, the outcome of which was a distinct segregation between the two classes, extended into daily life as well. Indeed, members of the citizenry of the Greek *poleis* (Alexandria, Ptolemais and Naucratis) were strictly forbidden to contract marriage with Egyptian "natives", though in reality not a few Greeks in the *chora* (mainly soldiers) did not adhere to the prohibition (cf. Fraser 1972, I, 71ff). Unfortunately, the judical status of those mixed marriages, as well as the legal position of the offspring born of them, is vague and unknown. It seems, however, that at least some of them were able to gain equality with the Greeks by receiving a proper (i.e. Greek) education (Davis 1951, 54ff).

4. Soldiers and *Politai*

The historical process of de-Hellenization in Egypt gathered momentum following the Battle of Raphia (217 BCE), as the Ptolemies were obliged to enlist a large number of "native" Egyptians into their army in order to cope with the severe problems caused by the lack of Hellenic manpower.[23] This being so, it is perhaps no wonder that an Egyptian "native" called Dionysus Petoserapis could be ranked among the "Friends" (*philoi*) of the royal court under Ptolemy VI Philometor, due to his military skills and talents (Diodorus Siculus 21,15a). Later, in the second half of the second century BCE, another Egyptian "native" named Paôs made even greater advance in his career, earning the title of "Kinsman (*syngenês*) and general (*stratêgos*) of the Thebaid".[24] The great boom of recruiting Jews to the Ptolemaic army since the days of Ptolemy VI Philometor is well in line with the picture described above. Many Jewish *metoikoi* and *laoi* from Alexandria, as well as many Jewish *laoi* of the *chora*, were welcomed into the Ptolemaic army; indeed, these Jews apparently constituted the lion's share of the units under the command of Onias IV and his sons Helkias and Ananias.

Military service, then, was undoubtedly a significant spring-board for "natives" seeking to raise their political and judicial status. The cases of the two above-mentioned Egyptians (Dionysus Petoserapis and Paôs) effectively prove this point; the careers of Dositheos and Onias IV, as well as those of Helkias and Ananias, probably fall into the same category (Josephus *c.Ap.* 2,49; *Ant.* 13,349, 354-55). Papyrological study supplies not a few instances corroborating this pattern. *CPJ* I no. 18 (dated 260/259 BCE), for example, clearly indicates that Jewish soldiers from Phebichis (Herakleopolites) shared an equal status with Greeks serving in the same unit—obviously an ethnically mixed cavalry unit named after its commander Zoilos (an eponymous officer)—which consisted of at least five sub-units, including a Jewish one. This picture is also reflected in several documents from the Fayûm area (such as *CPJ* I nos. 19, 22, 24, 25, 30, 31; *P. Gurob* no. 26; *P. Haun.* no. 11), all of which clearly indicate that there was no difference whatever between the legal status of Jewish and the Greek troops (Kasher 1985, 48ff). A document which casts even more light on the legal status of Jewish soldiers in the regular army is the above-mentioned *CPJ* I no. 19 from Arsinoë-Crocodilopolis in the Fayûm (dated 226 BCE). It contains an official report of a trial before the Court of Ten,[25] in which two "Jews" (*Ioudaioi*), a man and a woman, were involved. It is very significant for our study here to emphasize that the judges of that court were not those set over the "natives" (*laokritai*), nor those of the special court (*koinodikion*) who handled civil suits involving Greeks and "natives" (cf. *P. Ent.* no. 11), but those responsible for judging Greeks. The document under discussion is particularly important because of its judicial nature, the more so as it recalls the judicial norms customary in Alexandria (cf. Taubenschlag 1955, 508, 519). It should be kept in mind that the document was actually written in a court of justice, thus ensuring that the description of the litigants and the juridical terminology faithfully reflect the legal and judicial situation. The striking point is that both litigants involved were designated as

"Jews", and yet were simultaneously considered *politai* from the judicial point of view. This is clearly inferred from the fact that the *politikoi nomoi* ("Civic Laws") are mentioned as the basic supporting principles for the judgment taken by the court.[26] As these "Jews" could not be citizens of Alexandria, nor of any other *polis* in Egypt, the only logical and possible conclusion is that they were *politai* of a local *politeuma* in Arsinoë-Crocodilopolis.[27]

Before the Battle of Raphia the Ptolemaic army included mainly soldiers of non-Egyptian origin, the majority of whom were Greeks. They were allowed to form private associations of a religious, national or social character, and thus "to live by ancestral laws". Outside the three Greek *poleis* (Alexandria, Ptolemais and Naucratis), in the rural part of Egypt, these associations — the most prominent of which was the ethnic *politeumata* — were a kind of substitute for city-life.[28] Lesquier devoted considerable attention to this phenomenon and proved that, from the second century BCE on, several *politeumata* became pseudo-ethnic, enabling the alteration of ethnic designations for military purposes.[29] It appears that non-Greeks (Persians, Jews, and even "native" Egyptians) who joined such political frameworks of a clearly Hellenic character thereby changed their ethnic adherence and enjoyed complete naturalization. This could conceivably apply to the abovementioned case described in *CPJ* I no. 19. It seems, however, even more attractive to think that the case indicates the existence of a Jewish *politeuma* in Arsinoë-Crocodilopolis which was connected to the Jewish military unit serving there (Kasher 1985, 50-51, 141-42).

Another example of the same kind is probably that of the Jewish community in Leontopolis. A first-century inscription designates the members of that community as *politai* (*CIJ* II no. 1489); others describe them as *asteoi* (i.e. *astoi*) as distinct from *xenoi* ("foreigners") passing by.[30] It is quite obvious that those epithets did not refer to citizens of the three *poleis* in Egypt, but to *politai* of the local Jewish *politeuma* in Leontopolis. Apparently these inscriptions also reflect the situation which prevailed during the Ptolemaic period, when the Jewish military settlement of Leontopolis was established and enacted. Confirmation of this conclusion is provided by Strabo (as quoted by Josephus): "And only the Jews of the district named for Onias remained faithful to her (i.e. Cleopatra III Selene), because their fellow-citizens (*tous politas*) Helkias and Ananias were held in special favour by the queen". The terminological use of *politai* in this connection speaks for itself.[31] Another inscription, known as the "Helkias Stone",[32] though badly preserved, provides further information on the local community organization.

It takes the form of a honorary decision by the local "public" (*plêthos*), showing that the Jewish community in Leontopolis was an organized body empowered to make decisions (*psêphismata*). The use of the term *plêthos* is most illustrative, because of its perfect agreement with *Letter of Aristeas*, 310 regarding the Jewish *politeuma* in Alexandria,[33] as well as with *OGIS* no. 737 (line 6) regarding the Idumaean *politeuma* in Memphis.[34] The presence of a Jewish *politarchês* in Leontopolis, as mentioned in another first century inscription (*CPJ* III no. 1530A), also suggests that the local community was indeed organized as a *politeuma*.[35]

It is not impossible that a few more Jewish communities in Egypt may also have been organized as *politeumata*, particularly those connected to the military service. Unfortunately, the information at our disposal is very poor, and we are therefore not able to draw further conclusions.

5. The Alexandrian Jews

Our main interest, of course, lies in the Jewish community of Alexandria, which was both the largest and the most important. In our opinion, this community was a typical example of a recognized political body which emerged from a nucleus of military settlement; accordingly, its organizational framework was defined in *Letter of Aristeas* (308-10) as a *politeuma*.[36] The term corresponds perfectly with the official terminology used in Ptolemaic Egypt in relation to other foreign ethnic groups organized and recognized as legal entities, with certain judicial and political privileges.[37] It should be noted that the Jewish community of Berenice (in Cyrenaeca) was also called a *politeuma* in two inscriptions of the first century BCE.[38] The term was certainly a legacy from the Ptolemaic rule, the more so as a contemporary Greek author (Strabo) clearly states that "it has come about that Cyrene, which had the same rulers as Egypt, has imitated it in many respects, particularly in notably encouraging and aiding the expansion of the organized groups (*syntagmata*) of Jews, which observe the national Jewish laws".[39] In our opinion, the same applies to the Jewish *politeuma* of Alexandria; in fact, the inference from *Letter of Aristeas* 81 is that the term *politeuma* was applied to a group of people who ordered their lives according to the laws of their forefathers.[40]

This conclusion is also supported by another Alexandrian Jewish work, probably written in the Ptolemaic period. 3 *Maccabees*,[41] chapter 3, verse 4 describes the Jewish way of life in Alexandria as follows: "But reverencing God and conducting themselves according to his Law (*kai tô toutou nomô politeuomenoi*), they kept themselves apart in the matter of food, and for this reason they appeared hateful to some" (trans. H. Anderson). Indeed, the use of the verb *politeuô* reinforces the conclusion that there was in fact a Jewish *politeuma*, different from other political bodies, whose organizational basis leaned upon the laws of the Torah. The conclusion can find further support in 3 *Maccabees* 3,9 and 7,3, which refer to the Alexandrian Jewish community and to those in the countryside as *systêmata*.[42] The ordinary use of *systêma* was, in those times, simply "an organized body"; however, it was also quite commonly used in a military context, like *syntagma*,[43] and as such it well fits into our theme.

Josephus, the main source for the history of the Jews in Egypt, confirms the above picture perfectly. According to his statements, Jews had been settled in Alexandria by Alexander the Great, in reward for their military assistance;[44] the Ptolemies (probably Ptolemy II Philadelphus) were those who "assigned them a quarter of their own, in order that, through mixing less with aliens, they might be free to observe their rules more strictly".[45] This description also fits the information given by Strabo that "a great part (*meros*) of the city of Alexandria was separated (*aphôristai*) for this nation",[46] and that the Alexandrian Jews were presided over by an *ethnarches* of their own, who governed them "just as if he were the chief magistrate of an independent polity (*ôs an politeias archôn autotelous*)". The use of the term *politeia* in this context is very significant, and it is quite obvious (if not self-evident) that the reference is to the Jewish *politeuma*.[47] Consequently, the Jewish *politeuma* can be considered a city within a city, with its own authority and separate organization.[48]

One of the most important questions which arises in this context is undoubtedly related to the political stratification and judicial status of the Jewish population in Alexandria. In other words: did all Jews in that city enjoy the same status and privileges? Unfortunately, the information at our disposal does not allow us to draw any decisive conclusion. Some scholars have maintained that "the congregation of the Jews" (*to plêthos tôn Ioudaiôn*) mentioned in *Letter of Aristeas* 308, 310, is identical in meaning to, and therefore also synonymous with, "the people of the *politeuma*" (*hoi apo tou politeumatos*).[49] Others have contended that the *politeuma* was a limited group of privileged people within the broad Jewish "congregation" (*plêthos*).[50] The latter view can lead to the notion that the Jewish *politeuma* (like the *polis* of Alexandria) was composed of two circles, the inner made up of *politai* and the outer consisting of outright *metoikoi* and *laoi*.[51] This possibility is quite attractive, especially as it is supported by

Josephus' paraphrase of *Letter of Aristeas* (i.e. *Ant.* 12,107-108), in which *plêthos* and *politeuma* are not synonymous terms.[52] This way or another, when assuming that the Jewish community in Alexandria was organized according to common Greek standards, it is only natural and reasonable to think that the model was the Greek *polis* itself. Indeed, only a minority of the Greek population in Alexandria was entitled to enjoy full citizenship in the *polis*; some of the rest were "aliens" (*xenoi*) of Greek origin designated by external ethnics; and the majority were those called "Alexandrians" (*Alexandreis*), who were not registered in tribes or demes, and whose status is not clear enough, but can probably be compared with that of the metics (*metoikoi*) in Athens and other Greek cities.[53] In our opinion, quite a similar picture can be drawn in regard to the Alexandrian Jews, a picture which we shall try to advocate in the discussion below.

Philo and Josephus, though living in the Roman period, are still the main historical sources on that issue, and their writings often reflect the situation which was valid in the Ptolemaic period. It is very significant to point out that both of them, on several occasions, called all the Jews living in Alexandria "Alexandrians".[54] This designation, however, should not lead us astray, since there is no indication whatever that their intention was really to identify the Jews as citizens of the Greek *polis*. In actual fact, Philo called them "Alexandrian Jews" and clearly distinguished them from "the group of the other Alexandrians" (Kasher 1985, 234, 246ff). Josephus too used simultaneously, and on several occasions, terms like "Alexandrians", "the Jews in Alexandria", or just "the Jews", a fact which clearly shows that they could not be reckoned among the citizens of the *polis*, and that he himself did not define them as such. Furthermore, in other cases, Josephus made use of explicit terms like "the Jews residing in Alexandria" (*oi en Alexandreia katoikountes Ioudaioi*),[55] or "the Jewish people" (*to Ioudaiôn ethnos*),[56] which undoubtedly refer to the Jews as a distinct ethnic group—that is, an organized separate political entity. The same applies to the Jews of Antioch mentioned in his writings; they are called either "Antiochenes" or "the (Jewish) residents in Antioch", or simply "the Jews of Antioch".[57] To be more precise, Josephus says that "our residents in Antioch are called Antiochenes, having been granted *politeia* by its founder Seleucus" (*c.Ap.* 2,39). Indeed, one might think, at first glance, that the *politeia* in this context means citizenship in the *polis*; in fact, however, Josephus did not make any clear statement supporting such a conclusion. On the contrary, a much more persuasive inference is that the *politeia* he had in mind was the one related to the Jewish community.[58] Furthermore,

Josephus put it clearly enough that "similarly those (Jews) of Ephesus and throughout the rest of Ionia bear the same name as the indigenous citizens" (*ibid.*). The distinction which he made between Jews and Greek citizens is obvious and cannot be obliterated. The fact that Claudius' Letter to the Alexandrians (*P. Lond.* no. 1912 = *CPJ* II no. 153) contains a clear distinction between "Alexandrians" and "Jews" does not affect Josephus' terminology one way or the other, since the Edict cited by him also makes the same distinction (*Ant.* 19,281, 284) — the more so as Claudius in his Letter to the Alexandrians, which was an official document par excellence, also addressed the Jews directly (lines 80, 86ff), a most illuminating point indeed.[59]

One of the main reasons why modern scholarship rejects Josephus' statement that the "Jews of Alexandria (were) called Alexandrians" (cf. *Ant.* 19,281) is derived from papyrological evidence (*BGU* no. 1140 = *CPJ* II no. 151), in which the designation "Alexandrian" has been crossed out from the petition of the Jew Helenos son of Tryphon and replaced by "a Jew from Alexandria" (*Ioudaiou tôn apo Alexandreias*). But that document is actually a two-edged sword, since the term "Alexandrian" could not meet the legal requirements in regard to a citizen of the *polis*, as it was too general for that purpose. Whenever a full citizen applied to the authorities, he was obliged to comply with the lawful requirements and employ a complete and precise legal formula, including the specification of his deme and tribe (*P. Hamb.* no. 168, lines 5-8). As Helenos son of Tryphon could not add to the term "Alexandrian" any designation of an Alexandrian deme, he had to comply with the official requirement for precision in the designation form. In practice, there was no substantive difference between the two terms ("Alexandrian" and "a Jew from Alexandria"), since "Alexandrian" was apparently in daily use as a popular term designating *origo* (El-Abadi 1962, 122), and it was quite common as such in epigraphical evidence relating to Jews as well.[60] Furthermore, throughout the whole document Helenos' father was called "Alexandrian", and there is no indication whatever that his status was different from that of his son. As the term "Alexandrian" was not acceptable to the authorities in this case, the petitioner Helenos son of Tryphon needed to be more precise in order to use the right formula for his status. Indeed, the formula is here drafted in accordance to the pattern of *o deina tôn apo*, and thus points to a connection with a community body, which in this case was probably the Jewish *politeuma* (Kasher 1985, 200-203).

Admittedly, in calling the Jews of Alexandria "Alexandrians" or "Alexandrian *politai*" (cf. *Ant.* 14,188), Josephus seems to be misleading, but probably unintentionally so. It is not likely that he would have wanted to misinform his readers on a patently legal matter that could easily be verified. In our opinion, just as the term *politai* was used by Josephus and Philo in an ambiguous and rather imprecise way for both the citizens of the Greek *polis* and members of the Jewish *politeuma*, so was the term "Alexandrians". In addition, however, it also acquired in daily life the simple meaning of provenance (*origo*) in the common popular sense. In brief, the popular term "Alexandrians" was directed at Jews affiliated with the wide *plêthos* of permanent residents in Alexandria, whereas the semi-legal term "Alexandrian *politai*" was aimed at the narrow circle of the privileged members of the Jewish *politeuma*. Following the Greek pattern, the latter were apparently registered in *phylai* (tribes), one(?) of which was that of the Macedonians. As we see it, they should be reckoned as the Jewish aristocracy in Alexandria. The status of those Jews constituting the wide *plêthos* was, in our estimation, that of *metoikoi*, and perhaps also that of *laoi*, which, of course, ranked lower than that of the "Alexandrian *politai*" (cf. above notes 52, 53).

Josephus made several statements about the status and rights of Jews in Alexandria, most of which related to the Roman period, but were undoubtedly deeply rooted in the Ptolemaic period. In our opinion, all these statements should apply to the Jewish *politai* only—that is, to full members of the Jewish *politeuma*—and not to the Alexandrian Jews at large, as one might wrongly conclude from Josephus. In *c.Ap.* 2,35, for example, he wrote:

In fact, however, it (i.e. the Jewish quarter in Alexandria) was presented to them as their residence by Alexander, and they obtained privileges on a par with those of the Macedonians (*isês para tois Makedosi timês epetyxon*).

In *Bell.* 2,487 he wrote:

At Alexandria there had been incessant strife between the native inhabitants and the Jewish settlers since the time when Alexander, having received from the Jews very active support against the Egyptians, granted them, as a reward for their assistance, permission to reside in the city on terms of equality (*ex isomoirias*) with the Greeks.

As the term *isê timê* or *isotimia* is usually defined as "equality of rights", the term *Isotimoi* under the Ptolemies was applied to prominent persons whose status equalled that of various ranks of couriers such as "the King's kinsmen", "the first friends" etc.[61] The term *isomoiria* has a similar meaning: "equal part" or "equal share".

The statement in *c.Ap.* 2,35ff shows that Josephus only wished to present the Jews of Alexandria as having equal status, from the standpoint of their privileges, with the Macedonians. He endeavoured to prove it by emphasizing that, even in his time, there was still a "tribe" of Jews known as "Macedonians" (*ibid.* 36). The accuracy of this statement is definite, for such Jews are mentioned in Alexandrian papyri dating from the reign of Augustus.[62] However, Josephus' statement is somewhat exaggerated and may give the incorrect impression that all Alexandrian Jews were of that class and status (cf. also *c.Ap.* 2,35), which of course was not the case. Yet he did retain the Ptolemaic sense of the term *isotimoi*,[63] by which those Jews obtained their privileges and right to be called "Macedonians" (cf. *Bell.* 2,488). It is obvious that Josephus used the title to refer to a legal status deriving from its functional military denotation in early Hellenistic times, just as it is used in the papyri mentioned above and in other sources.[64]

Tcherikover (1977, 323f) contended that Josephus applied the term "Macedonians" to the citizens of Alexandria, and that he did not distinguish between "Greeks" and "Macedonians". His main authority for this view was *Bell.* 2,487-90 which refers to "Greeks" (*ibid.* 487, 490), "Macedonians" (488), and "Alexandrians" (490) in the same context. A careful study, however, shows that Josephus did not confuse the terms. The fact that he used the three of them in the same context indicates that, for him, the terms were not synonymous; had they been so, he could simply have written "citizens of Alexandria". In section 487 he said merely that the Jews were given the privilege "to reside in the city on terms of equality (*isomoiria*) with the Greeks". As he did not refer to any civic or political right, but only to the right of residence, there are no grounds for the claim that he identified the Jews with citizens of the *polis*. The *isomoiria* here means only that they were allotted "a quarter of their own", as were the Greeks. As such, they could be classified as at least ordinary *metoikoi*; otherwise, their stay in Alexandria would be limited to twenty successive days.[65] This very fact excludes, of course, the possibility that Alexandrian Jews were classified as the inferior *laoi* of the *chora*. Furthermore, any doubt about Josephus' construction of "Macedonians" is eliminated by *Bell.* 5,460, where the term clearly has a purely functional, military meaning, and no ethnic or political content at all. The Jews' equality to the "Macedonians" is no more than literal. In other words, Tcherikover's only conclusion should have been that the privileges of the

"Macedonian" Jews were the outcome of their military service, as were those of other "Macedonians", and as such they were placed outside the community of citizens (namely, the *polis*).[66]

The political status of the Jews in Alexandria, in comparison with the Greek sector of the city, is also indicated in Josephus' writings by the term *isopolitai* (*Ant.* 12,8). Modern scholarship has focused its main interest on this term, as well as on its derivative — *isopoliteia*[67] -, meaning respectively "citizens of equal rights", and "equality of civic rights". Adopting the method of historical analogy, some scholars attempted to project the Jewish "War of Emancipation" of the 18th and 19th centuries back into antiquity. Thus the Jews emerged as a national minority struggling for equal civic rights within the *polis*, while the Greeks kept their own ranks closed against Jewish infiltration.[68] The undesirability of such backward projection is evident. Phrases like "War of Emancipation" or "the Jewish Question" were the product of an alien and remote historical reality, and their application to classical antiquity distorts rather than clarifies.

Since political and municipal organization in ancient times was strongly linked with local cults, religious apostasy might be involved in obtaining full citizenship of a *polis*, and it is doubtful whether Jews were willing to surmount such an obstacle. We should be careful indeed in adopting rigid generalizations, since it is reasonable to assume that there were some Jews who wished to be wholly absorbed and integrated into the body of citizens. But their small number could not have presented a problem acute enough to draw the attention of kings and emperors, and such adaptable souls would certainly have been welcomed by the *polis* (cf. 3 *Maccabees* 2,30; 3,21-23). The Jewish struggle for equal political rights (namely *isopoliteia*), as recorded by Josephus, should not be interpreted as one for citizenship in the *polis*. The equality sought is rather to be conceived as that between two separate and coexisting political bodies, the Greek *polis* and the Jewish *politeuma*.[69]

The blurred ideas of modern scholarship on the civic status of Alexandrian Jews are probably derived from the vicissitudes of fate in the history of Jews in Egypt. According to Josephus, there were Jews who started as allies of Alexander the Great, served in his army and enjoyed equal rights with the Macedonians. Later, under the reign of Ptolemy I Soter, many of their brethren were brought to Egypt as captives and sold to slavery. From a juridical point of view, when liberated by Ptolemy II Philadelphus, they could have been classified as *laoi*; apparently, however, the majority of them were seemingly counted among the *metoikoi*, namely outlanders and settlers from abroad, or alien residents in a foreign city.[70] As such, they were free people who enjoyed the basic right of residence in Alexandria, as well as other personal rights on an equal footing with the *politai*. But, like other metics, they did not enjoy active political rights, and could not therefore be organized as a legal political entity of their own. As they could not integrate into existing political organizations as well, they could not even be full members of the Jewish *politeuma*. Unfortunately, we do not know how many were declared *laoi*, if any at all, through the decree of Ptolemy II Philadelphus.

In any event, Ptolemy IV Philopator tried to turn back the clock, so as to proclaim that "all the Jews will be degraded to the rank of natives and condition of servitude" and thus "be reduced to their former limited status" (3 *Macc.* 2,28-29; see Kasher 1985, 228ff). There is no clear indication in the sources for how long Philopator's decrees against the Jews were valid. Yet, according to the information of 3 *Macc.*, Ptolemy IV Philopator himself was the one to abolish his own decrees.

Later on, under Ptolemy VI Philometor, Cleopatra II, Ptolemy VIII Physcon (Euergetes II),[71] and Cleopatra III, during the second century BCE, Jews enjoyed great support from the authorities, to such an extent that we may speak of a "golden age" of the Egyptian Jewry. The massive enlistment of Jews into the Ptolemaic army in those days must have left its traces in their political and judicial status. It is simply illogical and almost impossible to imagine that high officers such as Onias IV, Dositheus, Helkias and Ananias would not take advantage of their high military positions to improve the status of their Jewish subordinates.

A period longer than half a century would be sufficient, in our estimation, to create a new political picture, according to which a great mass of Jews was gradually promoted to the status of *politai*. This change added fuel to the fire of hatred between Jews and Greeks in Alexandria, as the latter wanted to maintain in their city only one *politeia*, based on Greek elements and unquestionably identified with the Greek *polis*. It seems that the Greeks gained the upper hand under the reign of Ptolemy IX Lathyrus (89-80 BCE), if we may judge from the mid-sixth century, brief and vague evidence of Iordanes (*Rom.* 81.[72]).

The political anarchy which prevailed in Egypt between 58 BCE and the Roman conquest in 30 BCE can be compared to the swing of a pendulum in regard to the rights and status of the Jews. Thus, for example, Alexandrian Jews had not benefited from the distribution of free grain during the famine in Cleopatra VII's reign (Josephus *c.Ap.* 2,60). On the other hand, they were granted generous privileges by Julius Caesar in reward for their assistance in the Alexandrian War.[73] No wonder, therefore, that the Roman conquest of Egypt was marked from the very beginning by a tough struggle over the Jewish rights. It was first necessary for the Roman authorities to decide who of the Alexandrian Jews were entitled to be classified as *politai, metoikoi,* or *laoi.* Simultaneously, of course, they had to pay heed to the different meanings of equality (namely *isopoliteia, isoteleia, isonomia* etc.) which they bestowed upon the Jewish *politai* in comparison with the citizens of the Alexandrian *polis.* The imperial attempts to define Jewish rights on the basis of *status quo ante* called for trouble, since there was no decisive, unequivocal picture on that issue, and each of the parties involved (i.e. Jews and Greeks) did its best to pull the emperors to its own side.

6. Conclusion

The civic stratification of the Jews in Ptolemaic Egypt was legally determined by their affiliation to various political groups (slaves, natives, soldiers etc.) and these were socially and juridically defined to a large extent by functional criteria. Even the Alexandrian Jews were not homogenous at all from this point of view. The prominent sector among them were those reckoned *politai,* who were entitled to maintain a self-contained political community (*politeuma*) of their own. The very existence of such an independent and autonomous community within the territory of Alexandria, as well as the status of *politai* bestowed upon its members, were the major reasons for the prolonged conflict between Jews and Greeks citizens of the *polis* Alexandria. The latter refused to accept the existence of Jewish *politai* not affiliated with the *polis.* It seems that the lower classes among the Alexandrian Jews, namely those who were not *politai* but *metoikoi* and *laoi,* aggravated the conflict by their desire and efforts to achieve equal rights.

Notes

1. The main views stated in this article were first written in my Ph.D. dissertation (Kasher 1972). Later it took the form of a Hebrew monograph (Kasher 1978), and finally a revised English version (Kasher 1985).
2. For detailed information, see Taubenschlag 1955, 2ff.
3. For details, see Fraser 1972 I, 73; II, 156 (n. 251-52); Alberro 1976, 52-53.
4. Tcherikover, in: *CPJ* I 4 (n. 4); Kasher 1985, 3 (and n. 11), 42-43 (and n. 62); cf. Shutt 1985, 7ff. Alberro (1976, 36ff), however, tries unconvincingly to cast doubt on the credibility of *Letter of Aristeas.*
5. Josephus *c.Ap* 1,205-11; *Ant.* 12,5-6; Tcherikover 1977, 55-58; Stern 1974, 104-09.
6. Josephus *Ant.* 12,7. This seems to be his own interpretation, since it has no support in *Letter of Aristeas.*

7. See e.g. *Letter of Aristeas*, 12, 14-16, 20, 22-24, 33, 35; cf. Taubenschlag 1944, 50-51.

8. See Bouché-Leclercq 1907, IV, 121ff; Taubenschlag 1955, 53; Rostovtzeff 1941, 203, 1365-1366.

9. Cf. *Letter of Aristeas* 36; Josephus *Ant.* 12,45. Complementary information about military settlements of Jews in Cyrene, see Josephus *c.Ap.* 2,44; Applebaum 1980, 130ff.

10. See Liebesny 1936, 257-91; Wilcken 1937, 221-33; Westermann 1938, 1-30 (esp. 19ff); Préaux 1939 (1947), 313-15; Rostovtzeff 1941, 340ff; Fraser 1972 I, 74; cf. Alberro 1976, 48-50.

11. Gutman 1959, 67-68. I do not share Tcherikover's view about the Roman background of 3 *Maccabees*; for details, see note 41 below.

12. See Gauthiér & Sottas 1925, 23, n. 100; Abel 1952, I, 83. Despite the damaged text, which casts doubt on the identity of Eleazar the leader of the revolt (see the interpretation of Spiegelberg 1925), it is nevertheless reasonable to assume that these were acts of Jewish insurrection; see also Momigliano 1929, 180ff.

13. See: *M. Gittin*, iv 9; *J. Gittin*, 45d-46a; *B. Gittin*, 46b ff; *B. Kidushin*, 14b, 21a. There are several instances recorded in ancient Jewish epigrapy, such as *CIJ* I nos. 683, 690, 709-711; cf. also *CPJ* III no. 473.

14. On the meaning of the term, see Bickermann 1929, 232; Taubenschlag 1955, 590.

15. Indeed, there is mention of several of them in the testament (lines 13-14).

16. *SB* no. 6796 = *P. Cornell* no. 1 (dated 257 BCE); cf. *CPJ* I no. 7.

17. *SB* no. 6790 = *PCZ* no. 59076 (a+b) = *CPJ* I no. 4 (dated 257 BCE).

18. Tcherikover in: *CPJ* I 127. The boys' names can prove nothing, the more so as we are not able to trace their origin for sure, see: Tcherikover, *loc. cit.*

19. Those liberated in Alexandria could even gain the status of *metoikoi*, a matter which will be discussed later in this paper.

20. We know of Syrian villages in the Fayûm and the Heliopolitan regions and of those near Oxyrhynchus and Alexandria, in all of which considerable numbers of Jews were included among the local populations, see Kasher 1985, 44, 71, 89-90, 92, 122, 144-46.

21. For extensive information see Tcherikover in: *CPJ* I Section IV; Kasher 1985, 63ff.

22. See *P. Rev. Laws* cols. 41, 44 (259 BCE).

23. Cf. Polybius 5,107, 2-4; Jouguet 1928, 214-61. In the Battle of Raphia itself the numerical size of the "native" Egyptian sector (the *machimoi*) in the Ptolemaic army was 20.000 soldiers at least; for further details, see Rostovtzeff 1941, 1397, n. 126; Bar-Kochva 1976, 139.

24. He even took part in the suppression of a local uprising. See *W. Chr.* no. 101; Strack 1897, 257, no. 109.

25. In Greek *dikastêrion*; see Taubenschlag 1955, 484.

26. This conclusion can find more support in the fact that one of the litigants, a Jewess called Herakleia, appeared to the court with her guardian (*kyrios*) designated as "an Athenian of the Epigone" (line 38), who must have been of the same legal status; for further discussion, see Kasher 1985, 50-51.

27. The affinity of both terms is clearly indicated from the Cyrenean constitution (308/307 BCE), see: *SEG* IX no. 1 (lines 1-15), cf. Fraser 1972 I, 48; II, 132 (n. 101). The same applies also to *OGIS* no. 592; cf. Ruppell 1927, 288, 310ff; Taubenschlag 1955, 584; Smallwood 1981, 225-26. On the exact definition of *politeuma* and its implications, see later in the article.

28. We are familiar with several *politeumata* of that kind, such as the Idumaean (*OGIS* no. 737), the Phrygian (*OGIS* no. 658), the Cretan (*W. Chr.* no. 448 = *P. Tebt.* I, no. 32), the Boeotian (*SEG* II no. 871 = Bilabel & Preisigke 1915, no. 6664), the Cilician (*SEG* VIII 573 = Bilabel & Preisigke 1915, no. 7270), the Lycian (*SEG* II no. 848 = Bilabel & Preisigke 1915, no. 6025) and even more; cf. Kasher 1985, 179-180.

29. Lesquier 1911, 126, 150ff; cf. the reservations of Launey 1950 II, 1064-66, 1068-72, but see Lewis 1986, 89, 93.

30. *CIJ* II, no. 1513 (line 1); cf. also nos. 1490 (line 1); 1508 (lines 2, 10); 1509 (line 9). Indeed, the synonymity of the terms *astoi* and *politai* here has a purely rhetorical meaning, yet it is quite significant and illustrative.

31. Josephus *Ant.* 13,287. It is worthwhile noting here that it is Strabo too who employed the term *politeia* in regard to the Jewish community of Alexandria (*Ant.* 14,117), a matter which will be discussed later in this article.

32. *CIJ* II, no. 1450. The reference may be to the famous Helkias, one of Cleopatra III's commanders, or to his son or grandson. For further details see Tcherikover, in: *CPJ* I, 17, n. 45; D. M. Lewis, in: *CPJ* III, no. 1450; Kasher 1985, 123ff.

33. See Kasher 1985, 208-14; Schürer 1986, III.1, 88.

34. This incription includes a *psêphisma* bestowing honors upon the local *stratêgos* Dorion. Cf. also the use of *plêthos* in a Jewish inscription from Syrian Apamea (*CIJ* II, no. 804); for further details see Schwabe 1942, 85-93. One should not infer from this that *plêthos* is necessarily and always a synonym of *politeuma*. Here, however, it means an assembly of some association, corporation etc., the kind of which is mentioned above in *OGIS* no. 737 (second century BCE), as well as in *OGIS* no. 56 (from Canopus, third century BCE); cf. *PSI* V, no. 498 (third century BCE).

35. Robert 1940, 18-24; for further information, see Kasher 1985, 125ff.

36. The exact date of this Jewish Alexandrian composition is still controversial. The most common opinion attributes it to the middle of the second century BCE; see e.g. Wendland 1900, 3; Bickermann 1930, 280-98; Tcherikover 1960, 316-38; Fraser 1972 I, 689-99. Accordingly, Fraser (I, 55) dates the establishment of the Jewish *politeuma* in Alexandria to the day of Ptolemy VI Philometor, and not to the days of Ptolemy II Philadelphus. On the other hand, there are scholars who date it earlier, at the end of the third century BCE, such as Schürer 1901-1909 I, 608-09; Vincent 1908, 520-32; *idem* 1909, 555-75; Tramontano 1931; Pelletier 1962; cf. Rappaport 1970, 38-50. For recent opinions see Collins 1983, 81-86; Nickelsburg 1984, 75-80; Janowitz 1983, 347-57; Shutt 1985, 7-34. This is, of course, only a selected list of bibliographical references.

37. Smallwood gives an excellent definition: "A *politeuma* was a recognized, formally constituted corporation of aliens enjoying the right of domicile in a foreign city and forming a separate, semi-autonomous civic body, a city within a city; it had its own constitution and administered its internal affairs as an ethnic unit through officials distinct from and independent of the host city" (Smallwood 1981, 225). For detailed bibliography of similar definitions see, Kasher 1985, 39. n. 5. A complete denial of the existence of the Jewish *politeuma* in Alexandria (as elsewhere in Egypt) has lately been made by Zuckerman (1985/88, 171-85), but his presentation is an exceptional one, which completely deviates from the general opinion on this subject, not to mention the fact that it does not stand up to the test of scholarly criticism because of the clear data at our disposal in this matter.

38. See Roux 1942, 283, 290; and *CIG* nos. 5361, 5362.

39. Strabo *apud* Josephus *Ant.* 14,116. This piece of evidence will be discussed later.

40. This is inferred from the following wording: *tôn kat' auta pepoliteumenôn kai politeuomenôn andrôn*; cf. Josephus *Ant.* 12,38, and also 1,10.

41. Some scholars tend to date this book as late as the Roman period under Augustus, or even later; see Tcherikover 1961, 1-25. In contrast, Gutman (note 11 above) thought it was written in the Ptolemaic period, apparently in the second century BCE, and this date is, in our opinion, to be preferred, see Kasher 1985, 211ff; cf. Motzo 1934, 272-90 (reprinted 1977, 281-301). On

the various views on this matter, see Anderson 1985, 509-29; *idem* 1985a, 173-85; Schürer 1986, III.1, 537-42.

42. Version A (to 7,3) has *ta systêmata*, that is, the plural rather the singular. Josephus too employed the same term to denote Jewish communities in the diaspora (Josephus *c.Ap.*. 1,32).

43. See Liddell & Scott 1973, s.v. *systêma (3)*. Polybius, e.g. used this term for the "Macedonians" as well as for other military units. Cf. also 2 *Maccabees* 7,5 and 15,12. On papyrological use, see: Uebel 1968, 378. On the military significance of *syntagma*, see Lesquier 1911, 95-96.

44. Josephus *Bell.* 2,487; *c.Ap.*. 2,35, 37; cf. *Ant.* 12,8. This information is discredited by not a few scholars, the most prominent of whom was Tcherikover. They suspected Josephus of apologetic elaboration, and even blamed him with deliberate forgery; see: e.g. Tcherikover 1977, 272, 320ff; Fraser 1972, 54. In contrast, see Kasher 1985, 186ff; 262ff.

45. Josephus *Bell.* 2,488, 495; cf. *c.Ap.* 2,33-36. For its exact location see Alberro 1976, 29ff; Kasher 1985, 249ff.

46. *Apud* Josephus *Ant.* 14,117. Cf. the use of *meros* in *c.Ap* 2,34 as well. For the meaning of the verb *aphorizô*, Liddell & Scott 1973, s.v.

47. The same conclusion may be derived from the writings of Philo, see Kasher 1985, 233ff. This, of course, completely refutes the reservations of Zuckerman about the very existence of the Jewish *politeuma* in Alexandria (see n. 36 above). On the synonymity of *politeuma* and *politeia* in the writings of both Philo and Josephus, see Kasher 1985, 358-64.

48. Bell 1924, 10 ff; for more references, see Kasher 1985, 281, n. 56, to which add Alberro 1976, introduction iii, and 126, 234 and Otzen 1984, 55ff.

49. Schürer 1909, III, 72; *idem* 1986, III.1, 88; Tcherikover, in: *CPJ* I, 9 n. 24; cf. Fraser 1972 II, 139 n. 145.

50. Fuchs 1924, 89f; Ruppel 1927, 281; Tramontano 1931, 243; Box 1939, xxii (2), xxv.

51. Cf. Kasher 1985, 196-97, 239ff. In actual fact, we cannot tell who and how many were *metoikoi*, or who and how many were *laoi*, if any at all.

52. Against this, the synonymity of terms which might be inferred from the evidence relating to Leontopolis (mentioned above) may suggest a differrent conclusion; the same applies to the Idumaean *politeuma* in Memphis; cf. Thompson-Crawford 1984, 1069-75.

53. This view was highly contended by Bickermann, 1929, 226 (n. 1), 228; Rostovtzeff 1941, 1064; cf. for further discussion, see Fraser 1972 I, 38ff (esp. 47ff); Kasher 1985, 192ff.

54. Philo *In Flaccum*, 80, 123; *Legatio*, 194, 350; Josephus *Ant.* 14,188; 19,281; *c.Ap.* 2,38.

55. Josephus *c.Ap.* 2,7, 33, 44 (cf. also 55, 63); *Ant.* 14,113, 117.

56. Josephus *Ant.* 14,117-18; 19,278, 284, 285; cf. also *c.Ap.* 2,43; *Bell.* 2,487, 495.

57. Josephus *c.Ap.* 2,39; *Bell.* 7,44, 47, 54, 111.

58. In other words, *politeia* has in this context the same meaning as that mentioned by Strabo (*apud* Josephus *Ant.* 14,117. For a fuller treatment of this issue in relation to the Jewish community in Antioch, see Kasher 1985, 297ff.

59. Schubart 1925, 33 and Tcherikover (in: *CPJ* II, 49) admitted this, but made unconvincing attempts to explain it away.

60. *CIJ* I, nos. 644, 699; II, 918; *OGIS* no. 599; cf. Klein 1920, nos. 135, 137, 141, 154; *idem* 1939, nos. 4, 25, 26, 27. It is worthwhile noting that an unpublished Jewish tomb inscription in the Jaffa Museum of Antiquities also contains the form *apo Alexandreias*.

61. Rostovtzeff 1964, 166; Fraser 1972 II, 187, n. 73.

62. *CPJ* I, nos. 142-143. It is important to emphasize in this context that these Jews were land-owners in the *chora* of Alexandria, a privilege reserved for Alexandrian citizens only.

63. There are not a few instances of such usage in his works, see Rengsdorf 1975, 389, s.v. *isotimos*.

64. On the functional significance of the term "Macedonians" in the Hellenistic period, see Launey 1950, 321, 330, 353, 360ff. In Josephus *Bell.* 5,460 Josephus used the term "Macedonians" as a clearly military denotation which is therefore pseudo-ethnic in character. Arrian (7,6) too relates that Alexander the Great himself, while acting in Persia, recruited 30.000 youth who were "accoutred with Macedonian arms, and exercised in military discipline after the Macedonian system"; even Persian officers "were picked out and enrolled among the foot-guard in addition to the Macedonian officers" and "Macedonian spears were given to them instead of the barbarian javelins" etc. In view of this it can be deduced that as early as the time of Alexander the term "Macedonians" had a functional and pseudo-ethnic significance.

65. See *Letter of Aristeas* 110. On the credibility of this information, see Fraser 1972 I, 699.

66. It is worthwhile noting that Tcherikover himself maintained that the "Macedonians" were not citizens of the *poleis* next to which they were posted, see: Tcherikover 1931, 327ff (esp. 330). On the special status of the "Macedonians", see also Fraser 1972 I, 53, 80.

67. Cf. Josephus *Ant.* 19,281 (in relation to the Roman Period); also *Ant.* 20,173, 183 (in relation to Roman Caesarea Maritima).

68. In the eyes of Tcherikover, whose studies on this subject are the most comprehensive, this was the essence of "the Jewish Question" in those days. See: Tcherikover 1977, 310ff, 410ff; *idem* 1961, 247-49; *idem* 1963, 152, 155; *idem*, in: *CPJ* I, 60ff.

69. Cf. Alberro 1976, 129-30; I have, however, strong reservations with regard to the view that *isopoliteia* meant "honorary citizenship" (or rather "potential citizenship") in the city of Alexandria; for an extensive discussion, see Kasher 1985, 278ff.

70. See Tarn & Griffith 1952, 147ff. It is worthwhile noting that the captivity and exile of the Jews in Babylonia was described in the *Septuagint* by the terms *metoikesia, metoikia*, see: 2 *Kings* 24,16; cf.; *Jerem.* 20,3-4; *Ev. Matt* 1,11. As the *LXX* was written in Egypt, it is just logical to assume that the above mentioned terms reflect the norms familiar in Egypt.

71. On the short enmity of this king to the Jews and the reconciliation with them, see Kasher 1985, 8-9.

72. See also Porphyrius in: Jacoby, *FGrH* 260, F 2; cf. Tcherikover, in: *CPJ* I, 25 and n. 63; Applebaum 1980, 201ff; Fraser 1972 II, 168, n. 337.

73. Josephus *Ant.* 14,188-89; *c.Ap.* 2,37, 60. For detailed discussion see: Smallwood 1981, *passim*; Kasher 1985, 13-18, 186, 258.

PHILO AND THE JEWS IN ALEXANDRIA

Peder Borgen

1. Introduction

The topic of this paper, as stated in the title, needs to be defined. It may be understood to refer to the long debate about Philo's own place within Judaism. Was he basically a Jew, and if so how representative was he of Alexandrian Judaism? Or was he an intellectual pagan wearing a Jewish robe? In the present paper this question will be dealt with in an indirect way only.

The topic might also be examined from the perspective of the history of the Jews in Alexandria. How is Philo to be seen within this historical context? Since the Hellenistic period is to have the main focus of the paper, this perspective is especially relevant. However, the history of Alexandrian Judaism in the time after Philo should also be included.

The main emphasis is indicated by the organizers of the symposium, however: they wish the papers to illuminate tensions, conflicts, interaction and mutual influences, attitudes and stereotypes between the Jews and the non-Jews, as well as varieties and tensions within the Jewish community itself. The topic is very extensive, so that only some observations can be given as basis for further work. [1]

2. Historical perspective[2]

The first task is to sketch the historical perspective. During the Ptolemaic rule, Jews were settled all over Egypt. The largest Jewish community was the one in Alexandria. The Alexandrian literature, especially the translation of the Hebrew Bible into Greek, testifies to the strength and vitality of the Jewish community of Alexandria as early as the third century BC.

The main occupations of the Jews in Egypt were military service and agriculture. After the period of immigration and growth from the time of Ptolemy I Soter (304-284 BC) to Ptolemy V Epiphanes (204-181 BC), the Jews became a considerable military and political force from Ptolemy VI Philometor (181-145 BC) to the Roman conquest in 30 BC. During the period between 30 BC and 117

AD, three armed uprisings and revolts by the Jews demonstrate that the situation of the Alexandrian (and Egyptian) Jews was deteriorating: the armed uprising at the death of emperor Gaius Caligula in 41 AD, the impact of the Jewish war in Palestine on the tensions in Alexandria and Egypt, 66 and 70-73 AD, and the suicidal Messianic revolution of Jews in Cyrene, Alexandria and Egypt in the years 115-117 AD.

Philo's parents must have experienced the transition from Ptolemaic to Roman rule in 30 BC, and to some extent Philo represents a continuation of Ptolemaic Judaism within the new setting of Roman Egypt. Philo bases his works on the Septuagint translation of the Hebrew Bible. The translation was probably initiated under the reign of Ptolemy II Philadelphus (284-246 BC). Moreover, Philo brings together many of the elements found in Alexandrian Jewish literature:

1. The positive evaluation of the Ptolemaic rulers, found in the *Letter of Aristeas*, in the fragments of Aristobulus and the *Third Book of the Sibylline Oracles*, is also expressed by Philo in his praise of Ptolemy II Philadelphus in *Mos.* 2,28-31 and his positive evalutation of the Ptolemaic kings in *Legat.* 138-39. He extends this positive view to the Roman rulers Augustus and Tiberius (*Legat.* 141-61). This positive attitude is conditioned upon their recognition of the rights of the Jews to live in accordance with the Laws of Moses and worship the one God. Accordingly, the Roman emperor Gaius Caligula and the prefect Flaccus are under the judgement of God for abolishing the privileges of the Jews.[3]

2. Philo continues the approach, which has been seen in varying degrees in the *Letter of Aristeas*, in Aristobulus and the *Wisdom of Solomon*, to interpret the Laws of Moses and Jewish existence in general by means of Greek ideas and religious traditions. Of special importance is the circumstance that Aristobulus in his use of Greek philosophy and quotations and in his use of allegorical method represents a trend towards Philo's developed expositions. Like Philo, he stresses the cosmic significance of Judaism, and shows that Philo's philosophical exegesis was not an isolated case.[4]

3. The sharp polemic against polytheistic cult expressed in writings such as the *Third Book of the Sibylline Oracles*, the *Wisdom of Solomon* and the *Third Book of Maccabees*, is also found in Philo's writings.[5]

4. Philo continues the trend found in the earlier writings to see the Jews as a superior nation with a universal role to play.

5. Philo testifies to the continuation of ideological attacks on the Jews by non-Jews.

These similarities between Philo and earlier Jewish writings related to Alexandria, especially the interpretation of the Laws of Moses by means of Greek ideas and the stress on Jewish superiority, prove that he is not an isolated phenomenon or an outsider in the history of Alexandrian Judaism, but is an integral part of it. Throughout this literature attempts are made to combine an emphasis on what Jews and Gentiles have in common, with an underscoring of the distinctiveness of the Jewish nation.

The geographical context of this literature is on the whole the world of Hellenism. To a large extent, Philo also shares this perspective. Thus in a letter attributed to King Agrippa Philo gives the following picture of the Jews in Judaea and the Diaspora: Jerusalem is

the mother city not of one country, Judaea, but of most of the others in virtue of the colonies sent out of diverse times to the neighbouring lands Egypt, Phoenicia, the part of Syria called the Hollow and the rest as well, and the lands lying far apart, Pamphylia, Cilicia, most of Asia up to Bithynia and the corner of Pontus, similarly also into Europe, Thessaly, Boeotia, Macedonia, Aetolia, Attica, Argos, Corinth and most of the best parts of Peleponnese. And not only are the mainlands full of Jewish colonies, but also the most highly esteemed of the islands Euboea, Cyprus, Crete. I say nothing of the countries beyond the Euphrates, for except for a small part they all, Babylon and of the other satrapies those where the land within their confines is highly fertile, have Jewish inhabitants (*Legat.* 281-83).

It is interesting that in this survey of the Jewish Diaspora, no mention is made of the Jewish community of Rome, nor of the Jews in Italy as a whole, nor of the Jews in any other part of the western Mediterranean region.[6] The perspective is the world of Hellenism with its focus on the eastern Mediterranean.

In this world three centers are emphasized by Philo, Jerusalem, Greece, with Athens as the main city, and Alexandria and Egypt. Politically, Rome plays an important role in Philo's world, but Rome and Romans have no culture or learning of their own, but may serve as promoters of Greek culture or may follow Egyptian evil.[7] Philo thus sees Augustus as a promoter of Greek culture: he "enlarged Greece with many other Greek lands, ... and Hellenized the most important parts of the barbarian world" (*Legat.* 147).

3. Jews and non-Jews: separation and tension

Before pointing to aspects of the tension between Alexandrian Jews and the non-Jews some of the distinctive marks of the Jewish community should be listed.[8] Philo identifies himself as a member of the Jewish community. He offers glimpses from the structure of the community in Alexandria and some of the distinctive external marks. Philo tells that Augustus confirmed the rights of the Jewish community to live in accordance with their ancestral laws (*Flacc.* 50; *Legat.* 152-58). Augustus had appointed a council of elders to take charge of the affairs of the Jews (*Flacc.* 74 and 80). They had a large number of synagogues around in the city as centers for their communal life (*Legat.* 132-34; *Somn.* 2,127). Among the distinguishing marks of this community was the observance of the sabbath (*Legat.* 158; *Somn.* 2,123-32; *Migr.* 91), circumcision (*Spec.* 1,1-2; *Migr.* 92), the observance of dietary laws, such as the prohibition against eating pork (*Flacc.* 96; *Legat.* 361), the recognition of the Temple in Jerusalem, the payment of the Temple tax, and pilgrimages to Jerusalem (*Spec.* 1,78; *Legat.* 156; *Flacc.* 45-56; *Prov.* 2,64). Philo's works offer direct and indirect evidence for the celebration of various Jewish festivals, among which is one local festivals, the annual celebration of the Septuagint translation held on the island of Pharos (*Spec.* 2,39-222; *Mos.* 2,41-42). Some distinctive marks were of a more general nature, however, such as the attitude of superiority of the Jewish community, its stress on monotheism, etc., some of its ethical standards and aspects of its life-style.

There was in Alexandria a long history of tension between the Jewish community and some of the non-Jews. An anti-Jewish polemic was formulated by the Egyptian priest Manetho, about 300 BC. He gave a negative interpretation of the role of Moses, his laws and the history and practice of the Jewish people. He wrote that the Jews in Egypt swore to obey all the commands of Osarsiph (i.e. Moses), one of the priests of Heliopolis. By his first law he ordained that they should not worship the gods, and that they should have no connection with any save members of their own confederacy (*c.Ap.* 1,238-39 and 250). There are also reports on polemic offered by other persons familiar with the Jewish Diaspora, such as Apollonius Molon, Lysimachos and others. Moses and his laws are criticized and the Jews were accused of being atheists, since they did not join in the worship of the various gods around them, and of being misanthropists (*c.Ap.* 2,145-48). The rite of circumcision was ridiculed by Philo's contemporary, Apion, and many others (*c.Ap.* 2,137.142-43). Moreover, there is documentation for the criticism of the Jews for laziness because they abstained from work on the sabbath (Juvenal's Satire 14,96-106; cf. *c.Ap.* 1,209; Augustine, *De Civitate Dei* 6,11).

Philo writes explicitly that there were circles in Alexandria where such anti-Jewish traditions were nurtured and taught. With rhetorical force Philo addresses Gaius Caligula's slave Helicon in direct speech:

You have the false charges made against the Jews and Jewish customs, charges among which you grew up; you learnt them right from your cradle, not from a single individual but from the most garrulous section of the Alexandrian population. Show off your learning (*Legat.* 170).[9]

Such deep and widespread resentment against the Jews is also evidenced in the so-called *Acts of the Pagan Martyrs* and the strong anti-Jewish use of Jewish material in some of the Gnostic writings.[10] The attacks against the Alexandrian Jews in 38-41 AD have their general background in this atmosphere of tension and hatred between non-Jews and Jews.

At several points in his writings Philo defends the Jews against such criticism. To refute the charges of misanthropy, he refers to humane and philanthropic actions prescribed by the Laws of Moses. The Jews are told to be humane to fellow-human beings, also to enemies, and to show compassion even to flocks and herds (*Virt.* 141). According to Philo, even the universal call and role of the Jewish nation express this care of the Jews for all men:

...it astonishes me to see that some people venture to accuse of inhumanity the nation which has shown so profound a sense of fellowship and goodwill to all men everywhere, by using its prayers and festivals and first-fruit offerings as a mean of supplication for the human race in general and of making its homage to the truly existent God in the name of those who have evaded the service which it was their duty to give, as well as of itself (*Spec.* 2,167).

As for the sabbath, Philo writes: "On this day we are commanded to abstain from all work, not because the law inculcates slackness..." (*Spec.* 2,60). In *Hypoth.* 7,10-14 he tells about the sabbath gatherings with reading from the Laws of Moses and exposition, and asks: "Do you think that this marks them as idlers...?" (7,14). The sabbath and the sabbath gatherings were so essential to the Jews that they, according to *Somn.* 2,123-32, even firmly refused to yield to pressure from an official of Egypt who tried to force them to refrain from sabbath observance:

He tried to compel men to do service to him on it and perform other actions which contravene our established custom, thinking that if he could destroy the ancestral rule of the Sabbath it would lead the way to irregularity in all other matters, and a general backsliding (*Somn.* 2,123).[11]

Philo defends Moses against the accusation of being an impostor and mountebank (cf. Molon, *c.Ap.* 2,145) by referring to his success in bringing the whole people in complete safety amid drought and hunger and ignorance of the road and lack of everything, as easily as if there had been an abundance of everything (*Hypoth.* 6,3-4). Against those who ridiculed the rite of circumcision, Philo pointed to the fact that the Jews were not the only people who practised the rite. Among those who practised it were the Egyptians *(Spec.* 1,1-7; *QG* 3,47-48). Josephus uses a similar argument in *c.Ap.* 2,140ff. The practice of circumcision among Egyptians is documented in Herodotus 2,36-37 and 104, Diodorus 1,28; 3,32. As for the prohibition against eating pork, Philo answers the emperor in a diplomatic way: "Different people have different customs and the use of some things is forbidden to us as others are to our opponents" (*Legat.* 361-62).

Correspondingly, Philo follows the anti-pagan tradition of Judaism, with special anti-Egyptian focus, as also evidenced in Alexandrian Jewish writings from the Hellenistic period.[12] He offers criticism of polytheistic worship and is especially sharp and scornful in his criticism of Egyptian worship:

they have advanced to divine honours irrational animals, bulls and rams and goats ... And with these there might be some reason, for they are thoroughly domesticated and useful for our livelihood[13] ... But actually the Egyptians have gone to a further excess and chosen the fiercest and most savage of wild animals, lions and crocodiles and among reptiles the venomous asp, all of which they dignify with temples, sacred precincts, sacrifices, assemblies, processions and the like ... Many other animals too they have deified, dogs, cats, wolves and among the birds, ibises and hawks; fishes too, either their whole bodies or particular parts. What could be more ridiculous than all this? Indeed strangers on their first arrival in Egypt ... are likely to die laughing at it, while anyone who knows the flavour of right instruction, horrified at this veneration of things so much the reverse of venerable, pities those who render it and regards them with good reason as more miserable than the creatures they honour, as men with souls transformed into the nature of those creatures, so that as they pass before him, they seem beasts in human shape (*Dec.* 76-80).[14]

Philo here identifies the Egyptians with the deities they worship. Thus the dualism between monotheism and polytheism is also applied to a dualism between Jews and Egyptians.

For Philo the dualism between Jews and Egyptians serves as an interpretative category for understanding the conflict in Alexandria (and Rome) in 38-41 AD. The evil Egyptians were operative in the attack on the Jews in Alexandria:

> But Gaius grew beside himself with vanity, not only saying but thinking that he was god. He then found among the Greeks or the outside world no people fitted better than the Alexandrians to confirm the unmeasured passion which craves for more than is natural to mankind. For the Alexandrians are adept to flattery and imposture and hypocrisy, ready enough with fawning words but causing universal disaster with their loose and unbridled lips ... How much reverence is paid by them to the title of god is shown by their having allowed it to be shared by the indigenous ibises and venomous snakes and many other ferocious wild beasts (*Legat.* 162-63).

The Egyptians were active in Rome, too:

> The majority of these [Gaius' domestics] were Egyptians, a seed-bed of evil in whose souls both the venom and the temper of the native crocodiles and asps were reproduced. The one who played the part of chorus leader to the whole Egyptian troup was Helicon, an abominable execrable slave (*Legat.* 166).

The conflict between the Jews and the Egyptians was a dualism of principle. It was a sharp form of dualism between the Jews who worshipped the one true God and the Egyptians being "atheists" in their worship of the earthly animal gods. Gaius' claim to be worshipped as god belonged also to this earthly and atheistical form of religion. In this way the Alexandrian Greeks as well as Gaius were to be ranked among the Egyptians. It is therefore inadequate when E. M. Smallwood in her comments on *Legat.* 166 writes that Philo here uses the term "Egyptians" contemptuously to denote people who were in fact Greeks. To Philo the term "Egyptians" here expresses a basic theological dualism, and from this point of view the Alexandrian Greeks were "Egyptians". This interpretation was made all the more easy by the fact that Egyptian religious traditions and practices were mixed into the syncretism of the Alexandrian Greeks.[15] The Jewish nation was seen by Philo as being under God's providential care in spite of all misfortunes and sufferings, and indirectly in *Legat.* and explicitly in *Flacc.* it is stated that those who attack the Jews suffer punishment on the basis of justice and the principle of reversal. This principle of justice was at work when Flaccus was cut into pieces in his exile on the island Andros: "For it was the will of Justice that the butcheries which she wrought on his single body should be as numerous as the members of Jews whom he unlawfully put to death" (*Flacc.* 189). The understanding that justice and providence are at work in history is also found in the *Wisdom of Solomon*.[16]

The "atheism" of the Egyptians — that they worship creation and value earth and earthly deities above heaven (and God) and body above soul, etc. — is in several places criticized by Philo (see *Post.* 2; *Fug.* 180, 193 and 196; *Leg.* 3,112; *Her.* 203; *Fug.* 114 and 180; *Legat.* 77 and 163).[17] As for the charge against the Jews for misanthropy Philo turns the tables by stating that the many other nations are misanthropists when they practice the exposure of infants, not the Jews whose laws prohibit this (*Spec.* 3,110-19).

4. Mutual influence and interaction

There are not only attitudes of criticism and tension reflected in Philo's writings. Various forms of social and economic intercourse are seen, as well as cultural and religious influences and pressures. While the Jews in Ptolemaic time largely were found in military and agricultural professions, the situation changed in the Roman period. The Jews were eliminated as a military factor together with the Ptolemaic army. Philo then lists farmers together with some other professions, shippers, merchants and artisans (*Flacc.* 57). 'Capitalists' are also mentioned, probably persons who lend money to merchants and others.[18] In the area of social life, Philo's own participation is illustrative. He took part in banquets, frequented the theatre, and heard concerts; he watched boxing, wrestling and horse-racing (*Leg.* 3,155f.; *Ebr.* 177; *Prob.* 26 and 141; *Prov.* 2,58). In his writings Philo shows expert knowledge of details in athletics, so that Harris (1976) thinks that he must once have been an active athlete. Philo indicates a cautious attitude, however. To Philo the triennial festivals of wrestling, boxing, etc. organized by the cities occasion rivalry, anger and licentiousness. A Jew should try to avoid taking part, but if compelled to do so, should not hesitate to be defeated (*Agr.* 110-21). Although rabbinic writings reflect an even stronger reserve, *bGittin* 47a confirms Philo's statement in *Agr.* 110-21. R. Simeon ben Lakish is said to have once been a professional gladiator, which he justified on the ground of grim necessity. As for joining social clubs and paying the membership fee, Philo says: "...when the object is to share in the best of possessions, prudence, such payments are praiseworthy and profitable; but when they are paid to obtain that supreme evil, folly, the practice is unprofitable" and can lead to Egyptian animal worship (*Ebr.* 20ff and 95). In Egypt it is easy for Jewish youths to leave the ancestral way of life for alien ways, because the Egyptians deify things created and mortal, and are blind to the true God. When Philo reports on meals and table-fellowship, he seldom makes clear whether they take place in Jewish or non-Jewish settings, but he stresses the danger of excessive eating and drinking, and the danger of irregularities (*Spec.* 1,173-76) etc. It is interesting to notice that when Joseph gave a feast for his own family and the Egyptians, he feasted each party according to its ancestral practice (*Ios.* 202-26).

In Philo's writings we do not find much material which in a direct and explicit way tells about non-Jews who frequented the social and religious life of the Jewish community. The clearest example is the festival of the Septuagint:

Therefore, even to the present day, there is held every year a feast and general assembly in the island of Pharos, whither not only Jews but multitudes of others cross the water, both to do honour to the place in which the light of that version first shone out, and also to thank God for the good gift so old yet ever young. But, after the prayers and thanksgivings, some fixing tents on the seaside and others reclining on the sandy beach in the open air feast with their relations and friends, counting that shore for the time a more magnificent lodging than the fine mansions in the royal precincts (*Mos.* 2,41-42).

In a more general way, Philo states that the celebration of the sabbath made a strong impact upon the Greek and barbarian peoples:

They (the Laws of Moses) attract and win the attention of all, of barbarians, of Greeks, of dwellers on the mainland and islands, of nations of the east and the west, of Europe and Asia, of the whole inhabited world from end to end. For, who has not shewn his high respect for that sacred seventh day, by giving rest and relaxation from labour to himself and his neighbours, freemen and slaves alike, and beyond these to his beasts? (*Mos.* 2,20-21).

Josephus, in *c.Ap.* 2,282-83, describes in a similar way the broad influence of Judaism on the Gentile world. Among the observances kept by non-Jews, Josephus also lists abstention from work on the seventh day. Both Philo and Josephus exaggerate the impact of the sabbath on other peoples, but there are data which indicate that there was basis for their statements. V. Tcherikover points to the fact that personal names such as "Sambathion", etc. were used by non-Jews from the first century AD and onwards in Egypt and in other areas of the Mediterranean world. Tcherikover and others draw the conclusion that such names attest the adoption of sabbath observance by numbers of non-Jews.[19]

According to Philo, the circumstance that Ptolemy II Philadelphus (284-246 BC), a king of the highest distinction, initiated the translation of the Laws of Moses into Greek, showed that the laws were precious in the eyes of rulers (*Mos.* 2,25-43). Correspondingly, Philo also praises Augustus and the Roman official Petronius for their personal qualities and their favourable attitude to the Jews.

In contrast to Gaius Caligula, Augustus had recognized the rights of the Jews to worship and live in accordance with their ancestral laws and customs (*Legat.* 153-58), and he adorned the Jerusalem Temple and ordered that continuous sacrifices should be carried out every day at his own expense as a tribute to the most high God (*Legat.* 157). As for himself, he never wished anyone to address him as God (*Legat.* 154). He also praises Augustus for having established order and peace (*Legat.* 147).[20]

In his characterization of the Roman legate to Syria, Petronius, Philo brings him close to Judaism:

Indeed it appears that he himself had some rudiments of Jewish philosophy and religion acquired either in early lessons in the past through his zeal for culture or after his appointment as governor in the countries where the Jews are very numerous in every city, Asia and Syria, or else because his soul was so disposed, being drawn to things worthy of serious effort by a nature which listened to no voice nor dictation nor teaching but its own. But we find that to good men God whispers good decisions by which they will give and receive benefits, and this was true in his case (*Legat.* 245).

In Philo's view, the general attitude and policy of the Jews can be formulated in this way:

For all men guard their own customs, but this is especially true of the Jewish nation. Holding that the laws are oracles vouchsafed by God and having been trained in this doctrine from their earliest years, they carry the likeness of the commandments enshrined in their souls. Then as they contemplate their forms thus clearly represented they always think of them with awe. And those of other races who pay homage to them they welcome no less than their own countrymen, while those who either break them down or mock at them they hate as their bitterest foes (*Legat.* 210-11).

Philo's attitude towards encyclical education and political careerism in society at large is ambiguous. He has a concentrated discussion of the encyclical education in *De Congressu* and deals with it time and again in many of his other writings. The central Pentateuchal text for his discussion of education is *Gen.* 16,1-6 on Abraham's relationship to Sarah and Hagar. When Philo interprets Abraham's relationship in terms of educational ideas, he is dependent upon the allegorical interpretation of the figure of Penelope in Homer. For example Plutarch tells that those who, being unable to win philosophy, wear themselves out in the encyclical disciplines, are like the suitors of Penelope, who when they could not win the mistress, contented themselves with her maids. Correspondingly, when Abraham did not, at first, conceive a child with Sarah, he took the maid, Hagar, in her place.

This transformation of Penelope and her maids into Sarah and Hagar meant that Philo interpreted the allegory within a Jewish context, to express a Jewish point of view regarding encyclical education: the encyclical education is the school which the Jews have in common with their pagan surroundings. This is the reason why Philo often emphasizes that Hagar, i.e. encyclical education, was an Egyptian woman (*Congr.* 20ff; *QG* 3,19.21; *Abr.* 251). It may be used to serve Jewish ideals and wisdom (*Congr.* 74-76), or it can be misused so as to lead persons away from them (*Leg.* 3,167).

Philo draws extensively on Greek ideas and religious traditions in his writings and brings to a climax the tendency already present in the *Letter of Aristeas*, in Aristobulus and the *Wisdom of Solomon*. Like Aristobulus he has explicit quotations from Greek literature. Both use the allegorical method of interpretation, Philo in an even more developed form than that found in Aristobulus. In Philo's writings Stoicism and the Platonic and Pythagorean traditions predominate and are brought together in a way similar to combinations found in Middle Platonism and Middle Stoicism. Also other Greek schools of thought are referred to and discussed, such as Aristotelian views, Epicurean and Sceptic ideas, etc.

In his use of these ideas and traditions he, like Aristobulus, expresses sharp criticism at some points and draws positively on or re-interprets some other ideas. For example in *Opif.* 170-72a Philo criticizes Sceptic views that God's existence is doubtful, the Aristotelian view that the world is without beginning, and the Epicurean idea of a plurality of worlds and denial of providence. Positively, he uses and re-interprets the Platonic category of the intelligible world of ideas and the world of the senses, etc.

How did Philo evaluate these many traditions which he to a large degree draws on positively? And how did he look upon non-Jewish persons and groups who entertained them? Just as he can criticize in a dualistic manner certain aspects and certain groups, he can also express high esteem for other aspects and other non-Jewish groups. Nevertheless, for him Moses and his God-given Laws have the highest authority. At times he can say that what is good among non-Jews receives its full and authentic dimension in Moses and his followers. Thus in discussing the Stoic theme that the wise man is truly free, Philo states in *Prob.* 42ff that supreme freedom belonged to "him who was possessed by love of the divine and worshipped the Self-existent only, as having passed from a man into a god, though, indeed a god to men..." He quotes here *Exod.* 7,1: "And the Lord said to Moses: See I make you as god to Pharaoh", a text he often used elsewhere (*Leg.* 1,40; *Sacr.* 9; *Det.* 161f; *Migr.* 84 and 169; *Mut.* 19,125 and 128f; *Somn.* 2,189). The various levels of freedom of the good man receive their full dimension in Moses who worshipped the Self-existent only.

At times Philo entertains a concept also found in Aristobulus, that Greek philosophers derived their ideas from Moses. Philo says that Heraclitus derived his theory of opposites from Moses, or "snatched them from him like a thief" (*QG* 4,152; see also *QG* 3,5; cf. *Her.* 214); and that Greek legislators copied from the laws of Moses (*Spec.* 4,61). More cautiously he says that the Greek philosopher Zeno seemed to have learned from the Laws of Moses (*Prob.* 51-57).

5. Pluralism within the Jewish community

This presentation of relationships between Jews and gentiles must also examine the various attitudes and the tensions which existed within the Jewish community itself.

The Jews felt the pressure to integrate into the larger society. The danger of apostasy was therefore real. One outstanding example from the Ptolemaic period was the renegade Jew Dositheos, son of Drimylos. He served as one of the two heads of the royal secretariate, and later he was called to the highest priestly office in Egypt, that of being priest in the ruler cult. He served during the reigns of Ptolemy III Euergetes I (246-221 BC) and Ptolemy IV Philopator (221-204 BC).[21] In Philo's time, and in Philo's own family, the same occurred. Tiberius Julius Alexander, born c. 15 AD, the son of Philo's brother, Julius Alexander, left Judaism and had a public career which took him to the highest post of a Roman official in Egypt, that of prefect (66-70 AD). Philo seems to allude to this and similar cases in *Mos.* 1,30-31 which describes prosperous Jews who look down upon their relatives and friends and set at naught the laws under which they were born and bred, by adopting different modes of life.[22]

In Ptolemaic as well as Roman times, there were also Jews who had leading governmental positions without forsaking Judaism. The Jewish priest and military leader Onias and his sons Helkias and Ananias ranked high in the army of the Ptolemies, and also played a central political role.[23] Philo's own family also carried on traditions from earlier times, in so far as Philo's brother Julius Alexander was Alabarch (or Arabarch), that is, inspector-in-chief of the customs duties collected on the eastern borders of Egypt.[24]

There are passages in Philo's writings where he touches on the problems involved in building a career and having official positions. In *Leg.* 3,167 he tells about the wrong objectives of education:

Many, then, have acquired the lights in the soul for night and darkness, not for day and light; all elementary lessons, for example, and what is called school-learning and philosophy itself when pursued with no motive higher than luxurious living, or from desire of an office under our rulers.

The context shows that the point is not to prohibit the Jews from taking leading political positions, but to make certain that they are faithful to Jewish ideals and do not regard a successful career in itself as the aim of their education.[25] Similarily, in *Migr.* 172 Philo paraphrases Moses' prayer in *Exod.* 33,15 cited in *Migr.* 171, "If You yourself do not go with me on my journey, lead me not up from here":

But perhaps the meaning is something like this: 'Raise me not up on high, endowing me with wealth or fame or honours or offices, or aught else that is called good fortune, unless You Yourself are about to come with me.' For these things often bring upon those who have them very great losses as well as very great advantages, advantages when the judgement is under God's guidance; hurts, when this is not so.

Philo often refers to other exegetes and enters into debate with them. It is not possible to identify the different exegetical traditions with specific groups within the Jewish community, but they nevertheless indicate that there was some pluralism not only with regard to views, but also in attitudes and action. More work on this material is needed, but tentatively the following observations can be made.

Philo criticizes both literalists and allegorists. As for the allegorists, he tells that some among them went so far that they undermined central Jewish customs and institutions: "There are some who, regarding laws in their literal sense in the light of symbols of matters belonging to the intellect, are overpunctilious about the latter, while treating the former with easygoing neglect" (*Migr.* 89). Although they have the right understanding of the meaning of the observances, they do away with the outward observances themselves, such as keeping of the sabbath, the Feast, and circumcision; their neglect may even undermine the sanctity of the Temple (*Migr.* 91-92). Philo makes clear that those who entertain such attitudes have overstepped the borderline of the Jewish community and may suffer the censure of the many (*Migr.* 93). According to Philo the outward observances and the inner meaning should be kept together like body and soul (*Migr.* 93).

In the section on keeping the sabbath, Philo lists some specific points: to light fires, till the ground, carry loads, institute proceedings in court, act as jurors, demand the restoration of deposits or recover loans or to do anything else that one is permitted to do as well on other days (*Migr.* 91). The probable background for Jews who neglected these outward observances was the pressures felt when they wanted to function in society at large and discovered that such restrictions were obstacles which made social, economic and judicial life difficult.[26]

6. Cosmic and eschatological perspectives

The question of particularism and universalism has been much debated in Philonic research. Thus W. Bousset asked: How far has Philo overcome the Jewish particularistic religion and developed a true individualistic universalism?[27] The problem is formulated in the same way by U. Fischer in his book published in 1978 on eschatology in Diaspora Judaism.[28] Philo may seem basically to entertain such non-particularistic notions: according to him, the particular enactments of the Laws of Moses seek to attain to the harmony of the universe and are in accordance with cosmic law (*Mos.* 2,45-52 and *Op.* 3). On this basis it is logically possible to interpret Philo's presentation of the particular enactments only as illustrations of the universal cosmic principles at work among all human beings and in every individual.

There is an alternative understanding of universalism, however: a particular people and nation may be understood to have a universal and even cosmic role to play. In Philo's writings this way of reasoning is predominant, however: the general, universal principles are made manifest in the specific laws of the Jewish nation, and thus this nation is the center and the head of all nations. The eschatological expectation is then that all peoples are to recognize God's universal laws revealed in the Laws of Moses, and recognize the leading role of the Jewish nation (see *Mos.* 1,290-91; *Praem.* 79-97; *Mos.* 2,12-44).

Philo emphasizes the universal role of the Jews. God bestowed on Moses the kingship of a nation more populous and mightier than Egypt, a nation destined to be consecrated above all others to offer prayers for ever on behalf of the human race (*Mos.* 1,149). God judged him worthy to appear as a partner of His own possessions, and gave into his hands the whole world as his portion (*Mos.* 1,155-57). In the encounter with the Phoenicians, the superior and universal call of the Hebrew nation was made manifest. Moses mounted the neighbouring hill, and whenever his hands rose aloft, the Hebrews were made strong, but whenever his hands were weighed down the enemy prevailed. By symbols, God showed that earth and the lowest regions of the universe were the portions assigned to the Phoenicians, and the ethereal, the holiest region, to the Hebrews. Just as heaven holds kingship in the universe and is superior to earth, so the Hebrew nation should be victorious over its opponents in war (*Mos.* 1,217). The Hebrew nation was the heavenly people, while the other peoples belonged to the earthly region. Among the many other passages which deal with the superiority of the Jewish nation and her universal role one may refer to *Mos.* 2,12-65; 66-186; 187-291; *Abr.* 98; *Spec.* 1,97; 2,163 and 167; *QE* 2,42. The Jews are in true sense men (*Spec.* 1,303).

What is then the expectation for the future? On the basis of Philo's interpretation of the Bileam-prophecy in *Num.* 24,7 LXX, the expectation may be summarized in the following points: either by peaceful means or through war the Hebrew nation will be the rulers of the other nations (*Mos.* 1,289-91 and *Praem.* 93-97). Thus, although Philo's main emphasis is on gaining world power by peaceful means, there is in his writings an undercurrent of the militaristic tradition influenced by the fact that numerous Jews were soldiers in the Ptolemaic army. The transfer to Roman rule brought a change in this respect. The Jews were eliminated as a military factor together with the Ptolemaic army as a whole. The military tradition was carried on, however, as can be seen from the armed uprising by the Alexandrian Jews at the death of emperor Gaius Caligula in 41 AD, the uprising in 66 AD and the large-scale revolution of Jews in Cyrene and Egypt and Alexandria in the years 115-17 AD. Evidence for the existence of this war-tradition is also seen in the fact that the Romans demolished Onias' fortress-temple in Egypt after guerilla fighters (the *sicarii*) had fled from Palestine to Egypt in 73 AD and incited the Egyptian Jews to revolt.[29]

The cosmic and eschatological vision found in Philo's writings is then the expectation that the Jewish nation, to whom God's cosmic laws were revealed, should be the rulers of all nations. In this way the Jewish nation eventually would replace the Romans in being the empire-building nation. The Alexandrian Jews, although a (large) minority group in Alexandria, identified themselves with Jews everywhere and hoped for a period when their minority rôle would be changed into the rôle of world leadership. The establishment of a Jewish empire failed, however, and led instead to disastrous destruction of Egyptian and Alexandrian Jewry in 117 AD rather than to a new age with the Jewish nation as its leader.

Notes

1. My interpretation of Philo is especially seen in Borgen 2nd ed. 1981; in Borgen 1984, *CRINT* 2,2, 233-82; in Borgen 1984, *ANRW* 221,1, 98-154; Borgen 1987.
2. Concerning the Jewish settlement in Egypt prior to Alexander the Great, see especially Davies & Finkelstein 1986. For the history of the Egyptian Jews after Alexander, see the relevant sections of Tcherikover 1966; Tcherikover & Fuks 1957; the relevant sections in Fraser 1972; Kasher 1985; Borgen in *Anchor Bible Dictionary* (forthcoming).
3. Stemberger 1983, 43-48; Borgen 1987, 48-51.
4. See Borgen 1987, 1-16; Walter 1987, 83-85; Fraser 1972 I, 698-704; Kasher 1985, 208-11; Collins 1984, 357-81; Borgen 1984, *CRINT* 2,2, 274-79.
5. *Spec.* 1,54-55 and 315-15, etc.; Alon 1977, 112-24.
6. See Stern 1974, 118.
7. *Legat.* 147 and 162-66. See Smallwood (2nd ed). 1970, 229; cf. Palm 1959, 10-43 and 130-36.
8. Cf. Mendelson 1988.
9. Translation by Smallwood 1970 *ad loc.*
10. Musurillo 1954; Pearson 1984, 340-41.
11. For further analyses of *Somn.* 2,123-32, see Schwarz 1989, 62-69; Kasher 1985, 238 and 246.
12. See *Wisd.* 11,16; 12,24; 15,18.
13. A similar view is expressed by Hecataeus of Abdera in defence of Egyptian animal worship. See Fraser 1972 I, 503.
14. See further *Spec.* 1,79; 2,146; *Mos.* 1,23; *Cont.* 8-9; *Prov.* 2,65; *Legat.* 139 and 163; *QE* 1,8. In general, see Smelik & Hemelrijk 1984, 1852-2000.
15. Smallwood ad loc.; Pelletier 1972, 45-46; 165, n. 6; 187.
16. See Sowers 1967, 20-24. Cf. that Philo tells how a person who ridiculed the Jews, shortly afterwards hanged himself (*Mut.* 61-62).
17. Sevenster 1975, 97.
18. See Tcherikover & Fuks 1957, 1,48-50.
19. Tcherikover & Fuks 1957 1, 94-96 and 1964, 3, XIII. See also Eichhorn 1965, 35-47; Goldenberg 1979, 414-47.
20. See Delling 1972, 171-92.
21. Tcherikover & Fuks 1957, 1,230-236; Kasher 1985, 60.
22. Kasher 1985, 86-88.
23. Tcherikover 1966, 228-31; 276-84; Kasher 1985, 7-11.
24. Tcherikover & Fuks 1957, 1,49, n. 4; 1960, 2,188-90; Smallwood 1976, 257-59; Kasher 1985, 86 and 347.

25. See Borgen (2nd. ed.) 1981, 123-27; Mendelson 1982, 30 and 44-46.

26. In general, Roman law and Roman authorities helped the Jews in imposing the recognition of the sabbath at various places in the empire. The need for such assistance from the Romans proves that there was a strong resistance from the local populations and authorities against the privileges granted to the Jews in this way. In the period following the rebellion of Bar Kokhba (132-35) the Roman authorities suppressed the observance of the sabbath. Goldenberg suggests that *jHagigah* 2,1 77b, which cannot be precisely dated, most probably is to be placed in the last years of Hadrian. It is a weakness that Goldenberg in his discussion of the dating does not take into consideration the episode reported by Philo in *Somn.* 2,123. See Goldenberg 1979, 414-47.

27. Bousset (3rd ed.) 1926, 438-55.

28. Fischer 1978, 184-213.

29. See Borgen (forthcoming), "'There Shall Come Forth a Man'. Reflections on Messianic Ideas in Philo"; Hengel 1983   657-58. Cf. the Fifth Sibylline Book, written towards the end of the first century AD, which is openly hostile to the gentiles in Egypt and Rome.

JEWISH RESPONSES TO
HELLENISTIC CULTURE
IN EARLY PTOLEMAIC EGYPT

Carl R. Holladay

1. Introduction

In this paper we explore the themes of ethnicity and acculturation as reflected in Jewish writings in the early Ptolemaic period.[1] Specifically, the following questions inform our investigation: In what ways do these writings show Jewish authors assimilating various features of Hellenistic culture in the early Ptolemaic period? What is the relationship within these writings between cultural assimilation and ethnic identity? How do these texts show Jews establishing, maintaining, clarifying, or modifying their ethnic identity?

2. The Use of Greek Literary Traditions

To what degree did Jews during this period begin to adopt Greek literary genres, or to put it more broadly, relate to and appropriate Greek literary traditions, which were, in some basic sense, new to their tradition?

It is not altogether clear to what extent the adoption of identifiably new Greek literary genres is already evident in the *Septuagint*. There are well known instances where the translation accommodates to the new conditions and perspectives that developed in the Hellenistic period.[2] There may be instances where the translation and editing of historical portions of the *Septuagint* show traces of influence by Hellenistic historiography.[3] Certain *LXX* books make use of Greek literary traditions (*Wisdom of Solomon*) and in some cases the literary form of the entire work may be based on an essentially Greek genre (3 *Maccabees*, perhaps *Tobit*), but it is not at all clear that such cases occurred in Egypt in the early Ptolemaic period.[4] In any case, although the *LXX* is a product of Egyptian Jewry, and translated portions of the Pentateuch doubtless stem from our period, this body of writings poses its own set of problems that would require a separate investigation.

Once we get outside the *LXX*, however, and begin to look at those writings which, for the most part, are attributed to named Jewish authors, but which were not transmitted in canonical collections, as was the case with the so-called apocryphal writings, we find more clearly documented cases where Jews employ identifiably Greek literary genres.

The earliest instance is the historian Demetrius, usually designated "Chronographer", who likely flourished in the late third century BCE. In his work entitled *On the Kings in Judaea* he provided an apparently comprehensive treatment of Jewish history extending from the period of the patriarchs until the fall of Judah. His primary source is the Greek Bible, but his account is not merely a paraphrastic expansion of the biblical story. By employing the Greek literary device of *aporia-lusis*, he identifies problems in the text and proposes solutions.[5] Although he treats various logical and ethical inconsistencies in the text, he is primarily concerned to resolve chronological difficulties. So preoccupied is he with such textual difficulties that his account lacks the embellishments and heroizing tendencies often found in other Jewish "histories". Demetrius' approach to the biblical text reflects a level of critical awareness that leads Fraser to conclude that he was "fully alive to the requirements of scientific historical writing" and thus seriously engaging the Hellenistic historiographical tradition with "an originality and approach akin to that of Eratosthenes".[6] Wacholder is even more precise in proposing that Demetrius is an early representative of a "biblical chronographical school" that existed in Alexandria during the third century BCE.[7]

It is difficult to be as precise or definitive with respect to the other Jewish "historians", none of whom appears to relate to the Hellenistic historiographical tradition with the degree of sophistication found in Demetrius. Of these, Artapanus can be most confidently placed in an Egyptian provenance, and probably flourished in the mid-second century BCE. In his work *Concerning the Jews*, of which there are three surviving fragments devoted respectively to Abraham, Joseph, and Moses, he appears to have provided a running account of Jewish history based primarily on the biblical text, and in this respect he shares Demetrius' biblicistic interests. Yet he does not exhibit an interest in textual problem-solving as Demetrius does, nor does his work show the same kind of "scientific" restraint. Drawing more freely from non-biblical traditions, he produces a more highly embellished "haggadic" account. His aims are more overtly propagandistic than those of Demetrius; at least they surface in a different way.

If one seeks to identify the tradition, or genre, of writing with which Artapanus is most closely identified, it is most likely the tradition of popular historical romance.[8] Even if this is an accurate classification, one must then decide whether it represents a case of Jewish borrowing: is Artapanus, for example, clearly using a literary genre alien to the biblical tradition, or to other aspects of his Jewish historical tradition, or does his work stand in the same tradition as *Jonah*, *Susannah*, and *Tobit*? The strongest case for the former is made by M. Braun, who classified Artapanus within the tradition of popular, hero romance literature, and saw him portraying Moses in a manner similar to the way other heroic figures were portrayed in various cultures: Ninus and Semiramis in Assyria, Sesostris in Egypt, Manes and Metiochus in Phrygia, Cyrus in Persia, Alexander and Achilles in Macedonia.[9]

If it is difficult to determine relative degrees of literary appropriation with respect to the Jewish historians, this is certainly not the case with the Jewish poets of the Hellenistic period. Of the three whose works are known, albeit in fragmentary form, Ezekiel the Tragedian is the one we can most confidently place in an Alexandrian provenance within our period. He is usually thought to have flourished in the mid-second century BCE. Possibly Philo Epicus can be similarly placed, and there is a remote chance that Theodotus flourished in Alexandria, but this is a more disputed claim.

With Ezekiel the Tragedian we have an undisputed instance of a Jewish author appropriating identifiably Greek literary forms.[10] In this case, the literary form is Greek tragic poetry. The 269 lines of iambic trimeters that are preserved from Ezekiel's tragedy entitled *The Exodus* show that he clearly knows, and is directly influenced by, the Greek tragedians, most notably Euripides and Aeschylus. Yet it is also evident that he knew Homer, Sophocles, and even Herodotus.[11]

Although the case for placing Philo Epicus within an Alexandrian provenance is more difficult to make, it is likely enough to require that he at least be mentioned here. Like Ezekiel, he adopts a poetic genre, but stands within the tradition of epic poetry. The obscurity of his language and his ostensibly bombastic, pretentious style have long been noted, but these features are now seen as reflecting the tradition of Hellenistic epic. In particular, stylistic similarities have been noted between Philo Epicus and Apollonius of Rhodes' *Argonautica*, Rhianus of Bene's *Messeniaca*, and Callimachus' *Hecale*.[12]

In Aristobulus, who probably flourished in the mid-second century BCE, during the reign of Ptolemy VI Philometor, we have a Jewish author whom A.Y. Collins describes as "the first known Jewish philosopher" and "the earliest known theologian in the Judeo-Christian tradition engaged in the hermeneutical task".[13] The five surviving fragments of his exegetical work reflect his eclectic philosophical interests, but provide clear traces of interaction with Stoic and Pythagorean traditions. In spite of important differences between the way he read Moses and the way Stoics read Homer, his allegorical interpretation of scripture bears important resemblances with Stoic methods of allegorical exegesis that were developed and practiced in Alexandria and Pergamum. Even while recognizing the important differences between these two schools of interpretation, we can be fairly confident that Aristobulus' allegorical exegesis reflects awareness of both.[14]

Even though there are traces of allegorical interpretation in the earlier Jewish tradition (Isaiah's parable of the vineyard), the explicit use of this identifiably Greek form of interpretation occurs on a broad scale for the first time in Aristobulus. We find allegorical interpretation of the levitical food laws in the *Letter of Aristeas*, but it is minimal by comparison, nor does *Letter of Aristeas* systematically interpret the biblical text allegorically in the way Aristobulus does.

Whether, and to what extent, Aristobulus might have participated in philosophical and philological discussions in Alexandria is not known. Because of the philo-Semitic policies of Philometor and the opportunities for active, visible participation in Alexandrian life such favorable conditions created, it has been plausibly suggested that Aristobulus had direct contact with the Museum, and perhaps even some interaction with the king himself.[15]

Even though the date for the *Letter of Aristeas* is still seriously disputed, a good case can be made that it was written in the mid-second century BCE. Indeed, there are good grounds for thinking that its author and Aristobulus were contemporaries in Alexandria. This work, which ostensibly was written to provide an account of how the *Septuagint* came into being, provides an example of a Jewish author making sophisticated use of the Greek genre *diêgesis* (Lat. *narratio*).[16] The work throughout reflects awareness of rhetorical canons as outlined in the *progymnasmata*, and because the author successfully executed his work consistently sensitive to these canons, it is a "literary" achievement in a very real sense.[17] Oswyn Murray has shown the unmistakable connections between *Letter of Aristeas* and the kingship tractates that by this time had become well established features of the Hellenistic literary tradition.[18]

What distinguishes *Letter of Aristeas* from the other writings we are considering is that it does not develop a biblical theme, nor is it in some sense a midrashic treatment of the biblical text. Rather it presents a positive portrayal of Judaism using a completely new literary form, thus suggesting a significant level of independence. Here we find a Jewish author not only confident of his position in Alexandrian society but also of his mastery of Greek literary conventions, so much so that he is willing to depart from established practice.

The widespread use of Sibylline oracles in antiquity makes it difficult, if not impossible, to determine whether this was an originally Greek literary form.[19] In spite of the uncertain origin of this form and its notorious fluidity, the *Third Sibylline Oracle* that emerged from Jewish circles in Egypt in the mid-second century BCE is a clear instance where Jews made effective use of a well-established Greek genre. For all of the resonances between these oracles and prophetic oracles in the biblical tradition, attributing them to a pseudonymous sibyl represents a distinctive move surely calculated to inspire a level of awe and authority comparable to that found in non-Jewish circles.

While each of these writings represents a slightly different form of engagement with Hellenistic literary traditions, they are nevertheless instructive in several aspects.

First, we should note the sheer variety of literary traditions represented: critical historiography (perhaps more specific traditions and methods of chronography), historical romance, tragic and epic poetry, philosophical speculation, allegorical interpretation, rhetorically sensitive narrative, and sibylline oracles. In some cases these represent new ways of interpreting biblical materials and presenting traditional views. In other cases, they represent ways of resolving newly found problems within the biblical text. In still other cases, they provide new forms in which to recast biblical materials, which suggests new methods, and perhaps new contexts, of presentation. In at least one case, they represent significant departures from biblically based exegesis, at least in the willingness to incorporate non-Jewish traditions and legends.

Such willingness to experiment with new literary forms, especially to this extent, suggests a rather significant level of engagement with Hellenistic culture. While some of these writings still have the Bible as their chief point of orientation, others do not, at least not to the same degree. This in itself may represent an important shift if it means that Hellenistic culture is providing new ways for Jews both to understand and present their faith that are not as exclusively derived from the Bible.

Second, without denying the differences in levels of intellectual sophistication represented by these texts and without exaggerating their level of accomplishment, we conclude that these writings exhibit levels of Greek literacy that presuppose more than casual participation in the Greek educational system. They provide another form of indirect evidence that Jews in the Ptolemaic period were able to send their sons to Greek gymnasia.[20] If Greek schools had become well established in the countryside by the mid-third century, these writings may offer evidence that the Ptolemaic policy of providing education in Hellenistic culture was working in at least one ethnic group resident within Egypt.[21]

Or, at the more advanced level, they would appear to suggest significant levels of participation in Alexandrian intellectual life that spanned several decades. If Fraser is correct in suggesting that Demetrius exhibits genuinely "scientific" interests typical of Hellenistic historiography as practiced in Alexandria,[22] we should perhaps envision a social setting that gave him access to the Museum, both its archives and discussions. Given Eratosthenes' polymathic interests and his known openness to non-Greeks,[23] there appears to be no reason, in principle, why Demetrius could not have had some access to him.

If not as early as Demetrius, certainly 50 to 75 years later there seems to be the possibility that Aristobulus' philosophical appetite was being whetted by his participation in intellectual debates in and around the Museum, and that his intellectual achievements enabled him to have contact with official royal circles.[24]

Third, Jewish engagement with Hellenistic culture, as represented in these writings, represents both an exercise in ethnic promotion as well as ethnic self-preservation. To varying degrees, these texts exhibit what have variously been described as missionary, apologetic, or propagandistic tendencies. In spite of their various approaches, they all, most assuredly, write from a perspective sympathetic to the Jewish tradition. Their appropriation of these new forms suggests not only that Hellenistic culture was speaking *to* them, but that they were speaking *to* Hellenistic culture.

Yet these new literary forms are also serving to reinforce ethnic identity by providing ways for making both Jewish scripture and tradition more credible to Jews themselves. There is good reason to believe that Jews in Ptolemaic Egypt, for whatever reason, were beginning to read the Bible more critically and were beginning to ask questions of the text that required resolution before they could continue to find the text credible. In such cases, the methods of Greek chronography and allegorical interpretation provided needed solutions. Similarly, the decision to render the biblical story of the exodus in the form of Greek tragedy may have been a response to needs within the Jewish community. By the mid-second century BCE. it is fully conceivable that Jewish participation in the Greek educational system had occurred to such an extent that Jews began to wonder why the biblical tradition had nothing to compare with the Greek dramatic tradition, and that Ezekiel's *Exodus* is an attempt to show *Jews* that the biblical account can be made to be culturally respectable.

3. Attitudes Towards Hellenistic Religion and Culture

Because of Jews' well-known reputation in antiquity for being religiously and therefore socially exclusive, one way to determine degrees of acculturation is to ask to what degree these writings reflect a positive assessment of Hellenistic religion and culture, or at least an assessment that seems surprisingly tolerant, given the separatist attitude normally associated with the biblical tradition.

As scholars examine these texts more closely, it is becoming increasingly clear that one cannot proceed as if there were fundamentally two options: acceptance or rejection of Greek culture.[25] What one finds instead is a spectrum along which various authors may be placed, indeed along which different positions of a single author might be placed.

One of the most interesting cases is that of Artapanus.[26] Some of his most remarkable claims occur with reference to his portrait of Moses. He reports that Moses was called Mousaios by the Greeks and that he eventually became the teacher of Orpheus (Frg. 3,4). In depicting Moses as the cultural benefactor of Egypt, he includes among his activities the assigning of which gods (cats, dogs, ibises) were to be worshipped in each nome, the assigning of the sacred writings, as well as the distribution of land to the priests (Frg. 3,4). He further reports that because of these benefactions Moses received popular acclaim, and was given divine honors by the Egyptian priests who called him Hermes because of his ability to interpret the sacred writings (Frg. 3,6). He attributes the founding of Hermopolis to Moses and says that Moses and his companions consecrated the ibis there because of its reputation for protecting the citizenry from harmful animals (Frg. 3,9).

So astonishing are these claims that earlier scholarship doubted that Artapanus could have been Jewish, but because of his preoccupation with Jewish history and his tendency to present biblical personalities in glorified terms, there is no longer reasonable doubt.

In spite of what one makes of the various claims of Artapanus — and there are certain qualifications in his account — clearly, for him pagan religion is not antithetical to Jewish religion, nor does it pose a serious threat. Indeed, he presents Moses as ultimately responsible for organizing and solidifying Egyptian religion so that it could become a vital force within the country. Nowhere do we find Artapanus polemicizing against Egyptian religion, as, for example, Philo of Alexandria does much later in a manner much more in keeping with the biblical tradition.[27] Rather, for Artapanus Egyptian religion does not have a separate existence apart from Moses, and in this sense he may be said to subsume Egyptian religion under Jewish religion.[28]

At the other end of the spectrum representing a much more critical stance towards pagan religion and culture, stands *Third Sibylline Oracle*, which actually comprises five oracles.[29] In direct contrast to Artapanus, who praises Abraham for having taught the Egyptian king astrology (Frg. 1), the third oracle of *Third Sibylline Oracle* criticizes such practices as erroneous and worthless (vv. 220-30). Incorporating stock features of Jewish polemic against pagan worship, the fourth oracle (vv. 545-656) asserts monotheistic belief (629; also 760, 762-64), underscores the vanity of sacrificing to dead idols (vv. 547-49, 551-55), and praises the Jews for rejecting such palpably foolish forms of worship (vv. 586-90; also 605-07). Similar themes occur in the fifth oracle (vv. 721-23, 760). While there are important differences both in tone and content, this critique echoes the themes of the opening section (vv. 1-45), which may very well stem from the same setting.[30] This strongly negative position towards pagan worship is naturally closely aligned with the biblical tradition and anticipates the extended critique that occurs in *Wisdom of Solomon* 13-15,[31] which probably reflects an Egyptian setting in the late Ptolemaic or early Roman period.

Reinforcing this sharp polarization between Jewish and pagan forms of worship is a strong view of divine election. The third oracle recalls God's deliverance in the exodus and the giving of the Law on Sinai (248-58). In the section praising the Jews (573-600) in the fifth oracle, the sibyl emphasizes their special status as the sole recipients of God's special revelation (584-85) and contrasts the superiority of their ethical code to that of other nations (591-600; also 234-47). Torah is centrally important (580, 600), and the importance of the cult is strongly emphasized (575-79, 626-29).

Even with this sharply delineated critique, there are certain features of *Third Sibylline Oracle*, apart from the use of the genre itself, which reflect positive assessments of pagan thought and thus tend to dull the edge of the critique.[32] On the whole, however, these are outweighed by the more generally consistent negative critique. As Collins rightly concludes, in the end "the sibyl remains stubbornly particularistic".[33]

Midway between these two extremes, however, occur what are best described as mediating positions whose distinctive configuration of the elements of the Jewish tradition illustrate different responses to Hellenistic culture.[34]

The first of these to be considered is *Letter of Aristeas*, whose positive view of pagan culture results, on the one hand, in significant theological reformulation which represents genuine accommodation towards pagan religion, but which, on the other hand, stops well short of a sympathetic view of polytheism.[35]

In *Letter of Aristeas*, Jewish and Greek values are consonant with each other in fundamental respects, and at certain points they even converge. There is one God who extends protection and care to all of humankind (15-16), not to Jews exclusively, nor even to Jews in some special sense. In sharp contrast to *Third Sibylline Oracle*, no doctrine of election is articulated. The values promoted by the Mosaic law are the values esteemed by Greeks, such as the Aristotelian doctrine of the mean (122; see also 223, 256), or the more common virtues such as justice, temperance, and piety. In the table-talk section (187-300) the wisdom of the seventy-two translators echoes popular philosophical wisdom, especially the tradition of kingship tractates. What distinguishes their answers is the explicit theological warrant: as the ruler of all things (195), God is consistently made the reference point (see esp. 189, 200-201, 235). Throughout *Letter of Aristeas*, Greek wisdom is highly prized. Absent is the strident critique of (Greek) human wisdom one later finds in Paul (1 *Cor.* 1,18-26).

Yet, for all its appreciation of pagan culture and the universalistic tendencies this has produced, *Letter of Aristeas* finally draws a sharp line between Jewish and pagan religion. In its brief but pointed critique of pagan religion (134-38), *Letter of Aristeas* makes it clear that on the question of the one God there can be no debate. According to *Letter of Aristeas*, what distinguishes Jews from other peoples is their monotheism, and the various forms of polytheism, including Egyptian theriolatry, are misguided folly. Even though *Letter of Aristeas*'s critique would have won the assent of sophisticated pagans, including Egyptian priests,[36] what is significant here is that the critique is presented as essentially, if not exclusively, a Jewish position. He takes his stand against the majority view and does not reinforce his position by appealing to similar testimony from pagan authors.

Thus we find *Letter of Aristeas*, on the one hand, making certain concessions in terms of its theological outlook, and yet, on the other hand, stopping well short of complete accommodation.

We detect a similar ambivalence in the way *Letter of Aristeas* deals with the biblical food laws. Since Jewish dietary practices figured so prominently in establishing Jewish identity, both from the Jewish and gentile perspective, we can understand the importance attached to this issue in *Letter of Aristeas*. As we saw before in the formulation of its understanding of God, here again we see *Letter of Aristeas*, on the one hand, accommodating to pagan sensibilities, and yet, on the other hand, formulating an understanding of Jewish practice that would enable Jews to retain a well-defined sense of ethnic identity.

Letter of Aristeas insists that the presence of food laws in the biblical text requires them to be taken seriously.[37] But in what appears to be an accommodating move, it also insists that they are to be read allegorically, as symbols relating to appropriate ethical behavior, the real purpose of the Mosaic legislation. We may even be able to detect an apologetic note in *Letter of Aristeas*'s insistence that they are not inconsistent with the biblical view of creation: God did not create all things only then to designate some parts of creation clean, hence good, and other parts unclean, hence evil. The real point of the levitical food laws is to teach us how to behave appropriately, to be gentle like doves instead of aggressive like birds of prey. Thus, in one sense, *Letter of Aristeas* finesses the question of literal observance of biblical dietary laws, and in this way presents Jewish belief and practice in a way that would be much more palatable to cultured despisers, be they Greeks or Jews.[38]

Yet, as was the case earlier, here too cultural accommodation is only partial. *Letter of Aristeas*'s allegorical interpretation of the biblical food laws does not result in the blurring of distinction between Jew and non-Jews. Indeed, in one of the allegorical interpretations, *Letter of Aristeas* insists that the parted foot and cloven hoof not only signify the need to be discriminating in one's moral decisions, but also the need to be separate, to adopt a distinctive lifestyle (151-52). This conforms with the earlier insistence that Moses "fenced us about with impregnable palisades and with walls of iron, to the end that we should mingle in no way with any of the other nations" (130).

It should also be noted that *Letter of Aristeas*'s form of ethical allegory does not preempt the cult. To be sure, in the table-talk (234), we hear echoes of the biblical tradition that elevates "honoring God" above sacrificial offerings.[39] But this critique of the cult does not imply that it should be discontinued; sacrifices are to be practiced but their true symbolic significance must be properly understood (170). Thus tame animals are to be offered "so that those who offer the sacrifices, bearing in mind the symbolic meaning of the legislator, might be conscious of no arrogance in themselves" (170). Consistent with this view, Eleazar the high priest offers a sacrifice prior to sending the translators to Egypt (172).[40]

Thus *Letter of Aristeas* portrays a vision of Jewish faith and practice that is intended to be philosophically respectable. Its universal outlook displays remarkable latitudinarian tendencies. The Mosaic law and Greek wisdom go hand in hand. Those who specialize in the former are expected to be expert in the latter, and *Letter of Aristeas*'s hope is that the reverse will also be true. And yet, *Letter of Aristeas* holds out for a distinctive, clearly recognizable Jewish identity that does not simply merge with various forms of Greek and Egyptian identity: a monotheistic theological outlook; a consistent moral vision that results in a distinctive, commendable lifestyle; the performance of biblically prescribed religious practices whose true significance must be properly understood. *Letter of Aristeas* is unapologetically separatist, but not triumphalist, since it explicitly disallows attitudes of superiority and arrogant behavior (122).

Aristobulus displays neither the strong syncretistic tendency found in Artapanus nor the reactionary tendencies found in *Third Sibylline Oracle*. He exhibits a profound respect for Greek wisdom similar to that found in *Letter of Aristeas*, and like *Letter of Aristeas* presupposes the complementarity of Greek wisdom and Torah, but the response he formulates has a different configuration. Unlike *Letter of Aristeas* (and *Third Sibylline Oracle*), we find no explicit critique of pagan forms of worship such as idolatry or theriolatry. Like both of them, however, he emphasizes Jewish belief in monotheism (Frg. 4,5). The distinctive move he makes at this point, however, is not to affirm the uniqueness of Jewish belief in the Creator God, but to claim that respected Greeks, such as Pythagoras, Socrates, and Plato held a similar view, and, most significantly, that they derived the idea from Moses (Frg. 4,4; also Frg. 3,1). Aristobulus cites a pseudonymous text attributed to Orpheus (Frg. 4,5) and an authentic quotation from Aratus of Soli (Frg. 4,6) to show their dependence on Moses.[41]

Thus whereas *Letter of Aristeas* 312-13 acknowledges the Greeks' neglect of Moses (because of the sacredness of the Jewish scriptures), Aristobulus claims that Greeks had an impressive level of familiarity with the teachings of Moses. By employing this widely used argument for cultural antiquity (and therefore superiority), Aristobulus of course tacitly acknowledges the value and significance of Greek wisdom. So does *Letter of Aristeas*, but whereas his strategy is to argue for a *coordinate* role of importance for Greek wisdom, Aristobulus argues for a *subordinate* role. It is impressive, but derivative.

The degree to which Greek wisdom sets the agenda for Aristobulus is reflected in his hermeneutical approach to the biblical text. Like Demetrius, he reflects a critical self-consciousness towards the text, but rather than trying to resolve various kinds of inconsistencies *within* the text, he addresses interpretive problems that result when the reader brings wrong assumptions *to* the text. Against the literalists ("those devoted to the letter alone", Frg. 2,5), he argues for an allegorical approach which recognizes that Moses uses "words that refer to other matters" (Frg. 2,3). Accordingly, the reader must interpret the text "according to the laws of nature" (*physikôs*) and thus "grasp the fitting conception of God and not ... fall into the mythical and human way of thinking about God" (Frg. 2,2). Using this approach, he explains the true meaning of various anthropomorphic descriptions of God found in the Bible. Thus, the "hand of God" refers to God's power (Frg. 2,7-9a); God's "standing" refers to God's universal dominion (Frg. 2,9b-12a); God's "descent" to Sinai signifies God's ubiquity (Frg. 2,12b-17).

Aristobulus' philosophical interests are reflected in other ways as well.[42] The date for observing Passover is justified on cosmological grounds: it occurs at the time of the simultaneous solar and lunar equinoxes (Frg. 1,17-18). His explanation of Sabbath observance (Frg. 5) is especially illuminating because of the way it combines allegorical interpretation of the Jewish Bible and explanations of various Jewish traditions (wisdom) with appeal to various Greek philosophical traditions (Peripatetic, Pythagorean) and quotations from various Greek authors (Homer, Hesiod, Linus). What emerges is a vigorous effort to give philosophical respectability to two of Judaism's most cherished institutions.[43]

Aristobulus thus represents yet another form of response. Like *Letter of Aristeas* he has philosophical pretensions. His willingness to assert Moses' priority over the most respected names in Greek philosophy and literature displays an enviable level of confidence.[44] Yet it is a different kind of triumphalism from that of *Third Sibylline Oracle*. It is less harshly polemical, and it assumes a certain kind of philosophical discourse. Both are apologetically motivated, but whereas the oracle form of *Third Sibylline Oracle* is more in the nature of a monologue, a work dedicated to answering a king's questions (Frg. 2,1) suggests dialogue. His preoccupation with the biblical text aligns him with Demetrius, Artapanus, and to some extent *Third Sibylline Oracle*, but distinguishes him from Aristeas. In spite of his *bonafide* interests in philosophical questions, he is first and foremost a biblical exegete. At bottom, he is calling for a more responsible way of interpreting the Jewish Bible, confident that more philosophically appropriate ways of thinking about God are sure to follow.

Yet another mediating position is represented by Ezekiel the Tragedian who adopts neither Artapanus' strongly accommodating posture nor the hard-line position of *Third Sibylline Oracle*. Once again, the fragmentary nature of his work requires us to be somewhat tentative in trying to formulate his theological outlook, but the material that survives presents still another configuration of the Jewish tradition and consequently a response to Hellenistic culture that differs from the other texts.[45]

The decision to render the story of the exodus in the form of Greek tragedy is itself a significant move in the direction of Hellenistic culture. The real question is whether Ezekiel essentially uses a new form in which to recast a traditional understanding of the biblical tradition, or whether his recasting results in significant reformulation.

In many respects, his understanding of Judaism is closely aligned with the biblical tradition. Although he does not present an explicit view of election, his account of the exodus confirms the biblical view that God extends special protection to the Jews. This is underscored especially by the dramatic technique of having an Egyptian soldier articulate these views (Frg. 15). The speech of the Egyptian "messenger", on the one hand, attempts to capture the pagan point of view, and thus speaks of the Jews' prayer to "heaven, their ancestral deity" (vv. 212-13) and refers to the sun as "Titan Helios" (v. 217). Yet, the Egyptian messenger also unequivocally attributes the reversal of events to God who is "their helper" (vv. 236, 240), acknowledging him as "the Most High" (v. 239). Here we detect no universalist tendency to equate Yahweh with Zeus, nor to depict him as the God of all humankind.

Ezekiel conforms to the biblical account in ascribing great significance to the origin of Passover, devoting som forty lines to it (Frg. 13, vv. 152-74; Frg. 14, vv. 175-92). Faithful observance of the centrally important Jewish festival is fully expected by future generations of Jews (see esp. Frg. 13, vv. 170-74). Here we detect no ambivalence towards the cult comparable to that in *Letter of Aristeas*. Ezekiel makes no effort to justify its observance: it is part of the sacred story, and as such is binding.

Balancing these traditional viewpoints are some surprising omissions and inclusions. The storyline ends with the incident at Elim, and thus no attention is given to the giving of the Law at Sinai. In fact, apart from its focal interest in *Exodus* 1-15, there is no effort, as there is in *Letter of Aristeas*, to glorify the law or to present it as the embodiment of Greek ideals. Unlike Demetrius, in his account of Moses' marriage to Zipporah, Ezekiel makes no effort to present it as an endogamous marriage: Zipporah is an Ethiopian, from the land of Libya (Frg. 4, vv. 59-65; also Frg. 5, vv. 66-67).

One of the most unusual departures from the biblical account is the speech in which Moses rehearses a dream in which he is elevated to the throne of God and given universal dominion over heaven and earth (Frg. 6, vv. 69-82). As might be expected, widely different interpretations of this passage have been developed. Conceivably, Ezekiel is presenting Moses with images that recall Apollo, but there are elements of the speech that suggest connections with Jewish apocalyptic and mystical traditions.[46]

The inclusion of a description of a spectacular bird (Frg. 17, vv. 254-69), widely believed to be the phoenix, may be an instance where Ezekiel, in the spirit of Aristobulus, appropriates a tradition widely known in non-Jewish circles, but sets it in the time of Moses in order to establish its chronological priority to other traditions. But if so, it is certainly a much fainter form of the argument for cultural superiority than we find in Aristobulus.

Thus in Ezekiel Hellenistic culture is not envisioned as a defining norm to the extent that it is in *Letter of Aristeas* and Aristobulus. Perhaps the choice of tragedy as a genre as well as the choice of the exodus as the main theme made it impossible for Ezekiel to display a philosophical outlook comparable to that of *Letter of Aristeas* or Aristobulus. The closest he comes to displaying such an interest is the enigmatic reference to the "divine logos" that emanates from the burning bush (Frg. 9, v. 99). If the phrase is being used in a technical or quasi-technical philosophical sense, this would align Ezekiel more closely with Aristobulus (esp. Frg. 4), and might imply that he somehow equates the voice of God that finally came to expression in the Law with the "divine Logos" of the Greek philosophical tradition. If so, once again, it would be a form of the argument for cultural priority.

In summary, even within this limited number of Jewish writings, we find a considerably diverse set of responses to the Hellenistic environment of Ptolemaic Egypt. They each draw on the richly complex Jewish tradition in different ways. One writing may display an outlook in common with one or more of the other writings, but the patterns of convergence are not predictable.[47]

5. Ethnicity and Jewish Attitudes Towards Other Ethnic Groups

Yet another way of examining the theme of ethnicity as it is reflected in these writings is to look at the ways in which these authors give explicit attention to other ethnic groups and the attitudes taken towards them. Because of the Jews' status as a subject people under the Ptolemies, and the competitive relationship this created with the Egyptians, we are especially interested in the attitudes these writings display towards Egypt.

In Demetrius, there is very little explicit attention given to Egyptian culture. As noted earlier, his preoccupation with questions of chronology and genealogy may suggest some level of interaction with the Hellenistic historiographic tradition within Alexandria. There is no clear indication that the questions he addresses in the biblical text were raised specifically in reference to Egyptian culture. The one exception may be his discussion of Moses' marriage to Zipporah, in which he is especially concerned to show that she descended (through Jethro) from Abraham (Frg. 3,1-3). If the point of this exercise is to demonstrate that Moses did not marry a non-Jew, this may reflect Demetrius' response to intermarriage practices within the Jewish community.[48]

In the case of Artapanus, we see more explicit attention being given to Egyptians.[49] His treatment of the Jewish patriarchs Abraham and Joseph is focussed especially on their connections with Egypt (see Frgs. 1 and 2). Scholars have long held that Artapanus' highly embellished portrait of Moses was intended to respond to Manetho's uncomplimentary account of Moses, or a similar Egyptian tradition.[50] Indeed, the strong Egyptian cast of Artapanus' writings has long been recognized.[51] There are persuasive indications that he is not only responding to a literary tradition but that his writings reflect a social setting in which Judaism is experiencing competition with Egyptian mystery cults, specifically Isis.[52]

As was the case earlier when we examined Artapanus' attitude toward pagan religion, once again we find a remarkable degree of accommodation, yet not to the point where Jewish identity is fully neutralized. On the one hand, there is a distinctively pro-Egyptian perspective in Artapanus. He emphasizes the contributions Abraham, Joseph, and Moses have made to Egyptian culture, and his portrait of them as cultural benefactors of Egypt is rather consistent. In contrast to Demetrius, who appears to caution against intermarriage, Artapanus unhesitatingly reports that Joseph married Asenath, the daughter of a Heliopolitan priest, and fathered children by her (Frg. 2,3). Like Demetrius, Artapanus reports Moses' marriage to Raguel's (Jethro's) daughter, but makes no effort to demonstrate that she was Jewish (Frg. 3,19). Thus there does not appear to be the same preoccupation to maintain ethnic distinctiveness as we find in Demetrius.

But in spite of these accommodations to Egyptian culture, Artapanus maintains enough fidelity to the biblical account to present forthrightly the clashes between Jews and Egyptians that constituted an essential part of their sacred history. Taking up the story of *Exodus*, he reports that Palmanothes dealt meanly with the Jews (Frg. 3,2). He also describes Chenephres' jealousy of Moses and the plot to kill him (Frg. 3,5-20). Artapanus' description of Chenephres' death from elephantiasis conforms to the familiar pattern of divine retribution known in the biblical account and well-established among Hellenistic Jewish authors (Frg. 3,20).[53] His summary account of the exodus, even though it is embellished, retains the flavor of hostility between Jews and Egyptians found in the biblical account (Frg. 3,21-37). As noted earlier, Artapanus tells of the Jews' "procuring from the Egyptians many drinking vessels as well as not a little clothing and numerous other treasures" (Frg. 3,34). He also reports the biblical tradition that Pharaoh's armies died in the exodus (Frg. 3,37).[54]

Artapanus' account also exhibits the same spirit of triumphalism that we noted earlier. When the Egyptian king summoned Moses to inquire of him why he had returned to Egypt, Moses responded that he had come to liberate the Jews from Egypt because he had been so commanded by "the Lord of the universe" (Frg. 3,22). In one episode involving Moses and Chenephres the very name of God, perhaps scoffingly referred to by the Egyptian king, is powerful enough to be lethal (Frg. 3,23-26). Thus, what finally merges is a portrait of the Jewish God triumphant and the Jewish faith unscathed from its encounter with Egyptian power, religion, and culture.

Consistent with its generally negative portrait of pagan religion and culture described earlier, *Third Sibylline Oracle* sharply criticizes non-Jewish nations (199-210; 295-349; 489-544). The oracular woes against various nations are quite reminiscent of prophetic oracles in the Bible. But this is fully in keeping with the genre. Since these are stock themes for this type of writing, this probably tells us very little about the actual social setting of the writing. It may suggest that it derives from Jewish sectarian traditions in Ptolemaic Egypt, but this judgment has to be qualified. While *Third Sibylline Oracle* adopts a critical posture towards other nations, it is also self-critical. True to the prophetic tradition, *Third Sibylline Oracle* chastises disobedient Israel right along with the nations (e.g. 3,265-94).

It is very difficult to detect signs of anti-Egyptian hostility in *Third Sibylline Oracle*. If anything, some of the most pungent rhetoric is directed against Greeks (545-72; 732-40). In those instances where oracles are issued against Egypt, or where Egypt is warned of some impending disaster (e.g. 208, 314-18, 614), it is in a series of similar woes or warnings directed against other nations as well. Where one might expect explicit condemnation of Egyptian worship, e.g. in the polemic against astrology (220-30) and idolatry (279, 554, 586-90, 721-23), it is absent, and instead these vile deeds are either unattributed or attributed to nations other than Egyptians. Perhaps the one exception is the puzzling warning in 348-49: "know then that the destructive race of Egypt is near destruction and then for the Alexandrians the year which has passed will be the better one".

Several positive references are made to the "king of Egyptians", most notably the intriguing reference to the "seventh king" (192-93), probably a reference to Ptolemy VI Philometor, and the "king from the sun" (652-54), but of course these can only be construed as pro-Macedonian, or at least pro-Ptolemaic, and are doubtlessly politically motivated.[55] More than anything else, they reflect *Third Sibylline Oracle*'s optimistic views towards the Ptolemaic rulers of the mid-second century BCE.

Thus, ironically enough, the highly negative stance taken by *Third Sibylline Oracle* against the nations does not appear to translate into actual anti-Egyptian hostility. There are no clear indications within the work that Jews look with contempt on Egyptians *qua* Egyptians, nor any real signs of Jewish-Egyptian hostility. This is perhaps especially remarkable if the work stems from circles around Onias at Leontopolis.

With few exceptions, *Letter of Aristeas* takes the philosophical high road in the attitude it displays towards other peoples. Little attention is given to Egyptians or to aspects of Egyptian life. The overriding concern is to present a picture of harmony between Ptolemy II Philadelphus and his Jewish counterpart, the high priest Eleazar. The highly idealized portrayal of the world of the Ptolemaic court

Carl R. Holladay

and the world of Judaism suggests that two abstractions are being related to each other. The affected, courtly atmosphere is reflected in Aristeas' statement to Philocrates that he learned about the Jews "from the most erudite High Priests in the most erudite land of Egypt"(6).

Faint echoes of historical hostilities are heard, e.g. reference to the removal of Jewish slaves to Egypt (4, 12, 35). The rare references made to the Egyptian population are on the whole innocuous. In Ptolemy's letter to Eleazar we are told that the Jews had been given favored treatment "so native Egyptians might be in awe of them" (36). In the description of Jerusalem, a contrasting remark is made about Alexandria that is slightly disparaging toward the Egyptian population. The country folk who visited Alexandria and stayed longer than expected are said to be responsible for a decline in agriculture within the region (109). Similarly negative statements are made about Egyptian farmers and their agents (111).

The most negative statements about Egypt occur within discussions concerning moral behavior. The aforementioned passage polemicizing against pagan worship (134-38) is especially scathing in its denunciation of Egyptian theriolatry (138). In a similar vein, Jewish piety is said to have been recognized by Egyptian priests, and the Egyptian population, when compared with the Jews, are intemperate materialists (140-41). The discussion of food laws contains a contemptuous depiction of non-Jews resident in Egypt. The laws are said to have been given to keep Jews from being "polluted ... and infected with perversions by associating with worthless persons" (142). Compared with the Jewish morality, the "rest of mankind" is characterized as being sexually indulgent.

But here we recognize the rhetoric of moral superiority that derives from a well-developed sense of ethnic identity, and in this case is fed by the biblical tradition. These statements are primarily remarkable, given the length of the work, for their relative infrequency. They are also balanced with other statements, especially in the symposium section, in which flaunting one's moral superiority is eschewed (257) and which call for generous, civil deportment towards the rest of humanity.

Thus *Letter of Aristeas* tells us very little about Jewish attitudes towards Egyptians. The negative statements about the Egyptian populace are few but they do appear to reflect the conviction that Jews have now achieved a social status that sets them apart in conspicuous ways from other segments of the population.

With their exegetical interest and philosophical focus, the fragments of Aristobulus yield no significant information concerning his attitude towards other ethnic groups. Apart from two quotations from the *LXX* mentioning Egypt (*Exod.*

3,20; 13,9) and one brief reference to the Jews' exodus from Egypt, Aristobulus does not treat Egypt at all. The fragments do refer to Greeks in a thoroughly positive manner, but these are literary references.

For the most part, Ezekiel's attitude towards Egyptians is dictated by the *Exodus* storyline. Accordingly, he portrays the Egyptians, and especially Pharaoh, as the antagonists over which the Hebrews, under divine protection, triumph. There are some indications, however, that Ezekiel's retelling of the story casts the Egyptians in a slightly more positive light. The most conspicuous instance is his account of Moses' slaying the Egyptian (Frg. 2, vv. 42-58).[56] The biblical account places the blame squarely on the Egyptian who was "beating the Hebrew" (*Exod.* 2,11), and later Jewish rehearsals of this story (e.g. *Jub.* 47,10-12; Philo 5. *Mos.* 1.43-44) usually confirm or intensify this point of view. By contrast, Ezekiel neutralizes the blame, simply noting that Moses saw two men fighting, "the one a Hebrew, the other an Egyptian" (v. 42-43). In sharp contrast to Josephus, who omits the episode (*Ant.* 2,11,1), Ezekiel reports that Moses killed the Egyptian, and refers to his deed as "murder" (*phonos*, v. 47).

Since the extant fragments likely represent only about 25-30% of the whole, it is difficult to say whether Ezekiel's treatment of this episode suggests a pro-Egyptian *Tendenz*. It is worth noting, however, that his account of the plagues (Frg. 13), while obviously retaining many features of the biblical account, is, if anything, less harsh in its portrait of Pharaoh.

If these features of Ezekiel's account are in any sense typical, they may suggest that he has sought to make the biblical story of the exodus more palatable for an Egyptian audience. Similar openness may be reflected in his report of Moses' marriage (Frg. 3 and 4). Unlike Demetrius, Ezekiel does not try to establish the Jewish pedigree of Zipporah. Instead, without qualification he reports that Moses married the Ethiopian Zipporah, and in this respect his account more closely conforms to Artapanus, who reports Joseph's marriage to the Egyptian Asenath.

In summary, the outlook of these writings is heavily influenced by the generally negative portrait of Egypt in the biblical tradition. There are some indications that in defining their ethnic status within the multi-cultural setting of Ptolemaic Egypt, Jews are addressing questions of ethnic boundaries, such as the propriety of marrying non-Jews, the need to retain Jewish practices, e.g. food laws and religious festivals. While there are certainly clear indications that Jews are continuing to cultivate a sense of separateness, there is also some evidence that they are defining ethnic boundaries less rigidly. Thus Ezekiel can place great emphasis on the observance of Passover yet at the same time apparently demonstrate a more positive attitude toward Egyptians that actually runs against the grain of the biblical tradition. Similarly, *Third Sibylline Oracle* can maintain an almost sectarian stance towards other nations without being specifically critical of Egyptians.[57]

6. Conclusions

During the early Ptolemaic period there is clear evidence that Jews had begun to assimilate Hellenistic culture, and did so to significant degrees. In the Hellenistic environment of Ptolemaic Egypt they encountered new literary traditions and discovered new literary genres. These they readily adopted and began using to recast the biblical story. These new forms offered both possibilities and limitations, and form inevitably affected content. The recast versions of the biblical story we find emerging during this period often sing the same song but in a different key.

Nor should we see Jews' willingness to experiment with new literary forms as an effort merely to find new ways to tell the old story, for there are clear instances where the new forms assisted them in making the story more credible both to themselves and non-Jews. The methodological approach of Hellenistic historiography thus enable Demetrius to render a more scientifically respectable account of the biblical story. Using the allegorical method that had become well honed by Greeks in making Homer more palatable, Aristobulus (to a greater degree) and *Letter of Aristeas* (to a lesser degree) sought to make the biblical narrative more credible and Jewish practice more defensible.

The writings we have examined suggests that during the early Ptolemaic period Jews were engaging Hellenistic culture in a variety of ways and at a variety of levels. This appears to have occurred to an extent that requires some qualification to Rostovtzeff's judgment that "neither the Jews nor the Egyptians of Alexandria ever became Greek, either in spirit or in countenance".[58]

We certainly see Jews beginning to acquire a Greek countenance, and we have noticed some of the tensions that resulted from their efforts to become Greek in spirit as well. Not only that, we have identified some of the ways in which they began to reformulate their understanding of the Jewish tradition as they integrated various features of Hellenistic culture. While none of these authors "becomes Greek" in the sense that they abandoned the Jewish tradition entirely, they do begin to develop new ways of understanding Jewish identity.

Notes

1. For Fraser 1972 I, 687-716, the core of writings about which there can be little serious dispute consists of the following: *Septuagint* (including Greek translation of the *Hebrew Bible*, as well as the various apocryphal and "semicanonical" writings that are, in most senses, derivative from the Bible), Demetrius the Chronographer, Aristobulus, *Letter of Aristeas*, Artapanus, Ezekiel the Tragedian, and major portions of the *Third Sibylline Oracle*. In Schürer 1986, III,1, 470-74, all of these (with varying degrees of probability) are also placed within an Egyptian provenance during the Ptolemaic period, but in addition individual writings (some of which Fraser presumably includes within the category of "*Septuagint*") are also singled out as almost certainly in the same group: 3 *Maccabees*, *Joseph and Asenath*, *Wisdom of Solomon*. Others identified by Schürer as possibly in this category are: Cleodemus (Malchus), Pseudo-Eupolemus, *Testament of Job*, Philo Epicus (so Hengel 1981 I, 69), Theodotus, Pseudo-Hecataeus, Pseudo-Phocylides (=Ps-Phoc). With minor variations, Collins 1983 adopts a schematization that basically conforms to that in Schürer.

   For the purposes of this study, we have limited our investigation to those writings that can confidently be placed in an Egyptian provenance prior to the end of the second century BCE.: Demetrius, Aristobulus, *Letter of Aristeas*, Artapanus, Ezekiel the Tragedian, and the earliest portions of *Third Sibylline Oracle* (vv. 93-349, 489-829).

   These writings are available in English translation in Charlesworth 1983-85: Demetrius (2,843-54), Aristobulus (2,831-42), *Letter of Aristeas* (2,7-34), Artapanus (2,889-903), Ezekiel the Tragedian (2,803-19), *Sibylline Oracles* (1,317-472). Greek texts are available as follows: Demetrius and Artapanus in Holladay 1983; Ezekiel the Tragedian in Holladay 1989; Aristobulus in Holladay forthcoming; *Letter of Aristeas* in Hadas 1951; *Sibylline Oracles* in Geffcken 1902. For additional introductory information on these texts, see Schürer 1986, III,1 470-704, which comprises * 33A, "Jewish Literature Composed in Greek", also, see Denis 1970; Hengel 1981; Collins 1983.

   Any account of the writings must, of course, be correlated with the history of the Jewish community in Alexandria. In this paper, we assume the widely held view that the Jewish community in Egypt was relatively small and insignificant in the third century, but that it underwent a major transition during the mid-second century, when, under the reign of Ptolemy VI Philometor, it began to emerge as a much more significant force in Alexandrian society. See Tcherikover & Fuks 1957 I, 1-47; Tcherikover 1966, 269-87; Fraser 1972 I, 54-58, 83-85, 688-89; Smallwood 1981, 220-55, esp. 220-35.

2. For example, the rendering of the Hebrew plural *Elohim* with *Theous* in *LXX Exod.* 22,27, with the resulting command "Thou shalt not revile the gods" expressing a much more accommodating attitude towards pagan deities. See Tcherikover 1957 I, 42, also the literature cited on p. 31, n. 80, especially Dodd 1935.

3. On the complex question of the relationship between Greek and Israelite historiography, see van Seters 1983, 8-54.

4. On antecedent Greek traditions reflected in the Greek translation of *Prov.* 8,22-31, see Hengel 1981, 162-63. On the probable dating of Greek translations of various portions of the Bible, see Schürer, 1986 III,1, 476-477.

5. Fraser 1972 I, 693.

6. Fraser 1972 I, 692.

7. Wacholder 1974, 99. Wacholder, 104, speculates that "the chronological alterations adopted in the Septuagint version of the Pentateuch were a product of Demetrius' chronographic schemes". While admitting the possibility of influence from contemporary Alexandrian chronographic schools, Wacholder is finally disinclined to see direct, significant Hellenistic

influence on Demetrius.

8. This classification is now well accepted. See Holladay 1983, 190, 196 n. 16. Collins 1983, 33, prefers the category "competitive historiography", though he understands historiography in this case to include a "liberal component of legend and romance".

9. Braun 1938.

10. See Holladay 1989.

11. See Jacobson 1983.

12. See Fraser 1972 I, 624-49; Holladay 1989, 206, 219 n. 9 & 10.

13. See Charlesworth 1983-85 II, 834.

14. Walter 1964, 124-29.

15. Walter 1964, 39-40, 128-29; Tcherikover 1957 I, 20 n. 51.

16. Hadas 1951, 56-58.

17. Hadas 1951, 55.

18. Murray 1967.

19. See Collins, "Sibylline Oracles" in Charlesworth 1983-85 I, 317; also Collins 1983, 61-72, 148-51, 245.

20. At one point, Tcherikover 1957 I, 37-39, in trying to determine how Alexandrian Jews educated their children, offered two kinds of indirect evidence that Alexandrian Jews were allowed to send their sons to the gymnasia: (1) Since Jewish attendance of Greek schools was not expressly prohibited until the time of Claudius, most likely they were able to do so previously. (2) Since the gymnasia were privately run during the Ptolemaic period, entrance requirements were not based on ethnic status.

21. See D. Thompson, "Language and Literacy", this volume, pp. 39ff. It is worth asking whether the Jewish interest in Greek poetry, and knowledge of the Greek poetic tradition found in Ezekiel the Tragedian and Philo Epicus (perhaps Theodotus), may not derive from a curriculum such as the one described in the third century BCE handbook mentioned by Thompson in which reading extracts from Euripides and Homer, as well as Greek epigrams, figure centrally.

22. Fraser 1972 I, 690-94.

23. See Blomqvist, "Alexandrian Science: The Case of Eratosthenes", this volume, pp. 53ff.

24. See above n. 15.

25. The two options are sharply stated in Schürer 1986 III,1, 471-72.

26. See Holladay 1983, 1, 189-243.

27. *De Vita Contemplativa* 8-9. See, e.g., *Isa.* 40,18-20; 44,9-20; *Jer.* 10,1-16; *Ps.* 115,3-8.

28. See Collins 1983, 35.

29. Here I follow the analysis of the *Sibylline Oracles* in Collins 1974, the results of which are embodied in his introduction and translation in Charlesworth 1983-85 I, 317-472, esp. 354-80. Also see Collins 1983, 61-72. Collins dates the core of the *Third Sybilline Oracle* (97-349 and 489-829) to the period when Philometor was sole ruler (163-145 BCE) and proposes a Leontopolis provenance, specifically a context related to Onias, the founder of the Jewish temple there. Portions of the introductory section (1-96) he dates in the Roman period, although he leaves open the possibility that the section containing the polemic against idols (1-45) could be as early as the second century BCE. Collins sees the main corpus as containing five oracles: 97-161, 162-95, 196-294, 545-656, 657-808.

30. See note 29 above.

31. Compare esp. *WisSol.* 13,10; 14,12-20.

32. Collins 1983, 148-151, notes several of these accommodating features and indicates the points of resonance with various Graeco-Roman perspectives: elements of the ethical teaching, e.g. the denunciation of various sexual practices; God's giving the earth as the common possession

rehearsal of the battle of the Titans against Cronos (110-55) he sees as the author's "attempt to integrate Greek mythology into the overview of history", observing that "... the gods are demythologized in the euhemeristic fashion, (but) they are not simply dismissed as unreal" (p. 63).

33. Collins 1983, 151.
34. If one thinks of these responses as cases where an author is essentially drawing on the same elements of the Jewish tradition but configures them differently, depending on the way various elements of Hellenistic culture are assessed, then these different responses might be properly thought of as ethnic strategies. See Goudriaan, "Ethnical Strategies in Graeco-Roman Egypt", this volume, esp. pp.74ff.
35. See Hadas 1951, 59-66; also R. J. Shutt, "Letter of Aristeas" in Charlesworth 1983-85 I, 7-34.
36. Collins 1983, 180.
37. Eleazar's rather extended apology for the law in 128-71 is prompted by "our inquiries" (*ta di êmôn epizêtêthenta*), that is, those of Aristeas and his fellow Greeks, concerning the law. Rather than taking up a set of objections which are answered *seriatim*, it looks rather as if this apology is designed to answer one fundamental question, viz., why Jews observe food laws.
38. Compare the similar relaxing of dietary laws in Paul, e.g. *1 Cor.* 8,8; *Rom.* 14,14.20.
39. *1 Sam.* 15,22; *Ps.* 50,8-15; *Isa.* 1,10-17; *Jer.* 7,21-26; *Hos.* 6,6; also cf. *Matt.* 9,13; 12,7; *Heb.* 10,5-10.
40. These observations are made by Hadas 1951, 191 n. on * 234.
41. The fragment attributed to Orpheus is widely regarded as Jewish. Since it is quoted by Aristobulus, we can probably assume an Alexandrian provenance. It would technically constitute another writing in our corpus, but the textual tradition poses problems complex enough to justify our bracketing it for this investigation. See M. LaFargue, "Orphica", in Charlesworth 1983-85, 2, 795-801.
42. See especially Hengel 1981, 163-69.
43. Collins 1983, 178.
44. Hengel 1981, 169: "Behind these views there is no weakness which is prepared for assimilation, but a firmly based spiritual and religious self-awareness."
45. See Collins 1983, 207-11; also R. G. Robertson, "Ezekiel the Tragedian" in Charlesworth 1983-85 II, 803-19.
46. See Holladay 1989, 437-46.
47. It is instructive to note at least two other "mediating positions" both of which likely derive from the Roman period: 3 *Macc.* and Ps-Phoc. Though it describes events that purportedly occurred during the reign of Ptolemy IV Philopator (222-203 BCE), 3 *Macc.* represents a complex mixture of historical reminiscences and popular traditions. In contrast to *Letter of Aristeas*, 3 *Macc.* displays less explicit interest in Greek culture. Indirect appreciation of Greek culture is reflected in the author's sophisticated use of language, his attention to style, and his discriminating use of various Greek literary techniques and traditions (see Hadas 1953, 22-23). But such questions as how Jews should evaluate Greek culture, or whether they should assimilate or resist Greek values, are not explicit concerns in 3 *Macc.*, as they are, for example, in 1 *Macc.* and 2 *Macc.*, where the king's actions are integrally connected with his Hellenizing policies, and where Jewish fidelity is assessed in terms of whether, and how much, one accommodates to identifiably Hellenistic attitudes and forms of behavior.

With respect to its attitude toward pagan religion, the view of 3 *Macc.* is quite uncomplicated: pagan worship is clearly distinguishable from Jewish worship and the two are mutually exclusive. Not only is this straightforward position reflected in the Jews' stout resistance to the king's decree requiring them to become members of the imperially prescribed Dionysus cult (2,32-33), it is also seen in the brief section describing Philopator's worship of idols (4,16). Though less developed than the critique of pagan worship in *Letter of Aristeas* 134-38, the section is reminiscent of Dan. 5,4 and stands well within the tradition of Jewish polemic against idol worship as a remarkably foolish activity.

In 3 *Macc.*, the Mosaic law is of central importance and has its own independent status. Greek wisdom is not seen as a necessary complement of the law as it is in *Letter of Aristeas*, and a more literal view of the law is presupposed. In 3 *Macc.* there is no attempt to allegorize the requirements of the law, nor even to probe its deeper significance. Their import is assumed to be clear, and what is required is obedience rather than deeper understanding. Thus when Philopator threatens to violate the sanctity of the Temple, it is not a debatable issue. The Law was simply read to him (1,12). In the prayers of Simon and Eleazar, the law is drawn upon in a straightforward manner. It depicts the previous actions of God and these may be taken as indicative of God's future behavior. In the midst of the crisis, the Jews are described as continuing to revere God and "regulating their lives according to His Law" (3,4). Specifically this meant their continued adherence to the food laws, even though they recognized that the practice was odious to some of their non-Jewish neighbors. The critical importance of obedience to the law is further underscored by the chilling report that 300 Jews who had yielded to the king's decree were killed (7,10-16).

Combined with this view of the law is a strong view of election, certainly more sharply defined than one finds in *Letter of Aristeas*. Jerusalem is God's divinely chosen space and the temple is God's specially designated sanctuary (2,9,15). The God of 3 *Macc.* is a universal Creator God (2,2-3,7; 6,2), but not in the broad-minded sense of *Letter of Aristeas*. The outlook is more particularistic in that God extends special protection to Jews, especially in times of duress. Even Philopator himself is finally reported to confess that "God in heaven protects the Jews, being their ally always as a father to his children" (7,6). Accordingly, the theme of divine retribution against those who oppress the Jews is much more prominent in 3 *Macc.* (cf. 2,21-22; 5,6-8,13).

The Sentences of Pseudo-Phocylides, by contrast, display a quasi-accommodating attitude towards pagan religion. Standing within the gnomological tradition, the *Sentences* exude the spirit of wisdom literature, and for this reason, as van der Horst 1978, 67 notes, "we see a constant search for a universal ethics which shuns particularistic elements and is not averse to the good and useful elements in the ethics of the surrounding peoples." This may account for the relatively neutral position towards God reflected in Ps-Phoc., seen for example in the omission of the introductory formula, "I am the Lord, your God" in the author's appropriation of Lev. 19. A theology with some specific content emerges, but many of the claims made about God are commonplaces in both the Jewish and Graeco-Roman tradition. Monotheism is assumed, yet the *Sentences* contain several problematic verses that appear to move in the direction of polytheism. In two verses (75, 163), the author ascribes personality to heavenly bodies, but as van der Horst 1978, 68 notes, this is not unusual in Jewish texts. The most problematic instance occurs in vv. 103-104. "For in fact we hope that the remains of the departed will soon come to the light again out of the earth. And afterwards they become gods." Yet it is not at all certain that such a statement seriously conflicts with a monotheistic point of view. See van der Horst 1978, 187.

48. Collins 1983, 28.

49. See Holladay 1977, 212-14.

50. This position was argued by Freudenthal 1874-75, 161-62. Also see Braun 1938, 26-31; Fraser 1972 I, 706; Holladay 1983 I, 195 n. 10. A dissenting position is represented by Tiede 1972, 175-76, who proposes that Artapanus' reporting the Jews' theft of Egyptian goods prior to the exodus (Frg. 3,34-35) would merely confirm Manetho's charges. For a discussion of the grammatical problem, see Holladay 1983, 213 n. 89.

51.   Freudenthal 1874-75, 157-160 provides detailed analysis and notes specific instances of Artapanus' familiarity with Egyptian traditions, e.g. his use of the introductory formulas "the Memphians say" and "the Heliopolitans say" (Frg. 3,35). See Holladay 1977, 218-20.

52.   See Holladay 1977, 213-214.

53.   See Collins 1983, 35-36.

54.   See *Exod.* 14,28; *Ps.* 78,53.

55.   See Collins 1983, 64-70.

56.   See Holladay 1989, 425 n. 41.

57.   As noted earlier (see note 51 above), 3 *Macc.* offers an instructive example, probably from a later period. Ps-Phoc is less instructive in this regard.

      It should first be noted that the situation envisioned in 3 *Macc.* is clearly one of crisis: a Ptolemaic king has taken actions hostile to the Jewish community in Egypt, and these actions threaten to change its life dramatically. Through divine intervention, the crisis is successfully resolved and harmonious relationships, previously enjoyed, are restored. 3 *Macc.* is rather consistent, however, in portraying this episode as exceptional, not only to established Ptolemaic policy but to Philopator's own previous policy.

      To be sure, 3 *Macc.* acknowledges the severely strained relationship between the king and the Jews that have resulted from the crisis. Especially in the prayers of Simon the high priest (2,1-20) and Eleazar the priest (6,1-15) is the relationship between Jews and non-Jews presented as sharply polarized. But in neither instance is it implied that the relationship between Jews and non-Jews must be intrinsically hostile. Indeed, the Jews are presented as having historically supported the Ptolemies. Even under duress, they are said to have "continued to preserve their good will toward the royal house and their unswerving fidelity" (3,4).

      As for the relationship between Jews and other peoples resident in Egypt, it is especially striking how nuanced is the social setting depicted in 3 *Macc.* Although ambiguous in certain respects, it appears to reflect some of the complex social dynamics that doubtless existed at various times among the diverse populations of Ptolemaic Alexandria.

58.   Rostovtzeff 1954, 148.

NATIVE REACTIONS TO FOREIGN RULE AND CULTURE IN RELIGIOUS LITERATURE

Jørgen Podemann Sørensen

The historian of Ptolemaic Egypt faces the difficult task of reconstructing not only what actually happened, but also *to whom* it happened. How much of what we know to have happened, actually happened to the natives? And this question immediately raises another: How is it possible to trace native responses and reactions to the new institutions and the influx of foreign cultures imposed on them during the Ptolemaic period? There were insurrections, strikes, migrations, discontent — often sufficiently motivated by unbearable economic conditions. But what kind of cultural determinants were at work among the natives during a process involving both acculturation and resistance?

For the history of religions this question is of vital importance. A very large portion of the religions of Late Antiquity - mystery religions, Hermetism, Gnosticism - have roots in Egypt, and Alexandria was the melting-pot of Hellenistic religions and philosophies. The way Egyptian religious traditions met and intermingled with those of other cultures, notably the ruling Greeks and the Jews, is an important part of the Hellenistic process of syncretism and deserves closer study.

The native reactions to foreign rule and culture, or, more precisely, the Egyptian cultural determinants at work in the Hellenistic process of acculturation and resistance, can be studied in the *intertextuality* of prehellenistic and hellenistic Egyptian texts. Throughout the long history of ancient Egypt there are stories which are told again and again, and there are ritual traditions that are reproduced from the New Kingdom till the 7th century AD. On the basis of this imposing cultural continuity, changes can be observed and sometimes related to the historical and cultural circumstances of the period in which they occur. On the following pages I shall present such observations on changes related to the situation and the development in Ptolemaic Egypt within two literary *genres*: the *conte prophétique* and the *magical literature*.

A strange and untrue story of early Ptolemaic date may serve as our point of departure. It is told by Manetho in his *Aegyptiaca* (Fr. 54, Waddell 1980, 118ff) and preserved by Josephus (*c.Ap.* 1,26-31). The story was probably alleged by Manetho to have taken place in the 18th dynasty, but we shall content ourselves by noting that it was told as a story from Egypt's remote past, in a work intended to make the history and culture of Egypt known to the Greek-speaking world. It is about a certain king Amenophis, probably Amenophis III, who

conceived a desire to behold the gods, as Or, one of his predecessors, had done; and he communicated his desire to his namesake Amenophis, Paapi's son, who, in virtue of his wisdom and knowledge of the future, was reputed to partake in the divine nature. This namesake, then, replied that he would be able to see the gods if he cleansed the whole land of lepers and other polluted persons. The king was delighted, and assembled all those in Egypt whose bodies were wasted by disease: they numbered 80,000 persons. These he cast into the stone-quarries to the east of the Nile, there to work segregated from the rest of the Egyptians. Among them, Manetho adds, there were some of the learned priests, who had been attacked by leprosy.

The seer Amenophis, however, in whom we may safely recognize Amenophis son of Hapu, a wise official under Amenophis III and in Ptolemaic times a healing divinity, seems to have been shocked by the outcome of his prophecy; he added another prophecy "that certain allies would join the polluted people and would take possession of Egypt for 13 years." Then he took his own life. After some time the polluted people were released and permitted to settle in the old Hyksos town Avaris, since time immemorial dedicated to Typhon or Seth, the Egyptian god associated with strangers, the desert, and confusion. Having now a basis for revolt, they chose a former Heliopolitan priest as their leader. He framed many laws alien to Egyptian custom, of which a few are mentioned, viz.

that they should neither worship the gods nor refrain from any of the animals prescribed as especially sacred in Egypt, but should sacrifice and consume all alike, and that they should have intercourse with none save those of their own confederacy. (Waddell 1980, 126-27).

Making ready for war against king Amenophis, he sent for the shepherds, i.e. the Hyksos, in Jerusalem(!), and they all came, to the number of 200,000, to Avaris. Amenophis recalled the prophecy, gathered his men, instructed the priests to conceal the images of the gods securely, took into his charge Apis and the other sacred animals, and withdrew to Ethiopia. There he stayed for the thirteen years predicted by Amenophis son of Hapu and then returned and reconquered Egypt. In the meantime, the people from Jerusalem and the polluted Egyptians mistreated the people, destroyed towns, villages and temples, mutilated images of the gods, and blasphemously used the sanctuaries as kitchens to roast the sacred animals they had butchered, even compelling the priests to take part in this sacrilege. Their leader in all this, the former Heliopolitan priest, is said to have changed his name to Moses.

Already Josephus demonstrated that it is impossible to make any historical sense of this story; and modern egyptology could only add to his objections. Single historical persons and episodes may be identified in it (Meyer 1928 II,1, 420ff), but the way they interfere with each other is impossible. Our interest in the story, however, is not in its value as a source for Egyptian history, but in its tendency. What made it worth telling in the early Ptolemaic era were the themes of ethnicity and religion systematized in it. There is the anti-semitic theme which upset Josephus: the Jews (who were particularly opposed to Egyptian animal worship[1]) are identified with the Hyksos and associated with the lepers and the crippled. There is also the idea of a foreign *régime* in Egypt, destructive and blasphemously opposed to Egyptian religion. And in the very beginning, the purging, as it were, of Egypt of all its impure inhabitants is said to make the gods visible to the king. The rather luxurious aspiration of the king, "to become one who beholds the gods" (*theôn genesthai theatês*), reflects a longing for "ultimate reality" which is, as we shall presently argue, characteristic of the time. It is furthermore a point in the story, that an obstacle to full participation in this reality is the presence of 80,000 "wrong" persons in Egypt, and that these persons are later associated with foreigners.

Manetho's story is illustrative of Egyptian self-esteem in the beginning of the Ptolemaic era. It has no allusion to Ptolemaic rule, and the representation of the Jews seems to be the only element in it which could have a contemporary reference. Otherwise it draws on vague historical memory of other foreign dominations. Already Eduard Meyer (1928 II,1, 424ff) pointed out that the story reproduces an ancient literary tradition: Since the time of the Middle Kingdom, the prophecy of a temporary overturn of Egypt, in which foreigners mistreat the country, the social order is seriously disturbed, the gods neglected, and the sun does not shine like before, has been a literary and a religious motif. It is important that the disorder is only temporary, to be subdued by a saviour king who will dispel foreigners and let Egypt prosper under a righteous rule. The motif is intimately linked with royal ideology, and elements of it may occur in a royal accession decree even in times of peace and social stability.[2] The classical *exemplar*, as it were, of the kind of story told by Manetho is *The Prophecy of Neferti* (*AEL* I, 139ff). This Middle Kingdom story has a very obvious tripartite structure: The first part is the frame story, providing the circumstances under which the prophecy took place; the second part consists of prophetic lamentations, vividly depicting the future break down of order in nature and society:

> Lo, the great no longer rule the land,
> What was made has been unmade,
> Re should begin to recreate!
> The land is quite perished, no remnant is left,
> Not the black of a nail is spared from its fate.
> (Yet) while the land suffers, none care for it,
> None speak, none shed tears: "How fares this land!"
> The sundisk, covered, shines not for people to see,
> One cannot live when clouds conceal,
> All are numb from lack of it ... (*AEL* I, 141).

We cannot quote or even summarize the whole text, but it is important to note that along with the description of social *anomie*, foreigners in Egypt and human depravation, there are passages lamenting what we might call the absence of divinity:

> Re will withdraw from mankind:
> Though he will rise at his hour,
> One will not know when noon has come;
> No one will discern his shadow,
> No face will be dazzled by seing [him],
> No eyes will moisten with water.
> He will be in the sky like the moon ...
> (...)
> Gone from the earth is the nome of On,
> The birthplace of every god ... (*AEL* I, 142f).

Then follows the third part, the prophecy of king Amenemhat I who will put an end to foreign infiltration and let Order (*Maat*) "return to its seat, while Chaos (*jsft*) is driven away."

The prophecy of Neferti is a classical text of the Middle Kingdom,[3] known also in more than 20 fragmentary copies from the New Kingdom. We may regard Manetho's story as a late variation on a classical theme, in which important transpositions have taken place: The "absence of divinity" has become part of what corresponds to the frame story, and the prophetic theory of *anomie* has been doubled. No true Amenophis of the 18th dynasty could have longed to behold the gods; he saw the sun rise and set every day, and in all the temples of Egypt a priest would every morning open the *naos* and "see the god" on his behalf.[4] Manetho's Amenophis has assumed the colouring of a much later time. He is in search of a spectacular revelation, a particular dispensation from the normal and reluctantly accepted condition. But he is also characteristically aware that this condition has not always been prevalent; there was a time when "Or, one of his predecessors on the throne" was able to see the gods. A king of this name is mentioned in Manetho's account of the 18th dynasty, but as it stands it is more likely to refer to the god Horus as a mythical king of Egypt, i.e. to a primeval condition. It is this original condition of direct access to ultimate reality that Amenophis wants to have miraculously restored. This apocalyptic element in the story corresponds to an awareness of living in a decadent, if not a fallen, world: access to ultimate reality is barred by the presence of a great number of impure inhabitants.

It is in Amenophis's second prophecy that the theme takes on historical and relational proportions. Its framework is the traditional one of a temporary overturn of Egypt, in which the country is mistreated by foreigners. But in the way it is mistreated we can identify the contemporary serious religious dissent between Egyptians and Jews on animal worship and sacrifice pointed out by Smelik & Hemelrijk (1984, 1910f) On the whole, the prominence of religious matters - the care for the images of the gods and the sacred animals - in this expression of Egyptian self-esteem in the early Ptolemaic period is worth noticing.

Later in the Ptolemaic period, the story is told again, in the *Oracle of the Potter* (Koenen 1968, 178ff), this time with the Greeks as the foreign mistreaters of Egypt. Koenen argues that this text was composed "in the wave of Egyptian insurrection perhaps after 130 BC, but surely soon after 116 BC" (1968, 188ff; 1986, 317). The potter, a manifestation of the ram-god Khnum, predicts a time of hardships and foreign domination by "Typhonians" who have settled in Alexandria. Quite in accordance with the classical *exemplar*, Neferti, the text laments natural and social disorder: "The sun will be darkened, not wishing to behold the evils in Egypt" (transl. Griffiths 1983, 288). In the end, however, the goddess Isis will establish a king, Alexandria will become a desert, and its deities will go to Memphis. The prophecy is thus as clearly political as Neferti in its time, but it is no *vaticinium ex eventu*; it fixes no date for the overturn of Alexandria, but Koenen has shown that text variants bear witness to an interest in fixing the time or identifying the saviour king (1968, 188ff).

Still later, and probably for the last time, the story is retold as part of the Hermetic text Asclepius.[5] The apocalypse of Asclepius predicts a time when the gods of Egypt will be ridiculed and neglected, and the piety and devotion of the Egyptians will seem useless. Egypt, formerly the image of heaven and the temple of the whole world, will be deserted, and the gods shall withdraw from it. This is the *senectus mundi*, the end of religion, order, and rationality; but God will restore and renew the world, and even, it seems, found a new Alexandria (Koenen 1986, 320). No saviour king or any other "historical" event is expected; the perspective of national salvation is now transposed into a general eschatology. It is the hardships predicted that have historical reference: the passages about the gods of Egypt being ridiculed and religion punished as a crime (Ch. 24) very likely reflect the Roman attitude to Egyptian religion[6] and Roman legal measures restricting the movements of the Egyptian priesthood.[7] It is important to note that not only the traditional religion of Egypt, but also the *religio mentis*, i.e. Hermetism, is subject to persecution during the hardships to come (Ch. 25); the prophecy reflects the contemporary situation of the Hermetists as seen by themselves. The reference, finally, to the last of the Egyptians who shall be in their dealings like strangers (Ch. 24) reflects a state of advanced acculturation, but also a nativistic awareness.

From Manetho to Asclepius the same narrative framework registers the changing situation and exhibits the native reactions to it. The development from Neferti to Asclepius, from the idea of Maat returning to its seat to the futuric eschatology of a gnostic movement, is interesting in itself and has in fact been studied under various points of view.[8] But it is Manetho who has the key story. Its early date, at the very beginning of the Ptolemaic era, and the way it relates the foreigners, the leprous, and the primeval and the apocalyptic access to ultimate reality, make it a perfect illustration of a changing Egyptian attitude to the religious traditions of the past. In principle, the idea of a primeval golden age was never alien to Egyptian religion (Kakosy 1964), but primeval time was thought of as *sp tpj*, "the first occasion", as something to be reenacted in the worship and the festivals of the temples and realized anew by every royal accession (Hornung 1966). Even a late king like Taharka could have his reign recorded on a stela as a time when "the land was in abundance as in the time of the Lord of the Universe. Every man slept until daybreak and did not speak thus: "if only I had"..." (Kakosy 1964, 206). But Manetho's Amenophis is in serious difficulties; he lives in a polluted world, and access to the primeval condition and to ultimate reality is for him a matter of apocalypticism.

Modern anthropologists and sociologists (e.g. Worsley 1968, Wilson 1973) have called attention to the role of apocalypticism in "nativistic" movements in the Third World, as a response to cultural and social crisis, and Tord Olsson (1983) has applied this perspective to Iranian apocalypticism. The story of Manetho seems almost to anticipate these modern insights; the apocalyptic aspiration of Amenophis *is* a response to cultural conflict. It should be borne in mind, however, that Manetho was no sociologist; he establishes a relation between apocalypticism and cultural conflict on the level of religious ideas only, and no idea of social causes in the modern sense occurred to his mind.

Apocalypticism is indeed a salient feature in the literature of the natives in Hellenistic Egypt. And not only political apocalypticism as we find it most significantly in the *Oracle of the Potter*, but the general apocalyptic aspiration *theôn genesthai theatês*, to become a beholder of gods, to gain access to ultimate reality through vision and revelation. — It is a prominent theme in the Demotic cycle of narratives about Setne Khamwas, a legendary figure based on Prince Khamwas, the fourth son of Ramesses II.[9] In the first of these stories, preserved in a manuscript of Ptolemaic date, Setne finds in the tomb of a certain Prince Naneferkaptah a wonderful magical book, which Naneferkaptah himself has taken out of the water at Coptos, where it was guarded by serpents, scorpions etc. A priest had instructed him about the book "that Thoth wrote with his own hand, when he came down following the other gods", and how it could be found. Without betraying the plot, and still less the end, of this truly thrilling story, we shall consider the content of this magical book as described by the priest:

Two spells are written in it. When you [recite the first spell you will] charm the sky, the earth, the netherworld, the mountains, and the waters. You will discover what all the birds of the sky and all the reptiles are saying. You will see the fish of the deep [though there are twenty-one cubits of water] over [them]. When you recite the second spell, it will happen that, whether you are in the netherworld or in your form on earth, you will se Pre appearing in the sky with his Ennead, and the moon in its form of rising. (*AEL* III, 128f).

This is not the everyday magic of pharaonic spells against crocodiles, scorpions, and diseases; and it is also different from the miracles related in the classical Egyptian tales of wonder in *Pap. Westcar* (*AEL* I, 215ff). The book of Thoth stands out by its revelatory, apocalyptic character. Its spells enable its possessor to see what is hidden and behold the gods. As we shall presently see, the story of Naneferkaptah and the book of Thoth reflects the thaumaturgical and apocalyptical practices of the time, as we know them from Demotic and Greek magical papyri.

The second story of Setne has survived in a manuscript of Roman date only, and it is impossible to say how much of it goes back to the Ptolemaic period. It is a cycle of narratives about Setne's son Siosiris, a wonderful boy whose true descent we shall not betray. One of the wonders he works is to take his father to the netherworld. They have seen the funeral procession of a rich man and later a poor man being carried to the burial ground just wrapped in a mat; Siosiris wishes for his father the fate of the poor man in the hereafter, and as if to prove the filial piety of this strange wish, he takes Setne to a place in the western desert. A large lacuna keeps forever hidden the entrance to the netherworld and its first three halls. With the remaining four halls the divisions of the netherworld amount to the un-Egyptian number of seven. Other indicators of foreign influence are the Homeric punishments in the fourth hall, where people are plaiting ropes while donkeys are chewing them up; others are reaching out for bread and water above their heads while still others are digging holes under their feet. The painful fate of the rich man, whose misdeeds were found more numerous than his good deeds, and the exalted rank assumed by the poor man in the hereafter, may very well be developments of traditional Egyptian motives (Gressmann 1918), but the plasticity of the idea of individual moral retaliation in the hereafter is certainly a novel feature. Also the scenery of the netherworld in general is characteristically Egyptian, as we know it from the Book of the Dead and other Pharaonic sources. What is completely novel and highly significant is the revelatory framework that circumscribes the traditional motifs. The idea of a visit to the netherworld could easily be inspired by Greek literature, but we are not after the copyrights. What matters is that traditional Egyptian imagery, designed above all as a *ritual symbolism*,[10] has become the object of revelation, of subjective religious experience. The mortuary rituals of Pharaonic Egypt refer to ideas of the hereafter, but they never systematically describe the other world. The *Books of the Netherworld* in the royal tombs of the New Kingdom represent a more systematic approach to the beyond, and they are also said to represent the *knowledge* of the king.[11] For the king, this knowledge is a prerequisite for participation in the cosmic processes of the hereafter, but it is not a revelation; it has nothing of the spectacular breakthrough or the subjective experience we have found in Manetho and the Demotic narratives. Apocalypticism is a novel approach to age-old religious traditions.

Both the syncretism and the apocalyptic aspirations we have seen in the literary texts are also prevalent features of the Demotic magical literature and Greek magical literature of Hellenistic Egypt. Of this literature, little is left that can be dated to the Ptolemaic period — in fact just enough to show that the extreme syncretism we find in the many manuscrips of Roman date was well begun at least a century before.[12] The *genre* of Egyptian magical literature can be followed from about 1500 BC till the 7th century AD. In order to observe the changes that took place in the Ptolemaic period and are found accomplished in the papyri of Roman date, it is necessary to have an idea of the Pharaonic magical literature. In the following brief presentation[13] I shall try to point out cultural determinants for the later inclusion of non-Egyptian elements into the *genre*.

Pharaonic magical formulae have a very distinct *Sitz im Leben*; they are designed to ward off diseases, danger, enemies, evil dreams etc. In the ritual act of defeating these menaces it is the task of the formula to subject the situation to the rule of cosmology, to reduce or transscribe it into cosmological categories. Cosmology is a means of exerting ritual control, and it is the formula that puts this means to work. This is done in a rich variety of ways; most often by citing a mythical antecedent of the situation to be ritually controlled. The formula may relate a myth as *exemplar* of the case to be handled; the following spell against crocodiles thus treats the dangerous situation as a reflection of a mythical prototype:

Osiris is lying in the water, the Eye of Horus being with him and the great Sun-beetle spreading over him. Thou who art great through thy hand, who hast begotten the gods as a youth! May the one who is lying in the water get up safe! — If anything approaches what is lying in the water, it will approach the weeping(?) Eye of Horus (...) O ye who are in the water! Your mouth shall be sealed by Re, your throat shall be choked by Sekhmet, your tongue shall be cut out by Thoth, your eyes shall be blinded by Hike! Yonder four mighty gods who were in charge of the protection of Osiris, they are the ones who will be in charge of the protection of what is lying in the water, all men, all cattle that lie in the water, on this day of protection (Sander-Hansen 1956, 31-32).

This *epic* formula — a type also known from European folklore — relates a myth about its case and thus subjects it to cosmological and ritual control. The example chosen is particularly explicit on the relation between the myth related and the situation in question: It almost argues that the myth, as a rule or a precedent, is applicable to the case: the crocodile, which would approach the person in the water, would approach the Eye of Horus and expose itself to the four gods protecting Osiris. The primeval *exemplar* is only the *sp tpj*, the "first occasion", bound to be incessantly reiterated. Today is a day of protection, because it is ruled by a mythical precedent that sets certain limits as to what could happen.

The references to mythology and the continuity, which the formula establishes between the actual situation and a mythical pattern, are often of a more partial character: Sometimes the patient, or the magician, or another element in the magical act, is simply identified with a god or a mythical motif, without any story being told. And mythological references are not the only means to put cosmology to work on a case. Just as a formula may subject a situation to ritual control by placing it under the protection of a mythical *exemplar*, it may also reduce a case to its cosmological significance in a negative mode: by interpreting the danger or the disease as cosmologically impossible or at least unimportant. In a collection of spells for mother and child the following formula is addressed to a female demon causing illness in a child:

...You who spend your time making mud-bricks for your father Osiris! You who say against your father Osiris: "May he live from *d3js* and honey!" Run out, you asiatic woman who come from the desert, you negro woman who come from the wilderness! Are you a handmaid? — come in vomiting! Are you a noble woman? — come in his urine, come in the snot of his nose, come in the sweat of his body! — My hands are on this child — The hands of Isis are on him, as she lays her hands on her son Horus (Erman 1901, 50-51).

Osiris never had a daughter, and even if he had, she could hardly have been a maker of mud-bricks; it is a dirty job, not suitable for the daughter of a king. And as if this social *dérangement* was not a sufficient demonstration of her im-possibility, she is quoted for a statement of such world-overturning absurdity that there is no longer any doubt: she does not exist! That Osiris, who as a god lives on Maat, should nourish on *d3js*, a vomitive, which is, as an extra refinement, mixed in honey, is not only inconceivable; it cannot conceivably be said or proposed. Bringing *d3js* into a temple was considered a desecration. The disease is thus identified with an impossible mythical person, not unlike the second son of Mary in European magical formulae, a person who cannot exist at all.

Correspondingly, the disease is later called an asiatic woman from the desert and a negro woman from the wilderness. Geography is a cosmological discipline as well as mythology: The people who live in the desert and the wilderness, outside the cultivated Nile valley, are likewise cosmological outsiders and somehow less real than Egyptians. In this way the formula cuts off the disease, mythologically and cosmologically, but it ends up in a positive identification of mother and child with Isis and Horus.

These few examples may illustrate the central concerns and the typical features of Pharaonic magical literature. Its formulae reduce their case to cosmology, most often through mythological identifications, but also by interpreting danger and disease as something anticosmic or impossible. The last example also demonstrates that several different identifications or reductions may occur side by side in one and the same formula: The vicious daughter of Osiris, an asiatic woman, and a negro woman are parallel designations of the disease, in so far as they serve to cut it off from cosmology; but taken literally, they are mutually exclusive. And the positive mythological identification in the end is still another approach to the cosmological reduction of the actual situation. We are thus facing a specimen of what Henri Frankfort (1948a, 4; 1948b, 41) called "multiplicity of approaches". Frankfort's idea of "ancient thought" or "mythopoeic thought" as "admitting the validity of several avenues of approach at one and the same time" has been found particularly useful in the study of Egyptian ritual texts. In this literature it is not uncommon to find a series of parallel statements, each representing a definite approach. As we have just seen, such a series of concrete statements may be considered a paradigm expressing an abstract relation: the three identifications of the disease are mutually exclusive, but admitted side by side they express very well its anti-cosmic nature. In very much the same way several different mythological identifications may occur in the same formula; there is a Ramesside text, in which the user of the formula (the magician) identifies himself with six different gods.[14] As a formal characteristic of Egyptian magical formulae we shall name such a series of parallel mythological statements a *transmythological redundancy* — transmythological, because it combines different mythological contexts at liberty. It implies that several mythological identifications of different extraction may stand together, narratively unconnected, and with their reference to the situation as the only common denominator. Since they do not form a consistent narrative, they are interchangeable and may be replaced by other identifications.

The *genre* of Egyptian magical formulae was thus extremely flexible and open to new motifs, including features of foreign mythology. It is no mere coincidence that their Demotic and Greek successors in Hellenistic Egypt exhibit an almost breathtaking syncretism.

Most of the Egyptian religious literature of the Ptolemaic period - temple inscriptions, texts of temple rituals, funerary papyri, and other religious texts from tombs - seems to reproduce traditions already known from Pharaonic Egypt. Many rituals which are known to have existed or known only in fragments in earlier periods are extensively documented in Ptolemaic source material. It is fair to assume, however, that they are not radically different from the less known rituals of the New Kingdom. This does not mean that no changes are found or that an inert sacerdotalism had befallen the Ptolemaic priests. We can observe that the traditions are alive and intact, and traces of foreign cultural influence are extremely few.

Besides the more or less prophetic narratives, of which we have already considered some specimens, the one literary *genre* of Hellenistic Egypt that exhibits change and foreign influence is the magical literature in Demotic and Greek. In the Greek magical papyri, Nilsson (1948) found Egyptian, Greek and Jewish elements about equally numerous. Applied to the Demotic papyri, a similar statistical investigation is likely to yield very much the same picture, perhaps slightly in favour of the Egyptian element. The basis is, however, as also Nilsson seems to be aware, the Egyptian magical tradition. In a wilderness of gods, demons, and magical names of varied extraction, the Egyptian magical formula survives with its mythological identifications, no longer limited to Egyptian mythology. In a Demotic spell against a poisonous or bewitching potion the user identifies himself both with Horus and with Yaho, i.e. Yahweh.[15] Another formula, against the bite of a dog, is introduced as "the fury of Amoun and Triphis"; the bite of the dog is then mythologized as Seth against Osiris and Apophis against the Sun, and eventually the patient is identified with Horus the son of Osiris and Isis. But Horus is also called the founder of the earth, and in the end the names "Yaho, Sabaho (Sabaoth?), Abiaho" are addressed, probably as forms of Horus.[16] The transmythological redundancy of the Egyptian formula accommodates Jewish divine names side by side with the names of Egyptian divinities. Just as "Seth against Osiris" and "Apophis against the Sun" may stand as parallel mythological identifications of "the bite of the dog against the patient", thus "Horus who established the earth" may be connected in parallel with "Yaho".

Some of the most striking examples of syncretism in the history of religions are found in the Greek magical papyri. For the sake of brevity we shall use as illustration the following rather moderate eroticon:

Cup spell, quite remarkable: Say the spell that is spoken to the cup 7 times: "You are wine; you are not wine but the head of Athena. You are wine; you are not wine, but the guts of Osiris, the guts of IAO PAKERBETH SEMESILAM OOO E PATACHNA IAAA." [For *the spell of compulsion*: "ABLANATHANALBA AKRAMMACHAREI EEE, who has been stationed over necessity, IAKOUB IA IAO SABAOTH ADONAI ABRASAX"]

At whatever hour you descend into the guts of her, NN, let her love me NN, [for] all the time of her life (*PGM* 7, 643-51).

The common denominator of the head of Athena and the guts of Osiris and Iao may not be right at hand, but it is safe to assume that the three identifications make up a transmythological redundancy, this time spanning three cultures. "Guts" (*splagchna*) denotes those parts like heart and liver, that were considered the seat of feelings and sentiments, so that the parallel connection with Athena's head is not entirely out of place. Anyway, it is through these parallel divine identifications, that the wine is thought to intensify feelings in the person who drinks it.

In another spell, to be recited over an ointment, with which a man smears his private parts before having intercourse, it is said:

Let her, NN, love me for all her time as Isis loved Osiris and let her remain chaste for me as Penelope did of Odysseus (*PGM* 36, 283-94).

Examples could be multiplied, but at the moment we shall content ourselves with these few illustrations of the principle of transmythological redundancy and the way this salient traditional feature in Egyptian magical formulae accommodates foreign mythological motifs. Egyptian magical literature was able to absorb foreign mythological elements without changing the typical, basic structure of the formula. This implies, at least in principle, an acknowledgement on equal terms of the mythologies in question; but also that the different mythological elements are *subordinated* to this basic structure. The introduction of Athena and Yahweh side by side with Isis and Horus means a greater stock of mythology, not a new form of religion. Judged by the magical literature, the process of syncretism in the Ptolemaic period was to a very large degree governed by native cultural determinants admitting an unlimited inflow of foreign motifs, but at the same time preserving basic Egyptian structures.

The openness and the flexibility of the magical literature was, of course, also socially conditioned. It was not, like the temple literature, in the charge of institutions and hierarchies obliged to maintain traditional integrity. And in fact, the magical *genre* was not only open to motifs of foreign extraction, but also to new applications of magic — e.g. erotic magic, which is extremely frequent in the Greek papyri — and to those apocalyptic tendencies of the time, which we have already seen in Manetho and the Demotic narratives. The Demotic and Greek *grimoires* abound in the kind of "do-it-yourself apocalypticism" that Hopfner (1921-24) called *Offenbarungsmagie*. It is a kind of divination procedure, in which a god is made to appear, sometimes in a dream, sometimes in a vision, in order that he may answer questions. A few examples will illustrate the general character of this revelatory practice.

In a Demotic instruction to produce a horoscope by "the great god Iymhotep",[17] the magician is told to bring a stool of olive wood, clean and never used by any man on earth, put it in a clean place near his head and cover it with a cloth. He should also provide four bricks and a clay censer, on which to burn wild goose fat pounded with myrrh and a mineral, probably hematite. Then he should recite a spell in Greek for the horoscope and, "without speaking to anyone on earth", lie down and sleep. Then he will see the god "in the likeness of a priest wearing clothes of byssus on his back and wearing sandals on his feet." The god will speak with him about anything he might wish "with his mouth opposite your mouth". — In addition, the magician must prepare the tablet for the horoscope and write his business on a new roll of papyrus to be place on the tablet. "It sends your stars to you whether they are favorable for your business".

As we gather from the last instructions, the practical outcome of the procedure is a horoscope, related to a definite problem which the user is supposed to state in the Greek formula he recites, and again on the papyrus. This divination procedure has, however, an elaborate and dramatic framework, in which a face to face encounter between the god and the magician is arranged. The vision is a dream, but there is nevertheless a ritual to bring it about; and the ritual and divinatory procedure is reinforced by the subjective religious experience. The desire to behold the gods is not only a matter of political prophecy; apocalypticism has entered the private sphere of magic and divination.

The Demotic magical papyri give many similar instructions in the art of revelation and encounter with gods;[18] often a boy acts as an intermediary, who sees the gods and reports to the magician. There was probably always a practical divinatory purpose connected with the revelations, but this is not always expressly stated in the text. One formula has no other explicit purpose than the one given in its headline: "to see the bark of Pre".[19]

The Greek magical papyri offer a similar, but more varied picture. They have formulae for revelation,[20] sometimes through a dream,[21] and instructions and spells that produce a "direct vision"[22] or even a trance.[23] The formulae for direct vision often have a supplementary spell for the dismissal of the god, e.g. "Go away, Anubis, to your own thrones, for my health and well-being."[24] In a long and elaborate text[25] we may follow a full ritual structure, comprising a period of sacralization, a liminal period, and, as a desacralization, the dismissal of the god:

The sacralization that prepares the encounter with the god consists in the recitation of a hymnic prayer, first toward the sunrise, then to the lamp used in the ritual. In this way the lamp is associated with the sun. The magician must be dressed as a *prophêtês*, i.e. as an Egyptian high-priest (*hm ntr*), and wear a wreath of olive and garlic. Then he may address the lamp with a call for "light, breadth, depth, length, height, brightness" and ask for the god, "who is inside", to shine through.

The liminal character of the central part of the ritual is brought out by an intensified and alert ritual control: There is a "light-retaining spell" — "for sometimes when you invoke the god-bringing spell darkness is produced." In the god-bringing spell itself there is reference to the serpent Apophis, whom the Sun-god must defeat every day, lest he swallow up the sun. There are also instructions for retaining the god, in case he tends to pass away: "step with your left heel on the big toe of his right foot, and he will not go away unless you raise your heel from his toe and at the same time say the dismissal". These straightforward measures bear witness to the acuteness of the magician's task. And it seems that he faces not only the risk of failure, but also real danger: during the whole rite he must wear around his neck, "for the protection of your whole body", a phylactery, for which elaborate instructions are given.

The dismissal, finally, sends the god to his usual abode in heaven, and into his regular course as the sun. It is important to note that blessings are expected from the encounter with the god; the magician ends his spell of dismissal with the words: "Keep me healthy, unharmed, not plagued by ghosts, free from calamity and without terror. Hear me during my lifetime".

Side by side with the practical purpose of divination, there is in these instructions and spells an important element of self-initiation, of which the *Mithrasliturgie* is the most famous example. From the beginning to the end, the object of the ritual we have just surveyed is the magician himself. He is the person marked out for ritual, he is the one who beholds the god, and the one on whom the blessings of this spectacular revelation, this shocking experience of the real, are bestowed.

In the Demotic and Greek magical literature, this subjective, revelatory experience is an outstanding novel feature, continuous with the Hermetic and Gnostic currents of the 2nd to 4th centuries AD, but without precedents in Pharaonic magical literature. We have seen how the incorporation of foreign mythological elements into the transmythological redundancy of Egyptian formulae illustrates a process of easy acculturation without fundamental changes. The apocalyptic tendency does, however, represent a decisive innovation. In the development of ancient Egyptian religion there is an even more marked interest in personal religious experience, which reaches a culmination in the Ramesside period.[26] But it was never a visual experience; it was an experience of divine grace and help in distress, deeply felt, but not sensed and certainly not sensational like the apocalyptic *tours de force* we have surveyed. Compared with the Ramesside interest in religious experience, the apocalyptic aspirations of Hellenistic Egypt constitute a second and more decisive breakthrough.

A necessary precondition of apocalypticism is, in the words of a gnostic text from Nag Hammadi,[27] that "a veil exists between the World Above and the realms that are below". Of course, the pious Egyptian of the Ramesside period did not live with unlimited visual access to the vivid imagery of Egyptian mythology, whenever he lifted his eyes to the sky; not even the earliest kings of history did that. But there is a point in noticing that somehow Manetho's Amenophis believed they did. He has become aware of the veil that separates him from ultimate reality in a polluted world, and the story associates this polluted state with foreign rule and culture. His story is the literary expression of the relevance of apocalypticism in Ptolemaic Egypt.

Following Manetho, and more loosely the modern comparative evidence of dominated groups in the third world, I suggest that the prevalence of apocalypticism in the narratives and the magical literature of Hellenistic Egypt was a reaction to foreign rule and culture, i.e. both to cultural conflict and to the many and drastic social changes brought about by the Ptolemaic *régime*. As shown by Manetho, the religious and ideological pattern conditioning exactly such a reaction was ready from the very outset of the Ptolemaic period.

Notes

1. Cf. Smelik & Hemelrijk 1984, 1906ff.
2. Gardiner 1937, 86f. Transl. Caminos 1954, 323f.
3. See *LdÄ* 4, 380f for references.
4. Chapter 11 of the Daily Temple Liturgy: P.Berlin 3055, col. 4, 6-7.
5. Nock & Festugière 1972, II, 326ff.
6. Smelik & Hemelrijk 1984, 1920-1981, survey the almost unanimously negative attitude to the Egyptians and especially Egyptian religion in Roman literature.
7. Cf. Merkelbach 1962, 25f. and, more generally, Lewis 1984, 91ff.
8. Cf. Bergman 1983; Griffiths 1983; Assmann 1983; Koenen 1986.
9. Griffith 1900; transl. *AEL* III, 125-151.
10. For a further development of this point, see Podemann Sørensen 1989.
11. Explicitly in the title of the Amduat. Cf. Barta 1985; Assmann 1984, 77-84.
12. *PGM* CXVII, a fragmentary papyrus of the first century BC, has both Egyptian and Greek divine names. In the contemporary *PGM* XX Koenen (1962, 167-74) has detected an Isis-Horus motif in an otherwise Greek context.
13. For a more substantial account, see Podemann Sørensen 1984.
14. Borghouts 1971, 18, cf. Pl. 3.
15. *PDM* xiv, 568-74.
16. *PDM* xiv, 585-93.
17. *PDM* xiv, 93-114. Imhotep, the divinized architect of the Step Pyramid and high priest of Heliopolis in the Old Kingdom, the Egyptian personification of wisdom, was in the Ptolemaic period also a healing divinity. The Hermetic "Asclepius" is the *interpretatio Graeca/Romana* of Imhotep.
18. E.g. *PDM* xiv 93-114; 117-49; 232-38; 1078-89; PDM lxi 1-30; 63-78; PDM Suppl. 130-38; 149-62.
19. *PDM* xiv 295-308 (repeated in 805-16).
20. E.g. *PGM* II 1-64f; III 187-262; IV 1-25; XII 153-60.
21. *PGM* VII 664-85.
22. *PGM* III 633-731; IV 930-1114; V 54-69; Va 1-3; VII 319-34; VII 335-47; VII 727-39.
23. *PGM* IV 830-929.
24. *PGM* VII 319-34.
25. *PGM* IV 930-1114.

26. J.H. Breasted (1912, 344-65) saw the Ramesside period as "The Age of Personal Piety"; his beautiful collection of evidence in the form of translated texts is still valuable. More recently, Jan Assmann (1984, 258-85) has shown, within a comprehensive developmental synthesis, the connection between the Ramesside "personal piety" and the breakthrough of a transcendent notion of god.

27. The Hypostasis of the Archons, *NHC* II, 94, 9-10; transl. B. Layton in Robinson 1977, 158.

ABBREVIATIONS

AbhBerlin	Abhandlungen der Königlich Preussischen Akademie der Wissenschaften zu Berlin.
AEL	Lichtheim M. 1975, 1976, 1980 *Ancient Egyptian Literature* I-III Berkeley/Los Angeles/London
AJPh	*American Journal of Philology* Baltimore
ALGHJ	*Arbeiten zur Literatur und Geschichte des Hellenistischen Judentums* Leiden
ANRW	Temporini H. & Haase W. (eds.) *Aufstieg und Niedergang der römischen Welt. Geschichte und Kultur Roms im Spiegel der neueren Forschung* Berlin/New York
AOrientHun	*Acta Orientalia Academiae Scientiarum Hungaricae* Budapest
APF	*Archiv für Papyrusforschung* Leipzig
B	*Babylonian Talmud*
BASP	*Bulletin of the American Society of Papyrologists* New Haven, Conn. 1963-
BGU	*Berliner griechische Urkunden (Ägyptische Urkunden aus den Königlichen Museen zu Berlin)*, Berlin 1895-
CAH	*Cambridge Ancient History*
CE	*Chronique d'Égypte* Bruxelles 1925-
CIJ	Frey J.B. 1936, 1952, *Corpus Inscriptionum Judaicarum*, Città del Vaticano
CIG	Boeck A. *Corpus Inscriptionum Graecarum* Berlin 1828-77
Coll.Alex	Powell J.V. *Collectanea Alexandrina* Oxford 1925
CPJ	Tcherikover V. & Fuks A. & Stern M. (eds.) 1957, 1960, 1964, *Corpus Papyrorum Judaicarum* I, II, III, Jerusalem/London
CPR	Harrauer H. (ed.) 1987 *Corpus Papyrorum Raineri* XIII *Griechische Texte* IX 2. vols. Wien
CRINT	*Compendia Rerum Judaiocarum ad Novum Testamentum* Assen
FGrH	Jacoby F. (ed.) *Fragmente der griechischen Historiker* Berlin 1923-
GLAJJ	Stern M. 1964 *Greek and Latin Authors on Jews and Judaism* Jerusalem
GRBS	*Greek, Roman and Byzantine Studies* Cambridge, Mass. 1959-
HM	*Historia mathematica* New York/London

HR	*History of Religions* Chicago
HSPh	*Harvard Studies in Classical Philology* Boston 1890-
J	*Jerusalem Talmud*
JEA	*Journal of Egyptian Archaeology* London 1914-
JHAS	Journal for the History of Arabic Science Alep.?
JJP	*Journal of Juristic Papyrology* Warszawa 1946-
Josephus *Ant.*	Flavius Josephus *Antiquitates Judaicae*
Josephus *Bell.*	Flavius Josephus *Bellum Judaicum*
Josephus *c.Ap.*	Flavius Josephus *Contra Apionem*
JTS	*Journal of Theological Studies* Oxford
LdÄ	*Lexikon der Ägyptologie* ed. Helck W. & Otto E., Wiesbaden 1975
M	*Mishnah*
NTSup	*Novum Testamentum Supplements* Leiden
OGIS	Dittenberger W. (ed.) 1903-1905 *Orientis Graeci Inscriptiones Selectae* Lipsiae
PBA	*Proceedings of the British Academy* Oxford
P. Berlin	*Hieratische Papyrus aus den königlichen Museen zu Berlin* I, Leipzig 1901.
P. Cornell	Westermann W.L. & Kraemer C.J. (eds.) 1926 *Greek Papyri in the Library of Cornell University*, New York
PCPhS	*Proceedings of the Cambridge Philological Society* Cambridge 1892-
PCZ	Edgar C.C. 1925-1931 (ed.), *Catalogue général des antiquités égyptiennes du Musée du Caire; Zenon Papyri* Cairo
PDM, PGM	Betz H. (ed.) *The Greek Magical Papyri in Translation. Including the Demotic Spells I: Texts* Chicago 1986
P. Ent.	Guéraud O. (ed.) 1950 *ENTEUXEIS: Requêtes et plaintes adressées au roi d'Égypte au IIIe siécle avant J.-C.* Cairo
P. Gurob	Smyly J.G. (ed.) 1921 *Greek Papyri from Gurob* Dublin
P. Hamb.	Meyer P.M. (ed.) 1911-1924 *Griechische Papyrusurkunden der Hamburger Staats- und Universitätsbibliothek* Leipzig/Berlin
P. Haun.	Larsen T. (ed.) 1942 *Papyri Graecae Haunienses* Copenhagen
P.L.Bat.	*Papyrologica-Lugdono Batava* Leiden 1941-
P. Lille dem.	de Cenival Fr. (ed.) 1984 *Papyrus démotiques de Lille* III Cairo
P.Loeb dem.	Spiegelberg W. (ed.) 1931 *Die demotischen Papyri Loeb* München
P. Lond.	Kenyon F.G. & Bell H.I. & Skeat T.C. (eds.) 1893-1974 *Greek Papyri in the British Museum* London
P. Petrie	Mahaffy J.P. & Smyly J.G. (eds.) 1891-1905 *The Flinders Petrie Papyri*, Dublin
P.Rev.Laws	Grenfell B.P. (ed.) 1896 *Revenue Laws of Ptolemy Philadelphus* Oxford
Prosopographia Ptolemaica v. Peremans & Van't Dack 1968	

PSI	Vitelli G. & Norsa M. (et al.) (eds.) 1912- *Papiri greci e latini (Publicazioni della Società Italiana per la ricerca dei papiri greci e latini in Egitto)* Firenze
RBib	*Revue Biblique* Paris
RE	*Paulys Real-Encyclopäedie der classischen Altertumswissenschaft* Stuttgart 1894-
REG	*Revue des Études Grecque* Paris 1888
RhM	*Rheinisches Museum* Frankfurt
SB	Preisigke F. & Bilabel F. & Kiessling E. (eds.) 1915- *Sammelbuch griechischer Urkunden aus Ägypten* Göttingen/Strassbourg/Berlin
SBL	*Society of Biblical Literature Dissertation Series* (Missoula, MA) Atlanta, GA
SCI	*Scripta Classica Israelica* Jerusalem
SEG	Roussel P. & Salac A. & Tod M.N. & Ziebarth E. (eds.) 1923- *Supplementum Epigraphicum Graecum*, Leiden
SPA	*Studia Philonica Annual* Atlanta, Ga. 1989-
StAltägKul	*Studien zur altägyptischen Kultur* Hamburg 1974-
StPh	*Studia Philonica* Chicago
TAPhA	*Transactions and Proceedings of the American Philological Association* Boston 1869-
TU	*Texte und Untersuchungen* Berlin
UPZ	Wicken U (ed.) 1927 *Urkunden der Ptolemäerzeit (ältere Funde)* I Leipzig/Berlin
W. Chr.	Wilcken U. & Mitteis L. (eds.) 1912 *Grundzüge und Chrestomathie der Papyruskunde*, Leipzig/Berlin
ZÄS	*Zeitschrift für ägyptische Sprache und Altertumskunde* Leipzig, Berlin 1863-
ZNW	*Zeitschrift für die neutestamentliche Wissenschaft* Berlin
ZPE	*Zeitschrift für Papyrologie und Epigraphik* Bonn 1967-

BIBLIOGRAPHY

Acts of the Pagan Martyrs v. Musurillo 1954

Adorno Th.W. (et.al.) 1950 *Studies in Prejudice vol. I, The Authoritarian Personality* New York

Abel F.-M. 1952 *Histoire de la Palestine* I-II Paris

Alberro Ch.A. 1976 *The Alexandrian Jews During the Ptolemaic Period* Dissertation, Michigan State University

Almond G. & Verba S. 1963 *The Civic Culture. Political attitudes and Democracy in Five Nations* Princeton

Almond G. & Pye L. 1965 (eds.) *Comparative Political Culture* Princeton

Alon G. 1977 *Jews, Judaism and the Classical World* Jerusalem

Anderson B. 1983 *Imagined Communities. Reflections on the Origin and Spread of Nationalism* London

Anderson H. 1985 "3 Maccabees First Century B.C." in: Charlesworth 1985, 509-29

Anderson H. 1985a "Third and Fourth Maccabees and Jewish Apologetics" in: Caquot (ed.) *Littérature Intertestamentaire* Paris, 173-85

Applebaum 1980 *Jews and Greeks in Ancient Cyrene* Leiden

Aristotle, The Politics, translated by T.A. Sinclair, London 1962

Armstrong J. 1982 *Nations before Nationalism* Chapel Hill

Arnaldez R. & Pouilloux J. & Mondésert Cl. 1961- *Les oeuvres de Philon d'Alexandrie* Paris

Assmann J. 1983 "Königsdogma und Heilserwartung. Politische und kultische Chaosbeschreibungen in ägyptischen Texten" in Hellholm 1983, 345-78

Assmann J. 1984 *Ägypten. Theologie und Frömmigkeit einer frühen Hochkultur* Stuttgart

Aujac G. 1966 *Strabon et la science de son temps* Paris (thèse pour le doctorat)

Bagnall R.S. 1984 "The origin of Ptolemaic cleruchs" *BASP* 21, 7-20

Baines J. 1983 "Literacy and ancient Egyptian society" *Man* N.S. 18, 572-99

Baines J. 1988 "Literacy, social organization, and the archaeological record: the case of early Egypt" *State and society* ed. Gledhill J. & Bender B. & Trolle Larsen M., 192-214, London

Bar-Kochva B. 1976 *The Seleucid Army* Cambridge

Barraclough R. 1984 "Philo's Politics. Roman Rule and Hellenistic Judaism" *ANRW* 2,21,1, 417-53

Barta W. 1985 "Die Bedeutung der Jenseitstexte für den verstorbenen König" *Münchener ägyptologische Studien* 39, München

Barth F. 1969 (ed.) *Ethnic Groups and Boundaries. The Social Organization of Cultural Difference* Bergen/Oslo/London

Bateson G. 1942 "Morale and national character" reprinted in *Steps to an Ecology of Mind* New York 1972, 88-106

Bell H.I. 1924 *Jews and Christians in Egypt* London/Oxford

Bellah R. (et.al.) 1985 *Habits of the Heart. Individualism and Commitment in American Life* Berkeley

Benedict R. 1946 *The Chrysantemum and the Sword* New York

Berger H. 1880 *Die geographischen Fragmente des Eratosthenes. Neu gesammelt, geordnet und besprochen* Leipzig

Bergman J. 1983 "Introductory Remarks on Apocalypticism in Egypt" in Hellholm 1983 51-60

Bernhardy G. 1822 *Eratosthenica* Berlin

Bevan E.R. 1927 *A history of Egypt under the Ptolemaic dynasty* London (reprint Chicago 1968)

Bickermann E. 1929, 1930 "Beiträge zur antiken Urkundengeschichte. I: Der Heimatsvermerk und die staatsrechtliche Stellung der Hellenen im ptolemäischen Ägypten" *APF* VIII, 216-39; IX, 335-49

Bickermann E. 1930 "Zur Datierung des Pseudo-Aristeas" *ZNW* 29, 280-98

Bilabel F. & Preisigke F. 1915 *Sammelbuch griechischer Urkunden aus Ägypten* Berlin/New York

Bingen J. 1981 "L'Égypte Gréco-Romaine et la problématique des interactions culturelles" *Proceedings of the XVIth International Congress of Papyrology* Chico, 3–18

Blomqvist J. 1973-74 "Avvisandet av den heliocentriska världsbilden i antiken [with English summary: "The rejection of the heliocentric hypothesis in antiquity"]" *Lychnos*, 1–21

Boehm M.H. 1933 "Nationalism. Theoretical Aspects" in Seligman E.R.A. (ed.): *Encyclopedia of the Social Sciences* XI, 231-40

Borgen P. 1981 (2.ed.) "Bread from Heaven" *NTSup* 10 Leiden

Borgen P. 1984a "Philo of Alexandria" in Stone M. (ed.), *Jewish Writings of the Second Temple Period*, *CRINT* 2,2, 233-82

Borgen P. 1984b "Philo of Alexandria. A Critical and Synthetical Survey of Research since World War II" in *ANRW* 2,21,1, 98-154

Borgen P. 1987 "Philo, John and Paul" in Neusner J. (ed.) *Brown Judaic Studies* 131, Atlanta Ga

Borgen P. "The Jews of Egypt" in *The Anchor Bible Dictionary* Garden City NY (forthcoming)

Borgen P. "'There Shall Come forth a Man'. Reflections on Messianic Ideas in Philo" in Charlesworth J. (ed.) *The Messiah* Minneapolis, MN (forthcoming)

Borghouts J. 1971 "The Magical Text of Papyrus Leiden I,348" *Oudheidkundige Mededelingen uit het Rijksmuseum van Oudheden te Leiden* 51 Leiden

Boswinkel E. & Pestman P.W. 1982 "Les archives privées de Dionysios, fils de Képhalas" *Papyrologica Lugduno-Batava* 22 Leiden

Bousset W. 1926 (3.ed.) *Die Religion des Judentums im späthellenistischer Zeitalter* Tübingen

Bouché-Leclercq A. 1903-1907 *Histoire des Lagides* I-IV Paris

Box H. 1939 *Philonis Alexandrini In Flaccum* Oxford

Braun M. 1938 *History and Romance in Graeco-Oriental Literature* Oxford

Braunert H. 1964 *Die Binnenwanderung. Studien zur Sozialgeschichte Ägyptens in der Ptolemäer- und Kaiserzeit* Bonn

Breasted J.H. 1912 *Development of Religion and Thought in Ancient Egypt* New York

Bresciani E. 1978 "La spedizione di Tolomeo II in Siria in un ostrakon demotico inedito da Karnak" in Maehler, H. & Strocka V.M. *Das ptolemäische Ägypten* Mainz, 31-37

Bresciani E. 1984 "Testi lessicali demotici inediti da Tebtuni" *Grammata Demotica. Lüddeckens Festschrift* Würzburg, 1-9

Butler A.J. 1978 *The Arab conquest of Egypt* (2. ed. rev. P. M. Fraser) Oxford

Caminos R.H. 1954 *Late Egyptian Miscellanies* Oxford

Charlesworth J.H. 1983-1985 (ed.) *The old Testament Pseuepigrapha* I-II Garden City NY

Cimino M. 1982 "A new, rational endeavour for understanding the Eratosthenes numerical result of the earth meridian measurement" *Compendium in Astronomy. A volume dedicated to John Xanthakis* Dordrecht, 11–21

Collins J.J. 1974 *The Sibylline Oracles of Egyptian Judaism* (SBL Dissertation Series) 13 Missoula MT

Collins J.J. 1983 *Between Athens and Jerusalem: Jewish Identity in the Hellenistic Diaspora* New York

Collins J.J. 1984 "The Sibylline Oracles" in Stone M.(ed.) *Jewish Writings of the Second Temple Period CRINT* 2,2, 357-81

Crawford D.J. 1971 *Kerkeosiris. An Egyptian Village in the Ptolemaic Period* Cambridge

Dardel E. 1954 "The Mythic: According to the Ethnological Works of Maurice Leenhardt" *Diogenes* 7, 33-51

Davies W.D. & Finkelstein L. (eds.) 1986 *The Cambridge History of Judaism* I Cambridge

Davis S. 1951 *Race Relations in Ancient Egypt* London

de Meulenaere H. 1963 "La famille royale des Nectanébo" *ZÄS* 90, 90-93

Delling G. 1972 "Philons Enkomion auf Augustus" *Klio*, 171-92

Denis A.-M. 1970 "Introduction aux Pseudépigraphes Grecs d'Ancien Testament" *Studia in Veteris Testamenti Pseudepigrapha* I Leiden

Deutsch K.W. 1953 *Nationalism and Social Communication. An Inquiry into the Foundations of Nationality* Cambridge Mass. (2. ed. 1966)

Devauchelle D. 1984 "Remarques sur les méthodes d'enseignement du démotique" *Grammata Demotica. Lüddeckens Festschrift* Würzburg, 47-59

DeVos G.A. 1968 "National Character" in *International Encyclopedia of the Social Sciences* 11, 14-19

Dicks D.R. 1971 "Eratosthenes" *Dictionary of Scientific Biography* IV New York 388—93

Dodd C.H. 1935 *The Bible and the Greeks* London

Dragoni G. 1975 "Introduzione allo studio della vita e delle opere di Eratostene" *Physis* 17, 41—70

Dragoni G. 1979 "Eratostene e l'apogeo della scienza greca" *Studi di storia antica* 4, Bologna

Eichhorn D.M. (ed.) 1965 *Conversion to Judaism. A History and Analysis* New York

El-Abbadi M.A.H. 1962 "The Alexandrian Citizenship" *JEA* 48, 106-23

Engels D. 1985 "The length of Eratosthenes' stade" *AJPh* 106, 298—311

Erman A. 1901 "Zaubersprüche für Mutter und Kind" *AbhBerlin*

Finnegan R. 1988 *Literacy and orality. Studies in the technology of communication* Oxford

Firsov L. V. 1972 "Eratosthenes' calculation of the earth's circumference and the length of the Hellenistic stade" *Vestnik drevnej istorii* np. 121, 154—74 (Russian)

Fischer U. 1978 *Eschatologie und Jenseitserwartung in hellenistischer Diasporajudentum* Berlin

Fowden G. 1986 *The Egyptian Hermes: A historical approach to the late pagan mind* Cambridge

Frankfort H. 1948a *Ancient Egyptian Religion* New York

Frankfort H. 1948b *Kingship and the Gods* Chicago

Fraser P.M. 1970 "Eratosthenes of Cyrene" *PBA* 56, 175—207

Fraser P.M. 1972 *Ptolemaic Alexandria* I-II Oxford

Freeman D. 1983 *Margaret Mead and Samoa: The Making and Unmaking of an Anthropological Myth* Cambridge Mass

Freudenthal J. 1874-75 *Alexander Polyhistor und die von ihm erhaltenen Reste judäischer und samaritanischer Geschichtswerke* Breslau

Fuchs L. 1924 *Die Juden Ägyptens in ptolemäischer und römischer Zeit* Wien

Gans H.J. (et.al.) 1979 (eds.) *On the Making of Americans: Essays in honor of David Riesman* Pennsylvania

Gardiner A.H. 1937 "Late Egyptian Miscellanies" *Bibliotheca Aegyptiaca* 7. Bruxelles

Gardiner A.H. 1938 "The house of life" *JEA* 24, 157-79

Gauthiér H. & Sottas H. 1925 *Un décret trilingue en l'honneur de Ptolémée Philopator* Paris

Geertz Cl. 1973 *The Interpretation of Cultures* New York

Geertz Cl. 1983 *Local Knowledge* New York

Geffcken J. 1902 *Die Oracula Sibyllina* Leipzig

Gellner E. 1964 "Nationalism", in Gellner *Thought and Change* London, 147-78

Gellner E. 1973 "Scale and Nation" *Philosophy of the Social Sciences* 3, 1-17

Gellner E. 1983a *Nations and Nationalism* London

Gellner E. 1983b "Nationalism and the two forms of cohesion in complex societies" in *Proceedings of the British Academy* 58, 65-187; quoted from Gellner *Culture, Identity, and Politics* London 1987, 6-28

Geographi Graeci minores Rec. K. Müller I–II Paris 1855–1861

Glazer N. & Moynihan D.P. 1963 *Beyond the Melting Pot* New York

Glazer N. & Moynihan D.P. (eds.) 1975 *Ethnicity. Theory and Experience* Cambridge MA

Goedicke H. 1984 "Comments on the Satrap Stela" *Bulletin of the Egyptological Seminar* 6, 31-54

Goldenberg R. 1979 "The Jewish Sabbath in the Roman World up to the Time of Constantine the great" in *ANRW* 2,19,1, 414-47

Goldstein B.R. 1983 "The obliquity of the ecliptic in ancient Greek astronomy" *Archives internationales d'histoire des sciences* 33, 3–14

Goldstein B.R. 1984 "Eratosthenes on the measurement of the earth" *HM* 11, 411–16

Goody J. 1986 *The logic of writing and the organisation of society* Cambridge

Goody J. 1987 *The interface between the written and the oral* Cambridge

Gorer G. 1948 *The American People* New York

Gorer G. 1955 *Exploring English Character* London

Gorer G. & Rickman J. 1949 *The People of Great Russia: A Psychological Study* New York

Goudriaan K. 1988 *Ethnicity in Ptolemaic Egypt* Amsterdam

Gressmann H. 1918 "Vom reichen Mann und armen Lazarus" *AbhBerlin* 7

Griffith F.Ll. 1900 *Stories of the High Priests of Memphis* I-II Oxford

Griffiths J.G. 1983 "Apocalyptic in the Hellenistic Era" in Hellholm 1983, 273-94

Grosjean Fr. 1982 *Life with two languages* Cambridge Mass./London

Grønbech V. 1939 *Hellenismen* I–II København

Guéraud O. & Jouguet P. 1938 *Un livre d'écolier du IIIe siècle avant J.-C..* Cairo

Gulbekian E. 1987 "The origin and value of the stadion unit used by Eratosthenes in the third century B.C." *Archive for History of Exact Sciences* 37, 359–63

Gutman Y. 1959 "The Historical Value of III Maccabees" *Eshkoloth* III, 67-68 (Hebrew)

Hadas M. 1951 *Aristeas to Philocrates (Letter of Aristeas)* New York

Hadas M. 1953 *The Third and Fourth Books of Maccabees* New York

Hagedorn D. 1986 "Ein Erlass Ptolemaios' I, Soter?" *ZPE* 66, 65-70

Hammond N. G. L. 1990 "Royal pages, personal pages, and boys trained in the Macedonian manner during the period of the Temenid monarchy" *Historia* 39, 261-90

Handelman D. 1977 "The Organization of Ethnicity" *Ethnic Groups* 1,3, 187-200

Harbsmeier M. 1986 "Danmark: Nation, kultur og køn" *Stofskifte* 13, 1986, 48-73

Harris H.A. 1976 *Greek Athletics and the Jews* Cardiff

Harris N.V. 1989 *Ancient Literacy* Cambridge Mass./London

Hayes C. J. 1926 *Essays on Nationalism* New York

Hayes C.J. 1933 "Nationalism. Historical Development" in Seligman E.R.A. (ed.) *Encyclopedia of the Social Sciences* XI, 240-49

Hayes C.J. 1960 *Nationalism: A Religion* New York

Hellholm D. (ed.) 1983 *Apocalypticism in the Mediterranean World and the Near East* Tübingen

Hengel M. 1981 *Judaism and Hellenism: Studies in Their Encounter in Palestine During the Early Hellenistic Period* Philadelphia

Hengel M. 1983 "Messianische Hoffnung und politischer "Radikalismus' in der jüdisch-hellenistischen Diaspora" in Hellholm 1983, 655-686

Hiller E. 1872 *Eratosthenis carminum reliquiae* Lipsiae

Hobsbawm E.J. 1972 "Some reflections on Nationalism" in Nossiter T.J. & Hanson A.H. & Rokkan S. (eds.): *Imagination and Precision in the Social Sciences: Essays in memory of Peter Nettl* London, 385-406

Hobsbawm E.J. & Ranger T. (eds.) 1983 *The Invention of Tradition* London

Hobsbawm E.J. 1990 *Nations and Nationalism since 1780* Cambridge

Holladay C.R. 1977 *THEIOS ANER in Hellenistic Judaism: A Critique of the Use of this Category in New Testament Christology* (SBL Dissertation Series 40) Missoula, MT

Holladay C.R. 1983 *Fragments From Hellenistic Jewish Authors: Volume I: Historians* SBL Texts and Translations 20, Pseudepigrapha Series 10, Chico CA

Holladay C.R. 1989 *Fragments from Hellenistic Jewish Authors: Volume II: Poets* SBLTexts and Translations 30, Pseudepigrapha Series 12, Atlanta GA

Holladay C.R. *Fragments from Hellenistic Jewish Authors: Volume III* SBL Texts and Translations, Pseudepigrapha Series Atlanta GA (forthcoming)

Hopfner Th. 1921-1924 "Griechisch-ägyptischer Offenbarungszauber I-II" *Studien zur Paläographie und Papyruskunde* 21 & 23. Leipzig

Horst P.W. van der 1978 *The Sentences of Pseudo-Phocylides* Leiden

Howard J. 1984 *Margaret Mead. A Life* New York

Jacobson H. 1983 *The EXAGOGE of Ezekiel* Cambridge

Jacoby F. 1923- *Die Fragmente der griechischen Historiker* Berlin

Janowitz N. 1983 "Translating Cult: The Letter of Aristeas and Hellenistic Judaism" *SBL Seminar Papers* 347-357

Jouguet P. 1928 *Macedonian Imperialism and the Hellenization of the East* London

Kakosy L. 1964 "Ideas about the Fallen State of the World in Egyptian Religion: Decline of the Golden Age" *AOrientHung* 17, 205ff

Kaplony P. 1971 "Bemerkungen zum ägyptischen Königtum vor allem in der Spätzeit" *CE* 46, 250-74

Kaplony-Heckel U. 1974 "Schüler und Schulwesen in der ägyptischen Spätzeit" *StAltägKul* I, 227-46

Kasher A. 1972 *The Civic Status of the Jews in Egypt in Hellenistic and Roman Period* (Hebrew) Dissertation, Tel-Aviv University

Kasher A. 1978 *The Jews in Hellenistic and Roman Egypt* (Hebrew) Tel-Aviv

Kasher A. 1985 "The Jews in Hellenistic and Roman Egypt: The Struggle for Equal Rights" in *Texte und Studien zum Antiken Judentum* 7 Tübingen

Kautzsch E. (ed.) 1900 *Die Apokryphen und Pseudepigraphen des Alten Testaments* I-II Tübingen

Kedourie E. 1960 *Nationalism* London (rev. ed. 1985)

Keller G. A. 1946 *Eratosthenes und die alexandrinische Sterndichtung* (diss.) Zürich

Kemiläinen A. 1964 *Nationalism, Problems Concerning the Word, the Concept and Classification* Jyväskylä

Kemiläinen A. 1984 "The Idea of Nationalism" in *Scandinavian Journal of History* 9, 31-64

Klein S. 1920 *Jüdische-Palästinische Corpus Inscriptionum* Wien/Berlin

Klein S. 1939 *Sefer Ha-Yishuv* (Hebrew) Jerusalem

Knaack G. 1907 "Eratosthenes von Kyrene" *RE* 6, 358–88

Koenen L. 1962 "Der brennende Horosknabe *CE* 37, 167-74.

Koenen L. 1968 "Die Prophezeihungen des Töpfers" *ZPE* 2, 178ff

Koenen L. 1986 "Manichaean Apocalypticism at the Crossroads of Iranian, Egyptian, Jewish, and Christian Thought" *Codex Manichaicus Colonensis. Atti del Simposio Internazionale*, Cirillo L. (ed.), Cosenza

Kohn H. 1944 *The Idea of Nationalism. A Study in its Origins and Background* New York

Krois F.M. 1987 *Cassirer. Symbolic Forms and History* Yale

Langer S.K. 1949 "On Cassirer's Theory of Language and Myth" in Schlipp P.A. (ed.) *The Philosophy of Ernst Cassirer* Evanston

Launey M. 1949-1950 *Recherches sur les armées hellénistiques* I-II, Paris

Lesquier J. 1911 *Les institutions militaires de l'Egypte sous les Lagides* Paris

Lévi-Strauss Cl. 1962 *La pensée sauvage* Paris

Lewis N. 1984 *Life in Egypt under Roman Rule* Oxford

Lewis N. 1986 *Greeks in Ptolemaic Egypt* Oxford

Lichtheim M. 1975 *Ancient Egyptian literature, Volume I: The Old and Middle Kingdoms* Berkeley/Los Angeles/London

Lichtheim M. 1976 *Ancient Egyptian literature, Volume II: The New Kingdom* Berkeley/Los Angeles/London

Lichtheim M. 1980 *Ancient Egyptian literature, Volume III: The Late Period* Berkeley/Los Angeles/London

Liddell H. G. & Scott R. 1973 *A Greek-English Lexicon* (9. ed.) Oxford

Liebesny H. 1936 "Ein Erlass des Königs Ptolemaios II Philadelphos über die Deklaration von Vieh und Sklaven in Syrien und Phönikien (PER. Inv. Nr. 24. 552 gr.)" *Aegyptus* 16, 257-291

Lipset S.M. 1950 *Agrarian Socialism* Berkeley

Lipset S.M. 1960 *Political Man* New York

Lipset S.M. 1963 *The First New Nation. The United States in Historical and Comparative perspective* New York

Lipset S.M. 1976 "Radicalism in North America: A Comparative View of Party Systems in Canada and the United States" in *Transactions of the Royal Society of Canada* 14, 19-55

Lloyd G.E.R. 1973 *Greek Science after Aristotle* London

Lloyd-Jones *v*. Parsons 1983

Löfgren O. 1989 "The Nationalization of Culture" *Ethnologia Europaea* 19,1, 5-24

Lorch R. 1981 "A note on the technical vocabulary in Eratosthenes' tract on mean proportionals" *JHAS* 5, 166–70

Luce J.V. 1988 "Greek science in its Hellenistic phase" *Hermathena* 145, 23–38

Luedtke L.S. 1987 "The Search for American Character" in Luedtke (ed.) *Making America* Washington, 5-34

Luppe W. 1982 "Apeôsthê palin eis tous Lênaikous" *ZPE* 46, 147–59

Lynd R.S. & Lynd H.M. 1929 *Middletown: A Study of Contemporary American Culture* New York

Lynd R.S. & Lynd H.M. 1937 *Middletown in Transition: A Study in Cultural Conflicts* New York

Maass E. 1883 *Analecta Eratosthenica* Berlin

Mau J. 1975 "Eratosthenes 2" *Der kleine Pauly* 2, 344–46

Mead M. 1942 *And Keep Your Powder Dry* New York

Mead M. 1953 "National Character" in Kroeber A.L. (ed.) *Anthropology Today: An Encyclopedic Inventory* Chicago, 642-67

Mead M. 1961 "National Character and the Science of Anthropology" in Lipset, S.M. & Lowenthal L. (eds.) *Culture and Social Character: The Work of David Riesman Reviewed* New York. 15-26

Mead M. & Métraux R. 1953 (eds.) *The Study of Culture at a Distance* Chicago

McLuhan M. 1962 *The Gutenberg Galaxy: The Making of Typographic Man* Toronto

Mendels D. 1990 "The polemical character of Manetho's Aegyptiaca" *Studia Hellenistica* 30, 91-110

Mendelson A. 1982 *Secular Education in Philo of Alexandria* Cincinatti

Mendelson A. 1988 "Philo's Jewish Identity" in *Brown Judaic Series* 161, Atlanta Ga + C

Merkelbach R. 1963 "Die Erigone des Eratosthenes" *Miscellanea di studi alessandrini in memoria di A. Rostagni* Torino, 468–526

Merkelbach R. 1963-1964a "Origin and religious meaning of Greek tragedy and comedy, according to the Erigone of Eratosthenes" *HR* 3, 175–90

Merkelbach R. 1963-1964b "Tragödie, Komödie und dionysiche Kulte (nach der Erigone des Eratosthenes)" *Antaios* 5, 325–43

Merkelbach R. 1968 "Ein ägyptischer Priestereid" *ZPE* 2, 7-30

Merkelbach R. 1970 "Die Sphaerenharmonie auf einem ravennatischen Mystensarkophag" *ZPE* 6, 277–78

Meyer E. 1928 *Geschichte des Altertums* II,1 Stuttgart

Mitteis L. & Wilcken U. 1912 *Grundzüge und Chrestomathie der Papyruskunde* I–II Leipzig/Berlin

Momigliano A. 1929 "Il decreto trilinguo in onore di Tolemeo Filopatore e la quarta guerra di Celesiria" *Aegyptus* 10, 180-89

Mooren *v.* Peremans 1968

Motzo R.B. 1934 "Il citacimentao Greco di Ester e il III Maccbei" in: *Saggi de storia e letteratura Guideo-Ellenistica* Florence, 272-90 = reprinted in: *Richerche sull letteratura e la storia Guidaico-Ellenistica* Rome 1977, 281-301

Murray O. 1967 "Aristeas and Ptolemaic Kingship" *JTS* 18, 337-71

Murray O. 1980 *Early Greece* Glasgow

Musurillo H.A. 1954 *The Acts of the Pagan Martyrs. Acta Alexandrinorum* Oxford

Muwafi A. & Philippou A.N. 1981 "An Arabic version of Eratosthenes On Mean Proportionals" *JHAS* 5, 147–65

Newton R.R. 1980 "The sources of Eratosthenes' measurement of the earth" *Quarterly Journal of the Royal Astronomical Society* 31, 379–87

Nickolsburg G.W.E. 1984 "Stories of Biblical and Early Post-Biblical Times" in: Stone M.E. (ed.) *CRINT* 2 *The Literature of the Jewish People in the Period of the Second Temple and the Talmud* 2 *Jewish Writings of the Second Temple Period* Assen, 75-80

Nikiprowetzky V. 1977 "Le commentaire de l'Ecriture chez Philon d'Alexandrie: son caractère et sa portée; observations philologiques" *ALGHJ* 11. Leiden

Nilsson M. P. 1948 "Die Religion in den griechischen Zauberpapyri" *Kungliga humanistiska Vetenskapssamfundet i Lund. Årsberättelse / Bulletin de la Société Royale des Lettres de Lund* Lund, 59-93

Nock A.D. & Festugière A.J. 1972 *Corpus Hermeticum* II Paris

Oates J. & Bagnall R.A. & Willis W.H. 1978, "Checklist of Editions of Greek Papyri and Ostraca" (2. ed.) *BASP Suppl.* 1, Missoula.

Olsson T. 1983 "The Apocalyptic Activity. The Case of Jamasp Namag" in Hellholm 1983, 21-49

Orrieux Cl. 1985 *Zénon de Caunos, parépidemos, et le destin grec*, Centre de recherches d'histoire ancienne 64, Paris

Otzen B. 1990 *Judaism in Antiquity. Political Development and Religious Currents from Alexander to Hadrian* Sheffield

Palm J. 1959 *Rom, Römertum und Imperium in der griechischen Literatur der Kaiserzeit* Lund

Parsons E.A. 1952 *The Alexandrian Library. Glory of the Hellenic World. Its rise, antiquities and destructions* London

Parsons P.J. & Lloyd-Jones H. 1983 *Supplementum Hellenisticum* Berlin/New York

Paul A. 1984 "Les pseudépigraphes juifs de langue grecque" in: Kuntzmann R. & Schosser J. *Etudes sur le judaïsme hellénistique. Congrès de Strasbourg 1983* Paris, 71-94

Paul A. 1987 "Le Troisième Livre des Macchabées" *ANRW* 2,20,1, 298-336

Pearson B. 1984 "Philo and Gnosticism" in *ANRW* 2,21,1, 295-342

Pelletier A. 1962 *La Lettre d'Aristée à Philocrate* Paris

Pelletier A. 1972 (trans.) "Legation ad Gallum" in Arnaldez & Pouilloux & Mondésert

Peremans W. 1962 "Egyptiens et étrangers dans l'Egypte ptolémaïque" in "Grecs et Barbares" *Entretiens sur l'antiquité classique* VIII. Genève, 121-55, with discussion on pages 156-66

Peremans W. & Van 't Dack E. 1968 "Prosopographia Ptolemaica VI: La Cour, les relations internationales et les possessions extérieures, la vie culturelle" Peremans W. & Van 't Dack E. & Mooren L. & Swinnen W. (eds.) *Studia Hellenistica* 17 Louvain

Pestman P.W. 1980 *Greek and Demotic texts from the Zenon Archive*, *P.L.Bat.* 20, 2 vols., Leiden

Philippou, *v.* Muwafi 1981

Podemann Sørensen J. 1984 "The Argument in Ancient Egyptian Magical Formulae" *Acta Orientalia* 45, 5-19

Podemann Sørensen J. 1989 "Ancient Egyptian Religious Thought and the XVIth Hermetic Tractate" *The Religion of the Ancient Egyptians: Cognitive Structures and Popular Expressions* Englund G. (ed.). *Acta Universitatis Upsaliensis. Boreas* 20 Uppsala, 41-57

Potter D.M. 1954 *People of Plenty. Economic Abundance and the American Character* Chicago

Powell J.U. 1925 *Collectanea Alexandrina* Oxford

Préaux P. 1939 (1947) *L'économie royale de Lagides* Bruxelles

Préaux Cl. 1975 "Grandeur et limites de la science hellénistique" *CE* 50, 1975, 215–38

Préaux Cl. 1978 *Le monde hellénistique. La Grèce et l'Orient de la mort d'Alexandre à la conquête romaine de la Grèce (323–146 av. J.-C.).* I–II Paris 1978

Quaegebeur J. 1980 "The genealogy of the Memphite high priest family in the Hellenistic period" *Studia Hellenistica* 24, 43-89

Quaegebeur J. 1980/81 "Sur la 'loi sacré' dans l'Egypte gréco-romaine" *Ancient Society* 11/12, 227-40

Radice R. & Runia D.T. 1988 *Philo of Alexandria. An Annotated Bibliography 1937-1986* Leiden

Rappaport R. 1970 "When was the Letter of Aristeas Written?" (Hebrew) *Studies in the History of the Jewish People and the Land of Israel* I, 38-50

Rawlings D. 1982a "Eratosthenes' geodesy re-examined. Was there a high-accuracy Hellenistic astronomy?" *Isis* 73, 259–65

Rawlings D. 1982b "The Eratosthenes-Strabo Nile map. Is it the earliest surviving instance of spherical cartography? Did it supply the 5000 stades arc for Eratosthenes' experiment?" *Archive for History of Exact Sciences* 26, 211—19

Ray J.D. 1988 "Egypt 525-404 B.C." *CAH* IV (2.ed.), 254-86

Rengsdorf K.H.(ed.) 1975 *A Complete Concordance to Flavius Josephus* II Leiden

Riesman D. & Glazer N. & Denney R. 1950 *The Lonely Crowd: A Study of the Changing American Character* New Haven

Riesman D. 1958 "The Study of National Character: Some Observations on the American case *Harvard Library Bulletin* 13,1, 1959, 5-24 (reprinted in *Abundance for Whom?* New York 1964, 584-603)

Riesman D. 1961 *"1961 Preface" to The Lonely Crowd* New York

Robert C. 1878 (1963) *Eratosthenis Catasterismorum reliquiae* Berolini

Robert L. 1940 "Épigramme d'Egypte" *Hellenica* I, 18-24 Paris

Robinson J.M. 1977 (ed.) *The Nag Hammadi Library in English* Leiden

Rostovtzeff M.I. 1941 *The Social and Economic History of the Hellenistic World* I-III Oxford

Rostovtzeff M.I. 1964 "Ptolemaic Egypt" *CAH* VII, 109-154, 155-196

Roux J. & Roux G. 1942 "Un décret du politeuma des Juifs de Bérénice en Cyrénaïque au Musé Lapidaire de Carpentras (Planches III et IV)" *REG* LXII, 283, 290

Rubin J. 1968 *National bilingualism in Paraguay* Janua linguarum. Series practica 60 Haag/Paris

Ruppel W. 1927 "Politeuma - Bedeutungsgeschichte eines staatsrechtlichen Terminus" *Philologus*, LXXXII (N.F. XXVI), 268-12, 433-54

Samuel A.E. 1983 *From Athens to Alexandria: Hellenism and Social Goals in Ptolemaic Egypt* (*Studia Hellenistica* 26) Louvain

Sander-Hansen C.E. 1956 "Die Texte der Metternichstele" *Analecta Aegyptiaca* 7 København

Sandmel S. 1978 "Philo's Knowledge of Hebrew: The Present State of the Problem" *StPh* 5, 107-12

Sandmel S. 1984 "Philo Judaeus. An Introduction to the Man, his Writings, and his Significance" *ANRW* 2,21,1, 3-46

Sapir E. 1933 "Personality" in Seligman E.R.A. (ed.) *Encyclopedia of the Social Sciences* XII, 85-88

Schlesinger Ph. 1987 "On national identity: some misconceptions and misconceptions criticized" *Social Science Information* 26,2, 219-64

Schneider C. 1967-1969 *Kulturgeschichte des Hellenismus* I-II München

Schubart W. 1913 "Alexandrinische Urkunden aus der Zeit des Augustus" *APF* 5, 35-131

Schubart W. 1925 "H.I. Bell's *Jews and Christians in Egypt* London/Oxford 1924" *Gnomon* 1, 23-37 (recension)

Schürer E. 1901-1909 *Geschichte des jüdischen Volkes im Zeitalter Jesu Christi* (4. ed.) I-III Leipzig

Schürer E. 1973-1987 *The History of the Jewish People in the Age of Jesus Christ* I-III. Revised and edited by Vermes G. & Millar F. & Goodman M., Edinburgh

Schwabe M. 1942 "The Ancient Synagougue of Apamea in Syria" (Hebrew) *Qedem* I, 85-93

Schwarz D.R. 1989 "Philonic Anonyms of the Roman and Nazi Periods: Two Suggestions" *SPA* 1, 63-73

Schwarzenberg E. 1976 "The portraiture of Alexander" in *Alexandre le Grand. Image et réalité*, Fondation Hardt *Éntretiens sur l'antiquité classique* 22, 223–78. Vandouvres/Genève

Sethe K. 1904 *Hieroglyphische Urkunden der griechisch-römischen Zeit* II Leipzig

Sevenster J.N. 1975 *The Roots of Pagan Antisemitism in the Ancient World* Leiden

Shutt R.J.H. 1985 "The Letter of Aristeas" in: Charlesworth 1985, 7-34

Smallwood E.M. 1970 *Philonis Alexandrini Legatio ad Gaium* (2. ed.) Leiden

Smallwood E.M. 1976, 1981 *The Jews Under Roman Rule From Pompey to Diocletian: A Study in Political Relations* Leiden 1976 (reprint with corrections, Leiden 1981)

Smelik K.A.D. & Hemelrijk E.A. 1984 "Who knows not what Monsters demented Egypt Worships? Opinions on Egyptian Animal Worship in Antiquity as Part of the Ancient Conception of Egypt" in *ANRW* 2,17,4, 1852-2000

Smith A. 1971, 1983 *Theories of Nationalism* London 1971 (2. rev. ed. 1983)

Smith A. 1986 *The Ethnic Origins of Nations* London

Solmsen Fr. 1942 "Eratosthenes as Platonist and poet" *TAPhA* 73, 192–213

Solmsen Fr. 1947 "Eratosthenes' Erigone" *TAPhA* 78, 252–75

Sowers S. 1967 "On the Reinterpretation of Biblical History in Hellenistic Judaism" in Christ F. (ed.) *Oikonomia, Festschrift Oscar Cullmann*. Hamburg/Bergstedt, 20-24

Spiegelberg W. 1925 "Beiträge zur Erklärung des neun dreisprachigen Priesterdekretes zu Ehren des Ptolemaios Philopator" *Sitzungsberichte der Bayerische Akademie der Wissenschaften Phil.-hist. Abteilung* 4 München

Starobinski-Safran E. 1987 "La communauté juive d'Alexandrie a l'époque de Philon" *ALEXANDRINA. Mélanges offerts a Claude Mondésert* S.J. Paris 45-75

Steinmetz P. 1969 "Die Krise der Philosophie in der Zeit des Hochhellenismus" *Antike und Abendland* 15, 122–34

Stemberger G. 1983 *Die römische Herrschaft im Urteil der Juden* Darmstadt

Stern M. 1974 *Greek and Latin Authors on Jews and Judaism* I Jerusalem

Stern M. 1974 "The Jewish Diaspora" in *The Jewish People in the first Century, CRINT* I,1 Assen, 117-83

Strack M. L. 1897 *Die Dynastie der Ptolemäer* Berlin

Strecker K. 1884 *De Lycophrone, Euphronio, Eratosthene comicorum interpretibus* Gryphiswaldiae (diss.)

Supplementum Hellenisticum, *v*. Parsons & Lloyd Jones 1983

Swinnen *v*. Peremans & Van 't Dack 1968

Szabo A. 1980–1981 "Astronomische Messungen bei den Griechen im 5. Jahrhundert v. Chr. und ihr Instrument" *Platon* 32–33, 293–317

Taisbak C.M. 1984 "Eleven eighty-thirds. Ptolemy's reference to Eratosthenes in Almagest 1.12" *Centaurus* 27, 165–67

Tarn W.W. & Griffith G.H. 1952 *Hellenistic Civilization* London

Taubenschlag R. 1944 *The Law of Greco-Roman Egypt in the Light of the Papyri (332 B.C. – 640 A.D.)* Warszawa (2.ed. 1955)

Tcherikover V.A. 1931 *Jews and Greeks in the Hellenistic Period* (Hebrew) Tel-Aviv

Tcherikover V.A. 1950 "Syntaxis and Laographia" *JJP* 4, 179-207

Tcherikover V.A. 1960 *Jews in Graeco-Roman World* (Hebrew) Tel-Aviv

Tcherikover V.A. 1961 "The Third Book of Maccabees as a Historical Source of Augustus' Time" *Scripta Hierosolymitana* VII, 1-25

Tcherikover V.A. 1963 *The Jews in Egypt in the Hellenistic-Roman Period in the Light of Papyrology* (Hebrew) (2. ed.) Jerusalem

Tcherikover V.A. 1966 (2. ed.)1977 *Hellenistic Civilization and the Jews* Philadelphia

Tcherikover V.A. & Fuks A. 1957, 1960, 1964 *Corpus Papyrorum Judaicarum* 1-3. Cambridge, Mass

Thissen H.-J. 1980 "Chronologie der frühdemotischen Papyri" *Enchoria* 10, 105-25

Thompson Crawford D.J. 1984 "The Idumaeans of Memphis and the Ptolemaic Politeumata" *Atti del XVII Congresso Internazionale di Papirologia* Napoli, 1069-75

Thompson D.J. 1987 "Ptolemaios and 'The Lighthouse': Greek culture in the Memphite Serapeum" *PCPhS* 213 (N.S. 33), 105-21

Thompson D.J. 1988 *Memphis under the Ptolemies* Princeton

Thompson D.J. 1992 "Literacy and the administration in early Ptolemaic Egypt" in *Life in a multi-cultural society: Egypt from Cambyses to Constantine and beyond, Studies in Ancient Oriental Civilization* 51 Chicago, 335-38

Tiede D.L. 1972 *The Charismatic Figure as Miracle Worker* SBL Dissertation Series 1 Missoula, MT

Tilly Ch. 1975 (ed.) *The Formation of National states in Western Europe* Princeton

Tocqueville A. de 1835-40 *Democracy in America* Mayer J. P (ed.) New York. 1969 (vol. I, Paris 1835, vol. II Paris 1840

Tramontano R. 1931 *La Lettera di Aristeo a Filocrate* Napoli

Treu M. 1967 "Astronomisches in P.Ox. 2521" *RhM* 110, 84–93

Turner E.G. 1974 "A commander-in-chief's order from Saqqâra" *JEA* 60, 239-42

Uebel F. 1968 *Die Kleruchen Ägyptens unter den ersten sechs Ptolemäern* Berlin

van Seters J. 1983 *In Search of History. Historiography in the Ancient World and the Origins of Biblical History* New Haven, CT

Van't Dack *v.* Peremans

Varenne H. 1977 *Americans Together: Structured Diversity in a Midwestern Town* New York

Vatai F.L. 1984 *Intellectuals in Politics in the Greek World. From Early Times to the Hellenistic Age* London

Vincent H. 1908, 1909 "Jerusalem d'aprés la lettre d'Aristée" *RBib* V, 520-32; VI, 555-75

Wacholder B.Z. 1974 *Eupolemus: A Study of Judaeo-Greek Literature* New York

Waddell W.G. 1980 *Manetho with an English Translation* Loeb Classical Library London

Walter N. 1964 *Der Thoraausleger Aristobulos* Berlin, TU 86

Walter N. 1987 "Jüdisch-hellenistischer Literatur vor Philon von Alexandrien" *ANRW* 2,20,1, 83-85

Wendland P. 1900 "Der Aristeasbrief" in: Kautzsch 1900

Westermann W.L. 1938 "Enslaved People who are Free. Rainer Papyrus (PER) Inv. 24, 552" *AJPh* 59, 1-30

Wifstrand A. 1950 *Den grekiska kulturhistoriens faser* Stockholm

Wilcken *v*. Mitteis 1912

Wilcken U. 1937 (Reports) *APF* XII, 221-33

Will E. 1985 "Pour une 'anthropologie coloniale' du monde hellénistique" in Eadie J.W. & Ober J. *The craft of the ancient historian. Essays in honor of Chester G. Starr* Lanham/New York/London, 273-301

Wilson Br. 1973 *Magic and the Millennium* London

Wolfer E.P. 1954 *Eratosthenes von Kyrene als Mathematiker und Philosoph* Groningen

Worsley P. 1968 *The Trumpet Shall Sound* (2. ed.) New York

Youtie H.C. 1966 "Pétaus, fils de Pétaus, ou le scribe qui ne savait pas écrire" *CE* 41, 127-42 (= *Scriptiunculae* II no. 34, 677-93)

Youtie H.C. 1971a 'AGRAMMATOS': an aspect of Greek society in Egypt" *HSPh* 75, 161-76 (= *Scriptiunculae* II no. 29, 611-27)

Youtie H.C. 1971b "Bradeôs graphôn": between literacy and illiteracy" *GRBS* 12, 239-61 (= *Scriptiunculae* II no. 30, 629-51)

Zuckerman C. 1985-1988 "Hellenistic politeumata and the Jews. A Reconsideration" *SCI* VIII-IX, 171-85

Østergård U. 1988a "Er republikanske dyder det egentligt 'amerikanske' ved amerikanerne?" in Zetterholm S. (ed.) *Alexis de Tocqueville* Copenhagen, 145-202

Østergård U. 1988b *Hvad er en nationstat?* Aarhus

Østergård U. 1989 "Politikkens arena" in Hans Fink (ed.) *Arenaer - Om politik og iscenesættelse* Aarhus, 23-65

Østergård U. 1991a "Definitions of nation in European political thought" *North Atlantic Studies* 1,2, 51-56

Østergård U. 1991 "Feindbilder und Vorurteile in der dänischen Öffentlichkeit" in Trautmann G. (ed.) *Die hässlichen Deutschen?* 145-166, Darmstadt

INDEX OF PERSONS

INDEX LOCORUM

12,8: 115
12,10: 101
12,12-33: 101
12,107-08: 111
12,144: 103
13,287: 108
13,349: 107
13,354-55: 107
14,113: 111
14,117: 111
14,188: 113
19,281: 112
19,284: 112

Bellum Judaicum
   2,487: 110, 113
   2,487-90: 114
   2,488: 110, 114
   2,495: 110
   5,460: 114

Contra Apionem
   1,26-31
   1,209: 126
   1,238-39: 125
   1,250: 125
   2,7: 111
   2,28: 87
   2,28-32: 89
   2,29: 90
   2,33: 111
   2,35: 110, 113, 114
   2,36: 114
   2,37: 110
   2,39: 111
   2,44: 111
   2,49: 107
   2,60: 117
   2,63: 88
   2,29: 87

2,137: 125
2,140ff: 127
2,142-43: 125
2,145: 127
2,145-48: 125
2,282-283: 130

Juvenal
Satire
   14,96-106: 126

Livy
Roman History
   38,17,11: 95

Lucianus
Macrobii
   27, frg. 14 Berger, T 3 Jacoby: 71

Manetho
Aegyptiaca
   Frg. 21: 88
   Frg. 54: 165
   Frg. 164: 88
   Frg. 171: 88
   Frg. 172: 88
   Frg. 173: 88
   Frg. 176: 88

Marcianus of Heraclea
Geographi Graeci minores I.565, frg. 17
Berger: 70

Martianus Capella
   6.596: 65

New Testament
1 Cor.
   1,18-26: 147

Alexandria

Sais

Sebennytos

Mendes

Naucratis

Pelusium

Leontopolis

Leontopolis

Heliopolis

Saqqara

Memphis

Fayum

Arsinoe -
Crocodilopolis

Kerkeosiris

Oxyrhynchus

Akoris

Hermopolis

Lycopolis

Ptolemais

Nag Hammadi

Coptus

Thebes

Karnak